BROCK UNIVERSITY DISCARD

IEE COMPUTING SERIES 14
Series Editors: Dr. B. Carré
                Dr. D. A. H. Jacobs
                Professor I. Sommerville

ECLIPSE
An integrated project support environment

Other volumes in this series

Volume 1　Semi-custom IC design and VLSI
　　　　　P. J. Hicks (Editor)
Volume 2　Software engineering for microprocessor systems
　　　　　P. G. Depledge (Editor)
Volume 3　Systems on silicon
　　　　　P. B. Denyer (Editor)
Volume 4　Distributed computing systems programme
　　　　　D. Duce (Editor)
Volume 5　Integrated project support environments
　　　　　J. A. McDermid (Editor)
Volume 6　Software engineering '86
　　　　　D. J. Barnes and P. J. Brown (Editors)
Volume 7　Software engineering environments
　　　　　I. Sommerville (Editor)
Volume 8　Software engineering: the decade of change
　　　　　D. Ince (Editor)
Volume 9　Computer aided tools for VLSI system design
　　　　　G. Russell (Editor)
Volume 10　Industrial software technology
　　　　　R. Mitchell (Editor)
Volume 11　Advances in command, control and communication systems
　　　　　C. J. Harris and I. White (Editors)
Volume 12　Speech recognition by machine
　　　　　W. A. Ainsworth
Volume 13　Application of artificial intelligence to command and control systems
　　　　　C. J. Harris (Editor)

ECLIPSE
An integrated project support environment

Edited by Frank Bott

with a foreword by
Brian Oakley CBE

Peter Peregrinus Ltd., on behalf of the Institution of Electrical Engineers

Published by: Peter Peregrinus Ltd., London, United Kingdom

© 1989: **Peter Peregrinus Ltd.**

All rights reserved. No part of this publication may be reproduced, stored in a retrieval system or transmitted in any form or by any means—electronic, mechanical, photocopying, recording or otherwise—without the prior written permission of the publisher.

While the author and the publishers believe that the information and guidance given in this work are correct, all parties must rely upon their own skill and judgment when making use of them. Neither the author nor the publishers assume any liability to anyone for any loss or damage caused by any error or omission in the work, whether such error or omission is the result of negligence or any other cause. Any and all such liability is disclaimed.

This book was produced using the LATEX typesetting system; TEX is a trademark of the American Mathematical Society.

British Library Cataloguing in Publication Data

Eclipse: an integrated project support environment.—(IEE computing series; 14)
  1. Computer systems. Software. Development & maintenance management)
  I. Bott, Frank II. Institution of Electrical Engineers
  005.1

ISBN 0 86341 169 X

Printed in England by Short Run Press Ltd., Exeter

Contents

1 The Background to Eclipse   **1**
  1.1 HISTORICAL BACKGROUND 1
  1.2 SDS, FOUNDATION and GAMMA 3
  1.3 ADA AND THE APSE 4
  1.4 SOFTWARE DEVELOPMENT METHODS 5
  1.5 FORMATION OF THE ECLIPSE CONSORTIUM 6
  1.6 OTHER IPSE DEVELOPMENTS 7

2 Overview of the Eclipse Programme   **9**
  2.1 OBJECTIVES OF THE PROGRAMME 9
  2.2 IMPLEMENTATION ENVIRONMENT 10
  2.3 THE PUBLIC TOOLS INTERFACE 11
      2.3.1 The Two Tier Database 12
      2.3.2 Configuration Control 12
      2.3.3 The User Interface 13
      2.3.4 The Design Editor 14
  2.4 THE MAJOR TOOL SETS 14
      2.4.1 The MASCOT Tool Set 14
      2.4.2 The LSDM Tool Set 15
      2.4.3 The Ada Tool Set 15
  2.5 RESEARCH ACTIVITIES 16
  2.6 STATUS OF THE ECLIPSE PROGRAMME 16

3 The Management of Eclipse   **19**
  3.1 MANAGEMENT STRUCTURE 19
  3.2 REQUIREMENTS SPECIFICATION 20
  3.3 COMMUNICATION 21
  3.4 PLANNING 22
  3.5 MONITORING 22
  3.6 QUALITY MANAGEMENT 23
  3.7 CONTRACTUAL MATTERS 23

4 The Evolution of the Eclipse Kernel   **25**
  4.1 THE PURPOSE OF THE IPSE KERNEL 25
  4.2 INITIAL VIEW OF THE KERNEL 26
      4.2.1 Initial View of Data Representation 27
      4.2.2 Initial View of the User Interface 27

		4.2.3	Initial View of Distribution	28
	4.3	REFINED VIEW OF DATA REPRESENTATION		29
		4.3.1	Representing Detailed Data	29
		4.3.2	IDL and IDLE	30
		4.3.3	The Granularity Problem	30
		4.3.4	The Integrated Tools Interface	31
	4.4	REVISED VIEW OF THE KERNEL		32
		4.4.1	PCTE	32
		4.4.2	The Revised View of Data Representation	34
		4.4.3	Revised View of the User Interface	36
		4.4.4	Revised View of Distribution	36
	4.5	SUMMARY		36

5 The Eclipse Two-Tier Database 39

5.1	TWO-TIER DATABASE		39
5.2	THE FUNCTIONAL DATA MODEL		40
5.3	TYPES		41
5.4	IDLE		42
	5.4.1	Virtual Attributes	43
	5.4.2	Predefined Attributes	45
	5.4.3	Derived Attributes	45
5.5	FUNCTIONAL ANALYSIS OF PCTE		48
	5.5.1	Type Hierarchy	50
	5.5.2	Predefined Attributes	50
	5.5.3	USER DEFINED ATTRIBUTES	51
	5.5.4	Derived Attributes	52
5.6	THE ECLIPSE DATA MODEL		52
	5.6.1	Type Hierarchy	52
	5.6.2	Predefined Attributes	53
	5.6.3	User Defined Attributes	54
	5.6.4	Derived Attributes	55
5.7	THE DATABASE INTERFACE		57
5.8	NOTATION		59
5.9	BASIC DBI FUNCTIONS		60
	5.9.1	Root	60
	5.9.2	Creating Entities	60
	5.9.3	Reading and Writing Attribute Values	60
	5.9.4	Deleting Links	61
	5.9.5	Many-Valued Attributes and Iterators	61
5.10	OTHER DBI FUNCTIONS		62
	5.10.1	Manipulating Sequences	62
	5.10.2	Supporting Sets	63
	5.10.3	Copying Fine Structure	63
	5.10.4	Access to Type Information	64
5.11	CONFIGURATION CONTROL		65
5.12	CONCLUSION		67

CONTENTS

6 Interaction with Eclipse — 69
- 6.1 CONTROL PANELS — 70
  - 6.1.1 Control Panel Construction — 73
  - 6.1.2 Control Panel Implementation — 73
- 6.2 THE APPLICATIONS INTERFACE — 76
- 6.3 THE USER GUIDANCE SYSTEM — 78
  - 6.3.1 The Help System — 80
  - 6.3.2 Message Handling — 82
- 6.4 CONCLUSIONS — 84

7 The Design Editor — 85
- 7.1 INTRODUCTION — 85
- 7.2 GRAPHIC DESCRIPTION LANGUAGE — 86
- 7.3 THE SHAPES EDITOR — 89
- 7.4 THE DESIGN EDITOR (DE) — 90
- 7.5 DESIGN CHECKING — 92
- 7.6 DEVELOPMENT — 94

8 Eclipse as an APSE — 97
- 8.1 INTRODUCTION — 97
- 8.2 INTEGRATION — 98
- 8.3 THE CROSS-DEVELOPMENT SYSTEM — 99
- 8.4 A COMMON PROGRAM LIBRARY SYSTEM — 100
- 8.5 THE IADS TOOL — 102
- 8.6 CONFIGURATION MANAGEMENT — 103
  - 8.6.1 Derivations — 104
  - 8.6.2 Versions of program libraries — 104
  - 8.6.3 Sharing compilation units — 104
- 8.7 THE PROGRAM LIBRARY TOOL — 105
  - 8.7.1 Information Output — 105
  - 8.7.2 Modification functions — 106
- 8.8 FUTURE EXTENSIONS — 107

9 Development of the MASCOT 3 Tool Set — 109
- 9.1 INTRODUCTION — 109
- 9.2 HISTORY OF THE PROJECT — 110
- 9.3 OVERVIEW OF MASCOT — 111
  - 9.3.1 History — 111
  - 9.3.2 The Method — 111
  - 9.3.3 MASCOT 3 Representation — 113
- 9.4 SUPPORT FOR MASCOT 3 — 115
  - 9.4.1 Design Language — 115
  - 9.4.2 Scope of Method — 115
  - 9.4.3 Design Representation — 116
  - 9.4.4 Design Checking — 116
  - 9.4.5 Ada Generation and Compilation — 117
  - 9.4.6 Version and Configuration Control — 117

		9.4.7	Run Time Features	117
	9.5	MAPPING TO ADA		118
		9.5.1	Simple Template Implementations	119
		9.5.2	Subsystem Implementations	119
		9.5.3	System Implementations	120
	9.6	DESIGN OF THE MASCOT DATABASE		120
		9.6.1	MASCOT Database and Module Naming	120
		9.6.2	Module Representation	123
		9.6.3	Module Parts	125
		9.6.4	Ada Outputs	126
		9.6.5	Module Dependences and Participation	128
	9.7	THE TOOLSET		129
		9.7.1	Architecture	130
		9.7.2	User Interface	130
		9.7.3	Graphical Editing	131
		9.7.4	Locking	131
		9.7.5	The Tools	132
		9.7.6	Master Window Tool	133
		9.7.7	Display Tool	133
		9.7.8	Graphical Editor	136
		9.7.9	Textual Editor	138
		9.7.10	Status Control Tool	140
		9.7.11	Version/Configuration Control Tool	141
		9.7.12	Database Search Tool	141
		9.7.13	DRL Tool	142
	9.8	CONCLUSION		142
10	**The LSDM Tool Set**			**145**
	10.1	BACKGROUND		145
	10.2	WHAT IS LSDM?		145
	10.3	EARLY STAGES		148
	10.4	FACILITIES		148
	10.5	APPROACH		152
	10.6	LESSONS FOR TOOL BUILDERS		152
	10.7	THE TOOL BUILDER'S ENVIRONMENT		153
		10.7.1	Portable Common Tool Environment (PCTE)	153
		10.7.2	Two Tier Database	153
		10.7.3	Configuration Control	154
		10.7.4	Message System	154
		10.7.5	Applications Interface	154
		10.7.6	Help System	156
		10.7.7	Shapes Editor	156
		10.7.8	Graphical Description Language (GDL)	156
		10.7.9	Design Editor	157
	10.8	LIFE CYCLE SUPPORT		158
		10.8.1	Design	158
		10.8.2	Coding	159

CONTENTS ix

    10.8.3 Debugging 159
    10.8.4 Integration 160
    10.8.5 Validation 160
    10.8.6 Prototyping 160
10.9 SOME CONCLUSIONS 160

11 The System Structure Language   163
11.1 INTRODUCTION 163
11.2 THE LANGUAGE 164
    11.2.1 SySL and Configuration Descriptions 171
11.3 THE SySL TOOLKIT 172
    11.3.1 An Interactive System 174
    11.3.2 The SySL Language Browser and Structured Editor 175
    11.3.3 The SySL Build System 178
11.4 CONCLUSIONS 180

12 CDL and its Tools   181
12.1 BACKGROUND 181
12.2 GUIDELINES FOR REUSABILITY 181
12.3 THE COMPONENT DESCRIPTION LANGUAGE (CDL) 182
    12.3.1 CDL Version 1 183
    12.3.2 CDL Version 2 184
12.4 THE CDL TOOL SET 186
12.5 CONCLUSIONS 188

13 A Software Components Catalogue   189
13.1 INTRODUCTION 189
13.2 CLASSES OF SOFTWARE COMPONENT 191
13.3 COMPONENT INFORMATION BASE 192
    13.3.1 The cataloguing system 193
    13.3.2 Component Knowledge Representation 193
    13.3.3 Component Descriptor Frames 195
    13.3.4 The Catalogue User Interface 199
    13.3.5 Non-Functional Component Representation 201
13.4 SYSTEM EVALUATION 204
13.5 CONCLUSIONS 205

14 Distribution Issues for LAN Based IPSEs   207
14.1 IPSEs AND DISTRIBUTION 207
14.2 SUBSTRUCTURE REQUIREMENTS 208
14.3 PCTE DISTRIBUTION 209
14.4 ATOMIC TRANSACTIONS 210
14.5 IPSE TRANSACTIONS 210
    14.5.1 Long Term Transactions 211
    14.5.2 Nested Transactions 213
    14.5.3 Relationship with the IPSE Database 214
14.6 CONCLUSIONS 215

15 Distributed Systems Management and IPSEs   **217**
   15.1 BACKGROUND 217
   15.2 PCTE FROM A WAN VIEWPOINT 217
   15.3 IMPROVING PCTE DISTRIBUTION 218
   15.4 THE SIGDSM WORK 219
   15.5 MANAGING DISTRIBUTED SYSTEMS 220
      15.5.1 Review 221
      15.5.2 Services 221
      15.5.3 Domains 222
      15.5.4 Management Functions 225
      15.5.5 The Model 227
      15.5.6 Load Balancing 228
   15.6 SUMMARY 228

16 Achievements and Lessons   **229**
   16.1 COLLABORATION 229
   16.2 PLANNING 230
   16.3 TECHNICAL ACHIEVEMENTS 231
   16.4 CONCLUSION 232

Foreword

In some ways the Software Engineering part of the Alvey programme was the best. Certainly it had the best planned strategy. This was largely based on the work undertaken for the Alvey Committee, when a strategy was thrashed out in widespread consultation. Much of this strategy was implemented by the Directorate. Progress proved to be more difficult than in other parts of the programme, but the targets were more ambitious, and the work was at the frontiers of progress measured against the world scene.

Integrated Project Support Environments were a key element in the strategy; indeed the programme can claim to have popularised the use of the term IPSE. Eclipse was planned to represent something more advanced than the first generation of IPSE in the Alvey programme. Alderson and Bott place it in the second generation because it is based on a database and a distributed system of work stations linked by a local area network. A more advanced project, IPSE 2.5, was also planned but is still at a much earlier stage of development. Eclipse was able to take advantage of the emerging European software tool interface standard, PCTE, thus bringing welcome technical convergence of the Alvey and ESPRIT programmes.

I am very pleased that Frank Bott and his collaborators have put in the very considerable effort required to produce this book, for it is the first published record of all aspects of an Alvey project. It illustrates both the technical difficulties to be overcome and the significant advantages experienced in a cooperative effort for a project of this magnitude. Three firms and three universities were involved, making it one of the largest Alvey projects. This book makes a fascinating record of a cooperative project, demonstrating that with good management, progress can be made through cooperation that any one partner would have been quite incapable of achieving alone.

Brian Oakley

Preface

The Eclipse programme was established in 1984, as part of the Alvey Software Engineering Programme, with the goal of producing an experimental integrated project support environment (IPSE). The programme was led by Software Sciences Ltd (SSL); the other collaborators were CAP(UK) Ltd., Learmonth & Burchett Management Systems Plc (LBMS) and the Computer Science departments of the Universities of Lancaster and Strathclyde and of the University College of Wales, Aberystwyth (UCW).

The programme is now complete and, while many papers on individual aspects of the programme have been given at conferences or published in journals, the collaborators feel that it would be appropriate to publish a more complete and coherent view of the work that has been carried out — hence the present volume. It is intended primarily for workers in the field of software engineering environments and for those potential users of such environments whose interest goes beyond their functionality.

It should be emphasised that the Eclipse system described in this book is the system that was produced as a result of the Alvey project. Development of the system is continuing and commercially distributed versions are likely to have a wider range of tools and enhanced functionality in other ways.

A project like Eclipse does not spring to life from a void. Rather, it is the outcome of ideas, experiments and smaller, less ambitious systems which have either been originated by the participants or with which the participants are familiar from the literature. Many of the decisions made during the development of Eclipse can only be fully understood if viewed against this background — indeed the whole style of the project is a consequence of what went before. While much of this background is intangible, Chapter 1 presents the more concrete and more significant of the elements that led to the development of Eclipse.

Chapter 2 presents an overview of the Eclipse programme; it explains the objectives of the project and describes in outline the functionality of the system.

The management of a programme like Eclipse is a challenging task. The size of Eclipse was sufficient to ensure that all the traditional difficulties associated with large software projects would be present. The research element and the lack of a client in the traditional sense meant that the requirements specification was more than usually volatile. Six different organisations, all with different patterns of working, were involved; the three commercial partners each had their own legitimate commercial interests to protect. Chapter 3 describes the way in which the programme was managed, the difficulties encountered and the way in which these were overcome.

The next four chapters are concerned with the central facilities of Eclipse. Chapter 4 gives an overview of the architecture of the kernel and of the way in which it evolved during the course of the programme; it is the kernel which provides the fundamental mechanisms for achieving tool integration. The current version of Eclipse is built on PCTE (the ESPRIT funded Portable Common Tool Environment). However, the facilities provided by PCTE are at too low a level to be directly useful to most tool writers. Eclipse provides them with a higher level of interface, known as the Public Tools Interface (PTI); essentially this consists of a two tier database and a set of user interaction primitives. The two tier database is described in Chapter 5. From the users' point of view, a uniform style of interaction across all the tools is an important aspect of integration and the philosophy behind the Eclipse approach to the user interface is the subject of Chapter 6. Because the need to edit diagrams while maintaining constraints on their structure is a requirement common to many different design tools, a generic design editor was developed as part of the program; this is the subject of Chapter 7.

Chapters 8, 9 and 10 are concerned with the tools which constitute the basic Eclipse tool set. An IPSE which claims, as Eclipse does, to be language independent, should certainly be capable of functioning as an APSE. Ada development and cross development tools form part of the Eclipse tool set and are described in Chapter 8. In order to demonstrate how different methodologies can be supported effectively by the same IPSE, tool sets for MASCOT and LSDM (design methods oriented respectively towards embedded systems and information processing systems) were developed. Chapter 9 gives a detailed description of how the Eclipse facilities were used to produce a comprehensive MASCOT tool set; chapter 10 describes the experience of using Eclipse to produce the LSDM tools.

Other areas of work within the Eclipse programme were seen as primarily research areas, in the sense that they were not expected to produce more than prototype tools during the life time of the programme. The development of a language to describe the structure of large systems and of tools to support and use such descriptions is described in Chapter 11; tools to support and encourage the reuse of software are described in Chapter 12 and 13.

Work on distribution was originally expected to be very important in the implementation of Eclipse. The decision to base the project on PCTE, which already provides distribution mechanisms, albeit somewhat rudimentary, meant that this implementation work was no longer necessary. As a result, it became possible to carry out rather more fundamental work on distribution in IPSEs and this is the subject of chapters 14 and 15.

In the course of the programme, many of our ideas about IPSEs have changed. In the final chapter we attempt to evaluate the Eclipse programme and present the changes in our thinking to which it has led. The end of the Alvey programme is not, of course, the end of Eclipse. Eclipse is being used as a basis for other collaborative research projects, supported by the CEC, and there is substantial commercial interest in it. These developments too are briefly discussed in chapter 16.

Frank Bott

Aberystwyth

January 1989

Acknowledgements

The Eclipse programme would not have been possible without the generous support of the Alvey programme; our thanks are due to its Director, Brian Oakley, who has kindly contributed the foreword to this book, and to its successive Software Engineering Directors, David Talbot, Rob Witty and David Morgan. We owe a particular debt also to Howard Nicholls who was our main contact with the directorate throughout the life of the project.

The project was fortunate in having as Alvey monitoring officers three members of the National Computing Centre, Tony Ward (now of British Aerospace), Phil Mair and Reg Boot, all of whom showed great enthusiasm for the project and helped us in very many ways.

The project owes its birth and successful development to the vision of one man, David Rodway of Software Sciences. He was responsible for forming the consortium, for the initial negotiations with the Alvey directorate and for persuading Software Sciences to give the project their whole hearted support; throughout the project his wisdom prevented the inevitable differences between the partners from damaging the programme and his patience and light touch in negotiation enabled us to reach agreements with which everyone was content.

It is appropriate also to acknowledge here the role of Mike Falla (formerly of Software Sciences and now of the National Computer Centre); he was largely responsible for producing the very substantial proposal in numerous versions. Such was the expertise he acquired, that he turned gamekeeper and was seconded to the Alvey directorate.

The authors would particularly like to record their appreciation of the work of the late Bob Berry, whose untimely death robbed the programme of a popular and well liked figure, as well as a major technical contributor.

Very many people, too numerous to mention here, worked on Eclipse and their contributions to the project are gratefully acknowledged by the present authors.

List of Authors

A.Alderson	Software Sciences Ltd.
S.Beer	Strathclyde University
M.F.Bott	University College of Wales, Aberystwyth
J.Cartmell	Software Sciences Ltd.
D.Coffield	Lancaster University
A.Elliott	Software Sciences Ltd.
A.E.Elliston	Software Sciences Ltd.
J.Estdale	Learmonth and Burchett Management Systems
R.J.Gautier	University College of Wales, Aberystwyth
D.Hutchison	Lancaster University
M.Pickett	CAP (Scientific)
R.Pierce	Software Sciences Ltd
S.Potter	Software Sciences Ltd
M.B.Ratcliffe	University College of Wales, Aberystwyth
D.Shepherd	Lancaster University
J.Smart	CAP Group
I.Sommerville	Lancaster University
R.Thomson	Lancaster University
J.Walpole	Lancaster University
R.Welland	Glasgow University
M.Wood	Strathclyde University

Chapter 1

The Background to Eclipse

Albert Alderson and Frank Bott

The idea of an integrated project support environment cannot be ascribed to any individual or research group. Rather, it resulted from the coming together, on the one hand, of some 30 years of work in the development of programming methodology and operating systems and, on the other hand, a growing understanding and increasingly precise articulation of the needs of that part of the software industry which is concerned with the development of very large software systems. Equally, Eclipse was not conceived *de novo* but reflects both the experience and background of the partners and these wider ideas current in the software industry.

To understand why Eclipse is as it is and where it fits into the range of products which are described as IPSEs, it is necessary to understand something of the general historical background and something of the specific backgrounds of the partners.

1.1 HISTORICAL BACKGROUND

The earliest computers were not designed with the needs of the programmer in mind. Nothing more than the need to place programs into memory was accepted and this was met either by switches which allowed instructions, coded in binary, to be loaded laboriously one by one into memory, or by rudimentary binary loaders. The EDSAC 1 [136] was ahead of its time in 1949, in being equipped with a set of 'initial orders' which allowed programs written in a very simple form of assembly language to be loaded directly into memory.

By the end of the 1950s, two distinct threads became apparent in the development of the computer operating environment.

In higher education and in research organisations, programs are typically run only a few times once they have been developed. It is natural therefore for such organisations to place emphasis on easing the task of the programmer rather than on providing an efficient and robust environment for executing programs. Where such organisations had the expertise and the resources to develop their own systems, much effort was spent on the development of high level languages; hardware features to help in debugging were introduced; read-only memories were developed to make commonly used software such as assemblers and print routines easily accessible; and so on. The best known of these efforts was the Compatible Time Sharing System (CTSS) [23], developed as part of Project MAC at the Massachussets Institute of Technology. This type of system, essentially an environment oriented towards program development, has remained the model for the provision of computer services in higher education and research for over 20 years; only recently, with the availability of cheap, powerful work stations has this begun to change.

In the world of commerce and industry, it is normal for a suite of programs, once developed, to be run many hundreds of times, on a regular basis. The activity of production running dominates the use of the computer and usually takes precedence over new development. The need to get the most out of this very expensive machinery was therefore felt to be paramount — remember that, in 1960, a processor of the power of a VAX[1] 11/750 would cost over £1 million (1960 pounds!) — which meant providing an efficient, robust and reliable execution environment. The result was the development of operating systems which sought to optimise the use of processor time and memory, regardless of the inconvenience to the programmer. The later 60s and early 70s saw a consolidation of the work on commercial operating systems; such systems, if rarely elegant, became reliable and fairly efficient workhorses. Their effectiveness as software execution environments was greatly improved by the provision of teleprocessing monitors and database management systems; the use of high level languages, especially COBOL became normal.

In the industrial sector, a different style of execution environment was developed, the real time executive, and high level languages appropriate to this area, such as Coral and RTL2, became available.

All these developments helped to reduce the programming load — or, rather, helped to increase the programmer's effectiveness — but they were not aimed at assisting in the software development process as such. Under pressure from the need to sell to universities and research establishments, rudimentary time sharing facilities were grafted on to most commercially available operating systems but few of these were properly integrated into the main system; indeed, it sometimes happened that the time sharing facilities would not permit the development of programs to run in the main execution environment.

The idea that the software development environment and the execution environment need not be one and the same seems to be a very old one, albeit rarely mentioned in the literature. Normally it seems to have been viewed as a convenience (e.g. preparing software for a new machine on an existing one) rather than as desirable situation which could be exploited to improve the development process. Only in the mid 1970s was the desirability of working in this manner explicitly recognised; the classic paper is [58] which describes UNIX[2] as a 'programmers' work bench'.

The same period saw the development of CADES [115] which can fairly claim to be the first *project* support environment. This is a specialist environment supporting a large group of people working on ICL's mainframe operating system. It was ahead of its time in the sense that, with the hardware costs of the mid 70s and the comparatively unsophisticated software development methods of the time, it proved a very expensive system to run. Nevertheless, the high quality of the software produced with its aid

---
[1] VAX is a trademark of the Digital Equipment Corporation
[2] UNIX is a trademark of AT&T Bell Laboratories

1.2. SDS, FOUNDATION AND GAMMA

demonstrated the value of the idea. The development of PSL/PSA [122] took place at about the same time as CADES and demonstrated the potential for software tools to support the early phases of the life cycle.

The Stoneman report [15], articulated publicly for the first time the need for a software development environment, independent of any execution environment, to support the construction of very large, complex systems which were expected to be long lived. In the Ada[3] context such an environment was called an Ada Programming Support Environment (APSE). The need to replace the file store of the conventional time sharing system by a database was explicitly recognised; the need to support programming in the large and the need to provide support throughout the life cycle, from initial requirements determination to final phasing out, were emphasised. Three levels of provision were distinguished: the kernel APSE (KAPSE), which provides the support services needed by the tools; the minimal APSE (MAPSE), which provides a small tool set, adequate for developing systems (including itself) but no more; and the full APSE, which provides a tool-rich environment for developing high quality systems with high programmer productivity.

The Stoneman report stimulated an interest in support environments which has continued, at a steadily increasing level of activity, to the present. The word 'programming' has been replaced by 'project', as a result of the recognition that the APSE would support all aspects of a software development project; the reference to Ada has been dropped with the realisation that few of the characteristics of an APSE are specific to Ada while its replacement by 'integrated' emphasises the idea of tool cooperation. The result is the term 'IPSE'. The term 'software engineering environment' (SEE) has also come into use and is, more or less, synonymous with IPSE.

1.2 SDS, FOUNDATION and GAMMA

In 1972, with support from the Royal Radar Establishment (RRE, now the Royal Signals and Radar Establishment, RSRE), Software Sciences developed a specification for a system to provide integrated support for the development of large software systems [34]. The system was subsequently implemented jointly by RSRE and SSL and marketed under the name of the Software Development System (SDS); it was sold to a number of large organisations who used it successfully and was the subject of a STARTS debrief report [89]. SDS was essentially conceived as a single user system and much of its operation was in batch mode; it was followed by SDS-2 [2], a system with similar functionality to SDS but with multi-user, interactive operation. SDS-2 was developed with the aid of the National Computing Centre's Software Products Scheme.

SDS was designed around the idea of using a central database, based on the ERA (entity, relationship, attribute) data model, to record details about the products of the development process, to relate them to the recorded plan, and to relate both to details of staff. (The development products themselves were not held.) This approach had been successful but the need to hold the development products and to add configuration management was becoming clear.

Early in 1983, SSL, in collaboration with Aberystwyth, began work on a project

---

[3]Ada is a trademark of the US Government – Ada Joint Program Office

which was later to become known as Foundation [3]. The intention was to build, on top of SDS-2, the kernel of an IPSE, including facilities for automated configuration control and automatic system building. Existing SDS-2 facilities could be used to provide extensive project management capabilities. The configuration control and system building facilities were developed from ideas in Saviour [10], a prototype system developed at Aberystwyth in collaboration with SPL. Foundation was to run on VAX computers, using VMS[4] as the host operating system. Its development was supported by the National Computing Centre under the Software Products Scheme.

Foundation viewed the development process as a series of transformations carried out on successive representations of the developing system by applying tools. Some tools cause automatic transformations (e.g. compilers); some tools cause manual transformations (e.g. editors). The idea was that Foundation would automatically record the transformations as they were initiated by the user. A derivation network of relationships between development products would thus be captured. This would allow automatic recapitulation of the development process with consequent benefit to the maintenance function. It would also allow impact analysis for change proposals. Foundation also recorded the names of the files representing the life cycle products.

The automatic capture of the derivation network required that Foundation should be the means by which tools were invoked. The implication was that Foundation should be an *open* IPSE, in the sense that other tool suppliers would be encouraged to make their tools run under Foundation and would be provided with the facilities necessary to do this.

Closely related to the SDS-2 development was a programming language called Gamma [33] developed by SSL in the late 1970s, with some support from RSRE. This language had many of the features of Ada but was based more on Algol68 than on Pascal. Gamma was implemented in the form of a language specific, integrated support environment somewhat similar to Interlisp [123]. The source language components are held in a tree structured database which enables system building to be done automatically. Gamma was used to implement SDS-2.

1.3 ADA AND THE APSE

Following the adoption of Ada by the United States Department of Defense (DoD), a group of UK software houses, including Software Sciences, carried out, with support from the UK Department of Industry, a design study for an APSE, to include a production quality Ada compiler [128].

As a result of this work, Ada Group Ltd., a consortium made up of Software Sciences Ltd, Systems Designers Ltd, Systems Programming Ltd and ICL, started work on the development of the MCHAPSE, an APSE which was to include an Ada compiler and support for CHILL [12], the telecommunications programming language. This work was supported by a consortium of UK public bodies but the project had eventually to be abandoned due to lack of funding. Nevertheless, substantial progress had been made and the ideas developed in this project and in the APSE design study were to provide valuable input to the Eclipse design work.

---

[4]VMS is a trademark of the Digital Equipment Corporation

1.4. SOFTWARE DEVELOPMENT METHODS

One of the products of the MCHAPSE project, a tool called MIDL (Modified IDL, now the property of British Telecomm), was to prove more directly useful for Eclipse. IDL (Interface Description Language [90]) is a language for defining data structures; the IDL processor then generates access procedures to these data structures. MIDL was a modified and extended version of IDL from which Ada code could be generated. IDLE (IDL for Eclipse) was a further modification which was extensively used in Eclipse. The use of IDLE in Eclipse is described more extensively in Chapter 4.

Quite separately from these externally funded initiatives, CAP were working on retargeting the Telesoft Ada compiler to produce code for the Intel[5] 80286 processor and on the development of supporting cross-development tools.

1.4 SOFTWARE DEVELOPMENT METHODS

The need to impose a discipline and a structure on the process of software development has been recognised for very many years. The 1970s saw the development of many so-called 'structured methods' which aim to do precisely this. A number of such methods have achieved widespread use and can reasonably claim to be successful. A major difficulty in adopting such methods is the administrative burden of keeping the very many products of the development process up to date and in step with each other; the difficulty is exacerbated by the fact that many of these products take the form of diagrams.

It was natural to look to the computer itself to assist in overcoming this difficulty and tools were developed for many of the major methods to do just this. The arrival of comparatively cheap, powerful work stations with bit mapped displays and pointing devices was a major advance since it allowed diagrammatic material to be maintained on the computer. Such tools can only be fully effective if they are capable of interworking, that is, if they use common data formats; it is also very desirable that they should have a common user interface so as to avoid placing a heavy burden on the memory and learning capacity of their users. These needs were part of the motivation for articulating the concept of an IPSE and the provision of tools to support structured development methods was an objective of Eclipse from the start.

All three industrial partners were able to bring to Eclipse extensive and relevant experience of software development methods. SSL and CAP had both used MASCOT [111] extensively and SSL had developed a set of MASCOT support tools for a client; work had also been carried out on tailoring SDS2 to support software development using JSD [60]. CAP had been a member of the AUGUSTA consortium which had carried out a major study of the use of software development methods with Ada, on behalf of the UK Department of Industry [127]. LBMS had developed a very successful database design method in 1977/78. This was expanded into SSADM (Structured Systems Analysis and Design Method) [78] in a joint development with the UK government's Central Computer and Telecommunications Agency (CCTA) during 1981. LSDM (the LBMS Structured Development Method) was developed from SSADM as LBMS' own commercial offering. By 1984 LBMS had already developed some prototype support tools for LSDM.

This experience, together with their dominant position in the UK IT industry, led

---

[5]Intel is a trademark of the Intel Corporation

to the choice of LSDM, MASCOT and JSD as the methods for which tool support in Eclipse would initially be provided.

Also relevant to this area is the work that CAP were carrying out on the development of a user interaction manager [113]; this product was ultimately used as part of Eclipse.

1.5 FORMATION OF THE ECLIPSE CONSORTIUM

The Alvey programme was initiated in the latter half of 1983 and the document 'Alvey Software Engineering — a Strategy Overview' was published in November 1983. It was clear from this document that the work on Foundation lay firmly in the integration area of the Alvey Software Engineering Strategy; further, collaboration with other companies and other academic institutions, with support from the Alvey programme, offered the possibility of extending Foundation so as to produce something approaching a full IPSE, rather than just a kernel. SSL accordingly decided to take the lead in forming a consortium.

Discussions began immediately with SPL International. Although SPL and SSL were competitors, relations between the two companies were good; SPL were able to offer both parallel experience in areas such as Ada and the APSE and complementary experience in MASCOT and in knowledge based techniques. LBMS and SSL had already had some preliminary discussions about the possibility of a joint venture to develop tools; their inclusion in the consortium meant that Eclipse would be able to include tools suitable for information system development as well as embedded systems and was also in accordance with the Directorate's policy of encouraging smaller companies to participate in the programme.

Aberystwyth's participation as one of the academic partners was a natural consequence of the collaboration on Foundation. Strathclyde's interest in, and experience of, MMI research and software development methods made them also natural participants. SSL already had contacts with Lancaster in other areas and were happy to be able to bring their expertise in distribution into the consortium.

In the spring of 1984, the consortium was shaken by the news that the owners of SPL, Western Broadcasting of Canada, had sold the company to Systems Designers Ltd. Since System Designers was already the managing partner of an Alvey project concerned with research in IPSE technology, it asked the other members of the Eclipse consortium to release SPL from its obligations. This was done but created the urgent need for another partner. CAP(UK) was approached and agreed to join the consortium. Inevitably, however, this involved major changes to the proposal; CAP's interests were different to SPL's and had to be accommodated. The major change was that an Ada development system would become part of the Eclipse tool set, replacing some of the tools which SPL would have contributed.

The final version of the proposal was completed and submitted in May 1984 and approved by the Alvey Directorate early in July. Contract letters were sent by the Directorate to the industrial partners in August allowing a start date for charging purposes of 1.7.84. Funding for the academic partners had to be routed through the Science and Engineering Research Council who were, unfortunately, unable to match the commendable despatch of the Directorate; contract letters to the academic partners were not sent until January 1985, with the start of the contract back-dated to 1.10.84. Given that the academic partners needed to recruit staff to work on the project, this meant that much of the academic work was very late in starting.

1.6 OTHER IPSE DEVELOPMENTS

The Alvey software engineering strategy envisaged three generations of IPSE development. The first generation would be file based systems, essentially sets of cooperating tools running under UNIX. The second generation would use a database (network, relational or ERA) in place of a file system and would include support for distributed working. The third generation would be knowledge based and include 'intelligent tools'.

A recent review [112] suggests that there are over 100 software project support environments being developed, in experimentation or being sold. The Alvey classification into generations is still useful, although there are important characteristics that it fails to address.

The first generation of environments is available in the market place. Typically, the range of tools is very restricted and the user interface is fairly primitive; in many cases, there is little evidence of real integration. Despite these limitations, such environments can be valuable and the commercial success which some of them have achieved demonstrates that a need exists; furthermore, their comparative lack of sophistication means that less effort is needed to bring them into productive use. Typical examples of such IPSEs are BIS/IPSE [109], an IPSE oriented towards information systems development, ALS [124], strictly speaking an APSE rather than an IPSE, and GENOS [52], a first generation IPSE with a well integrated user interface. CASE (Computer Aided Software Engineering) workbenches can usually be regarded as also falling into this category.

A second generation IPSE is essentially the product specified in Stoneman and Eclipse falls into this category, along with ASPECT [48]. The only second generation IPSEs such products available commercially at the time of writing (January 1988), so far as the authors are aware, are the Rational APSE [5] and the Apollo DSEE [72]. They are true second generation IPSEs so far as the use of the database is concerned, but in other ways they are very limited, particularly in their support for distribution.

ISTAR [119] and IPSE 2.5 [94], [137] exhibit features which are not addressed by the Alvey classification. ISTAR provides good support for a limited form of distributed development; it also incorporates a model of the software development process which serves as another axis of integration. IPSE 2.5 is taking the notion of process modelling much further; instead of the single model built into ISTAR, facilities are provided to allow an organisation to define its own model or models. ISTAR and IPSE 2.5 are *active* IPSEs, in the sense that they lead the user through the tasks he must carry out. Other important characteristics of IPSE 2.5 are its support for formal methods and its use of a fine-grained database.

Work on knowledge based IPSEs, the Alvey third generation, is still very much at the research stage; the Alvey ISM project falls into this category and [98] indicates one way in which research on intelligent tools might proceed.

Given this plethora of IPSE developments, the tool supplier is in a difficult position; how does he overcome the difficulty of interfacing his tools economically to all these IPSEs or how does he decide which IPSEs will be commercially successful. There is a clear need for a standard for the *tool support interface,* the interface which an IPSE offers to the tools which it supports.

There are two distinct efforts in this area.

In the United States, as a result of an initiative from the DoD's Ada Joint Program Office, a joint service team, known as the KAPSE Interface Team (KIT) and a complementary KAPSE Interface Team from Industry and Academia (KITIA) were formed to work towards a set of APSE interface standards to permit the sharing of tools and other software between DoD supported APSEs. This set of standards is known as the Common APSE Interface Set (CAIS). The first version of CAIS was published as 'proposed DOD-STD-1838 (CAIS)' in 1987. A number of prototype implementations of this version of CAIS have been produced. In parallel with the definition of the first version of CAIS, KIT/KITIA established a set of Requirements and Design Criteria (the RAC) for APSE interfaces. A second version of CAIS, known as CAIS-A, is being developed to meet the RAC.

In Europe, a project with the title 'A Basis for a Portable Common Tool Environment' was initiated by a consortium of six European computer manufacturers, under the CEC's ESPRIT programme, in 1983. The tool interface itself has become known as PCTE and its specification [96] is now relatively stable. PCTE is technically more advanced than the first version of CAIS and meets most of the requirements of the RAC, except in the area of security. The French government have sponsored a project (Emeraude) to produce a production quality implementation of PCTE and the ESPRIT programme has funded the porting of this implementation to a variety of machines, including Sun/UNIX, [6] VAX/UNIX, VAX/VMS and IBM/PC, as part of the Sapphire project [121]. The current version of Eclipse is based on PCTE and so will be all future versions.

More details of PCTE and CAIS, together with a comparative analysis, will be found in [80] and [81]

---

[6]Sun, Sun Workstation and SunWindows are trademarks of Sun Microsystems, Inc.

Chapter 2

Overview of the Eclipse Programme

Albert Alderson and Frank Bott

2.1 OBJECTIVES OF THE PROGRAMME

The purpose of the Eclipse Programme was to develop an Integrated Project Support Environment (IPSE) of the kind described in the US DoD Stoneman document [15] to populate it with tools to support several software development methods and to support Ada. The features which characterise such an IPSE are its use of a database to hold all data relating to a project, and its provision of a kernel of facilities supporting the development of tools. Such a kernel should provide for all of a tool's requirements with respect to execution, inter-process communication, input-output and database access (at least). Provided that tools use only the defined interface to the kernel, they will be portable to other implementations of the same interface.

The intention was to develop the underlying support facilities and then build tools which would demonstrate how such facilities enable integrated tools to be built. It was not our intention to develop a complete IPSE product. The programme has not concerned itself with tools for project management, at Alvey's request. Rather, it has concentrated on tools for the software development life cycle in a configuration controlled environment. Omitting such a large area of potential tool development has forced us to consider how to integrate existing tools and how to enable third parties to develop integrated tools for Eclipse. These considerations have had a considerable impact upon the direction of the programme, leading us ultimately to base our work on PCTE (see below), and strongly influencing the design of the interface to our kernel facilities, the Public Tools Interface (PTI).

The word 'integrated' in the term IPSE is susceptible of various interpretations. One interpretation is exemplified by systems such as Interlisp. [123] or POPLOG [50]. In effect, such systems consist of a single tool which allows the user to invoke any action at any time; the effect depends on the current state of the user's environment. In a sense this is the ultimate integration. However such systems seem to be designed to support programming in the small rather than programming in the large; furthermore, it is usually difficult to add new facilities or to use existing tools without having access to the kernel.

Stoneman has a different interpretation of 'integrated'. Tools cooperate with each other by sharing data structures which are held in a common database. The procedures which provide access to this database are responsible for maintaining consistency and for enforcing, for example, appropriate version control disciplines. At a very primitive level, it may be said that UNIX adopts this interpretation of 'integrated'; the common database is the UNIX file store and the shared data structures are byte strings.

Integration in the Stoneman sense was one objective of Eclipse. However, it was also our objective to build an environment which was integrated in a different but equally important sense — consistency of the user interface — an idea present implicitly in Stoneman but never really developed there. Obviously the user interface to a graphical design editor and an Ada compiler cannot be identical, but we can require the principle of minimum surprise to hold. Pressing the same button on the mouse or keyboard should have a predictably similar effect and two things that look the same should have the same properties; if an item is to be selected from a menu, the choice should always be indicated in the same way.

It was not our intention, nor would it have been possible within our time and resource constraints, to construct an IPSE of full production quality. Nevertheless, to provide a convincing demonstration of the effectiveness of our approach, it was necessary that the kernel facilities be implemented to something approaching production quality and that the tools themselves should be something better than mere prototypes; as a result substantial efforts have been expended in quality control.

2.2 IMPLEMENTATION ENVIRONMENT

Eclipse was always intended to form the basis of a range of commercially exploitable products; it was therefore essential the hardware and software environment on which it runs should have a long life ahead of it. A major concern was to provide user interaction modes more sophisticated than the usual textual representation of data and commands. This led us to decide that we should use bit-mapped screen technology with a pointing device such as a mouse. The computational load and memory requirements of such devices demand the provision of personal work stations. This decision immediately forced us to consider networks of such work stations and the implications of distributing an IPSE over such a network.

A substantial amount of effort was expended at the start of the programme in deciding on the choice of work station and of local area network (LAN) technology. At the time the effort seemed excessive but with hindsight it was well worthwhile; the final choice — Sun Microsystems work stations with Ethernet technology for the LAN — has been abundantly justified by developments in the marketplace over the past three years. Our original plans envisaged a Digital Equipment Corporation VAX computer as being, in some sense, the centre of the network but the development of high performance machines by Sun and the spectacular improvements in their price/performance ratios has rendered this unnecessary.

The choice of operating system was somewhat easier. UNIX was already part of the

2.3. THE PUBLIC TOOLS INTERFACE

SERC Common Base Policy and therefore very acceptable to the academic partners. Its increasingly important position in the market place, its portability and the wide range of tools available to run under it made it equally acceptable to the industrial partners. Which version of UNIX to choose was more difficult. The availability and widespread use of Berkeley 4.2bsd made it the obvious choice but it was recognised that System V would be important in the longer term.

The first version of Eclipse was based on Berkeley 4.2bsd and SDS2 (see chapter 1) but it rapidly became apparent that the Portable Common Tool Environment (PCTE, [96]), a development financed by the European Community's ESPRIT programme, was likely to provide a *de facto* standard as base for future IPSE developments in Europe and that it would therefore be appropriate, for both technical and commercial reasons, to use this as the basis for all future versions of Eclipse. The only production version of PCTE under development was being developed by the French group GIE Emeraude using UNIX System V on a Bull SPS7 work station. Three of the Eclipse partners (Software Sciences, CAP and Aberystwyth) have collaborated with GIE Emeraude in an ESPRIT funded project, one part of which has involved the porting of this PCTE implementation to the Sun. It is this which now forms the base layer on which Eclipse is implemented.

It was originally intended that most of the implementation of Eclipse would be carried out in Ada. Unfortunately, the quality of the Ada compilers available at the time, together with the difficulties of accessing facilities on the Suns from Ada, made this impracticable and it was reluctantly decided that most of the system would be written in C. The situation regarding Ada compilers is now (January 1988) much improved.

2.3 THE PUBLIC TOOLS INTERFACE

Technically PCTE offers much of the kernel interface required to produce the Public Tools Interface. It provides database and user interface facilities upon which the Eclipse facilities can be built. It provides a mechanism, albeit limited, for local area distribution. It also gives a simple way of incorporating non-Eclipse tools. The latter is particularly significant in view of the extensive range of software engineering tools being developed to run under PCTE. However, the facilities of PCTE are at a fairly rudimentary level — there are no configuration control facilities, for example — and a substantial amount of work is required to make these facilities readily usable by the tool builder.

In order to provide kernel facilities at a level convenient for the tool builder and ensure consistent patterns of user interaction and database usage, we have built a second layer on top of PCTE and the interface which this presents is known as the Public Tools Interface (PTI), already referred to. Most of the tool development within Eclipse uses the PTI and its specification [28] is available to anyone considering building tools to run under Eclipse. However, the standard PCTE and UNIX interfaces are available so that tools using these interfaces directly can also run under Eclipse.

2.3.1 The Two Tier Database

Perhaps the major distinguishing feature of Eclipse is its database interface. In PCTE and in various commercially available IPSEs such as ISTAR [119] and BIS/IPSE [109], the objects held in the database are treated as simple files; while the objects themselves are regarded as entities with attributes and relationships, nothing is said about the structure of their contents. This presents the tool builder with a dilemma. If more than one tool is to manipulate the same class of object then either the physical structure of the objects must be built into the tool, with a consequent loss of all the advantages of using a database, or the objects must be broken down into atomic items and these items treated as individual database objects, leading to unacceptable performance problems.

In our view this is a major weakness. The means of integrating tools is to be through access to common structures in the database, but the majority of data is being treated as having no structure. This is plainly not the case. Contents frequently have a well defined structure. For example a design diagram consists of nodes and arcs, and a document consists of chapters, sections, paragraphs, figures, cross-references etc.

This problem has been overcome in Eclipse by using a two tier database. The first tier represents objects just as in PCTE. The second tier represents entities within the contents of objects. From the point of view of the individual tool, however, this division is invisible.

We have also introduced the notion of versioning of objects into our database. This is done by introducing an item of which certain objects are versions. Special facilities are provided for introducing new versions and for selecting the required version of an item. Unless specific action is taken the database will always select the latest version of an item.

Allowing objects to be structured internally is however only part of the solution. If we consider an object representing a document, for example, it is likely to contain cross-references to other documents and perhaps to other chapters, sections or figures in those documents. Similarly a diagram may be part of a hierarchy of design information; a node on such a diagram may be further defined by other diagrams or documents or program text, etc.

In the Eclipse database we allow relationships to exist between entities in the first or the second tier and other entities in the first or second tier. These relationships can relate to specific versions or can be indirect via the item. The latter possibility allows the particular version of interest to be selected using the configuration control facilities, described below.

2.3.2 Configuration Control

In Eclipse configuration control is concerned with identifying which versions of which items are to be utilised in a particular circumstance. The system is based on a configuration object which has references to a subset of versions of items. When following a relationship involving versions, the database chooses the latest version of the item from the current configuration. Any number of different configurations may be created.

When a user is developing some item, versions are created which must remain private until they are of adequate quality. When a version reaches this state it is

2.3. THE PUBLIC TOOLS INTERFACE

'published'. Once published the version cannot be modified. Others may now use the version but they are not compelled to do so. If they wish to use it in some configuration then they 'acquire' it into that configuration. If they no longer wish to use it they 'release' it from that configuration. When no other user has the version acquired, the owner may 'withdraw' it. He then has the right to modify or destroy it.

2.3.3 The User Interface

The Eclipse user interface is designed to utilise bit-mapped screens with both mouse and keyboard input. It offers multiple windows each of which may display multiple frames. The frames may be text, graphics, control panel or message frames. The windows may be iconised. The interface handles the full range of interactions from text to graphics.

In designing the user interface for a set of integrated tools, the first need is to establish some guiding principle or metaphor for the pattern of interaction. Many systems intended for use in an office environment use a desk-top metaphor, for example. In Eclipse we have chosen a control panel metaphor, as being more appropriate to the environment in which it is expected to be used. We treat the interface to a complex piece of software in a similar way to the interface to a complex piece of hardware. The user has various interaction possibilities such as buttons, indicator lights, menus, and signs. The latter are areas of the frame with a title. These can be used for both display and input of values. Such values may be selected from fixed or dynamically created menus.

The control panel metaphor establishes a framework for communication between the user and the system but it is not enough, by itself, to ensure a consistent user interface; standards are required for the presentation of data and for interaction with the system. The best way to ensure that such standards are adhered to is to provide a library of software components which implement them; this has been done in Eclipse. The same technique has been used to ensure consistency in the provision of help facilities and the display of messages.

The control panel metaphor, together with the standards and conventions governing the way in which it is used constitutes the Eclipse .ul house style; the software which implements the house style constitutes the Eclipse Applications Interface (AI). The AI is designed as a communication channel between the user and the tool.

The result of this approach is that the tool is not concerned with the manner of presentation of data. It needs to provide values for the user to see and it needs to get values from the user. However the precise nature of the interaction is not important to the tool. For example, where a tool wishes the user to select a value from a set, the user could be asked to choose from a menu with all options on display, or cycle through a set with one at a time on display, or type a value which is checked to confirm it is a member of the set. How the value is obtained and which part of the window is used in the interaction is not important to the tool; these decisions are handled by the AI.

The actual presentation to the user is however important and getting the total image which is presented to the user 'just right' can involve a lot of tinkering. We have chosen therefore to describe the interaction style and layout by means of a language called FDL, Format Description Language. The description can be altered independently of the tool. It is possible for each user to have his own description of the interface to a tool — this is valuable since 'good user interface' is very subjective. A careful balance has to be drawn between the advantages of total uniformity on the one hand and tailoring the interface to the nature of the individual tool on the other.

2.3.4 The Design Editor

The great majority of methods in use in software engineering employ diagrammatic notations. Any tool set for such a method clearly needs a diagram editor; it should be capable not only of maintaining neat diagrams but also of checking that the diagram being produced conforms to the rules of the method. Rather than produce a separate editor for each method, it was decided to produce a generic diagram editor that could be parameterised by definitions of the graphical representations and the semantics of any method.

This definition is in two parts. A graphic description language, GDL, is used to define the semantics, while the symbols used are designed using the Shapes Editor. Our approach is based on the premise that a design diagram is a directed graph which can be represented by nodes and links. From these two basic types of entity, most design diagrams can be constructed.

2.4 THE MAJOR TOOL SETS

The Eclipse programme has developed three major tool sets. Two of these support design methods — LSDM and MASCOT 3 — while the third supports the Ada programming language. Together they span a large part of the software development cycle: LSDM addresses the phases from requirement specification to physical system design, MASCOT 3 addresses primarily the detailed design phases leading to a physical system design, and the Ada facilities address implementation; we have not directly addressed testing.

2.4.1 The MASCOT Tool Set

The MASCOT 3 tool set in Eclipse is aimed at the production of systems written in Ada using the MASCOT 3 method. The MASCOT 3 support consists of tools which allow the design to be captured, manipulated and checked using the standard MASCOT 3 diagrammatic representations. During the checking phase, Ada packages corresponding to the design can be generated automatically and the necessary compilation operations initiated.

The tool set is controlled by the user from a master window. From this window, the user sets various global values and invokes the tools of the tool set.

The MASCOT view of configuration management is different from the Eclipse view described above but the Eclipse kernel is sufficiently flexible to accommodate it. A status control tool is used to maintain the three possible status levels: registered, introduced and enrolled. It causes the necessary checking to be undertaken and, where appropriate, causes Ada packages to be generated and compiled. A configuration control tool is provided which uses the PTI configuration control facilities and the

2.4. THE MAJOR TOOL SETS

MASCOT 3 status information to control the production of versions of the design and the implementation.

Tools are also provided to produce textual versions of the design, using the standard MASCOT 3 textual design representation language, and to allow the MASCOT design database to be interrogated.

The MASCOT 3 tool set makes use of the Eclipse Integrated Ada Development System to control and compile the Ada source and to manipulate its Ada program libraries.

2.4.2 The LSDM Tool Set

LSDM is a data driven, requirements analysis and system design method; it uses such concepts as entity models, dataflow diagrams, entity-event matrices and entity life histories to develop a logical system design consisting of database schemas and process specifications. The LSDM tool set is designed to support the major elements of the systems analysis part of LSDM. It aims to reduce the analyst's work load by managing the data as it is collected and providing easy access for recording, reviewing and updating it. This data may be captured as diagrams or on the Eclipse equivalent of paper forms.

The LSDM tool set enables users to develop LSDM diagrams of three types: dataflow diagrams, logical data structures and entity life histories. Each is supported by an instance of the Eclipse generic design editor. The applications interface is used directly to provide a variety of LSDM forms. Relevant ones can be accessed from within the design editor. A master window tool acts as a control panel for the tool set, specifying the design model to be accessed and invoking other tools. All design data is held in the two-tier data base.

(LSDM itself goes beyond the logical system design to handle some aspects of physical design but tools to support these activities are not included in Eclipse.)

2.4.3 The Ada Tool Set

Eclipse provides an integrated tool set for the development of Ada programs, known as IADS (Integrated Ada Development System). The facilities provided are based on the Telesoft Ada compiler for the Sun work station and the Telesoft-INTEL 80286 cross development facilities being developed by CAP.

IADS is a tool which provides control panel access to the Ada development facilities of Eclipse. It enables the user to select a step in the development of Ada programs and supply the required parameters. IADS creates the various database objects required by the Ada tools and maintains the relationships between them.

The steps that IADS supports are:

- creation and editing of Ada source;

- creation of program libraries;

- Ada compilations;

- Ada linking;

- cross-assembly of INTEL 80286 assembler;
- linking and creation of target images and PROM burning;
- host execution of Ada programs;
- target execution of Ada programs;
- host and target symbolic debugging;
- version controlled program library maintenance.

The system is designed in such a way as to enable further targets to be readily accommodated and also to allow other Ada compilers to be easily integrated.

2.5 RESEARCH ACTIVITIES

In addition to the work so far described in this chapter, work of a more speculative research character has been carried out within the programme, largely by the academic partners.

Software reuse is an area of software engineering whose importance is widely recognised and to which the programme has devoted significant efforts. The problems we have addressed are the cataloguing of components so as to facilitate their retrieval for reuse and the assembly of such components to produce complete systems or subsystems. This latter aspect of the work has a strong emphasis on interfaces and because of this, and in keeping with the rest of the work in the programme, we have concentrated on components written in Ada. The work is based on a component description language, CDL, and on the use of diagrammatic techniques to assemble components described in CDL, from which the Ada text of the complete system is generated. Related work has developed a notation for describing the structure of complex systems and produced tools to process such descriptions.

Research on development methods has been pursued in two areas. The first is the development of the generic design editor, already referred to; the success of this work is evident from the fact that it has been possible to incorporate the design editor in the Eclipse kernel but there remain aspects which are still the subject of research. The other area of research on development methods is a study of how sequences of methods can be created with automatic transformation between outputs and inputs.

Research on user interfaces is concerned with evaluating the Eclipse user interface with a view to improving it and, more generally, discovering principles which can be applied to the design of user interfaces for complex software systems such as IPSEs.

The distribution work is considering the problems of wide area communication between IPSEs such as would occur between contractors on a large project. The utility of intermittent connection by mail systems is of particular interest.

2.6 STATUS OF THE ECLIPSE PROGRAMME

At the time of writing (January 1988), the Eclipse programme is close to completion. A complete version of the system as described in sections 2.3 and 2.4 above has been

2.6. STATUS OF THE ECLIPSE PROGRAMME

demonstrated publicly on a number of occasions. The research work is scheduled to continue until the end of September 1988 and some of the results of this work, in particular the work on software reuse will be integrated into the Eclipse system.

Where we go next with Eclipse will be determined by many factors, not least the interests of potential users. However the work we have already done indicates a number of possible directions and some of the research work is continuing with the support of other government and EEC programmes.

There would be value in providing support for further methods. A limited tool set for JSD was developed for the first version of Eclipse and we are therefore well placed to develop a more comprehensive one for the current version. We have studied CORE and have produced a very detailed draft design for its support. In both cases the generic facilities of Eclipse allow a basic level of support to be developed very quickly.

Document preparation is a very important area which we have yet to address. We would wish to enable documents to be represented as structures within the Eclipse database. The interaction between documentation and design and implementation information could then be modelled. This in turn would permit the provision of quality control facilities based on the cross-referencing of design and implementation with requirements, design, test and change control documents. However we would wish to provide document hard copy production by interfacing to some system such as Fortune [84].

The industrialisation of successful products of research is part of the planned programme. In particular we expect that the software reuse work will produce interesting tools.

Chapter 3

The Management of Eclipse

Frank Bott and Tony Elliston

Looking back to the start of the Eclipse project, one can see all the ingredients for a classic software engineering disaster. The scale of the project was large — some 200 man years spread over three and a half years of elapsed time — and the activities were dispersed over six organisations and seven or eight geographically separated sites; in addition, it was a technically complex development, with a large research element, and there was no detailed requirements specification. In retrospect, starting such a project at all looks foolhardy.

Nevertheless, the project proved to be a success. While this success is in very large measure due to the hard work and technical insight evident in the following chapters, it could only have been achieved within a framework of effective project management, which this chapter describes.

Effective project management depends ultimately on planning, monitoring and quality control and these will be dealt with individually in the later sections of the chapter. However, in the special circumstances of Eclipse, the need to establish a management and reporting structure, the need to define more clearly the goals of the project and the need to set up effective communication mechanisms were essential preliminaries.

3.1 MANAGEMENT STRUCTURE

As envisaged in the Eclipse proposal and confirmed in the collaboration agreement between the partners, the programme was under the overall control of the Eclipse Steering Group. This was chaired by SSL's Software Technology Director and consisted of the Manager of SSL's Software Engineering Business Centre, the Programme Manager, the Chief Designer and a senior representative of each of the other Partners. The Steering Group met quarterly to receive a report on progress and to discuss strategic issues, particularly potential exploitation of Eclipse, relationships with the Alvey Directorate and contractual and financial matters.

Although SSL was the leader of the consortium, the relationship between SSL and the other partners was never conceived as being that which normally holds between a prime contractor and subcontractors; indeed, such a relationship would not have been within the spirit of the Alvey programme. Many matters which a prime contractor would handle without consulting subcontractors were therefore agreed at the Steering Group.

The Steering Group was not, of course an executive body and so an executive management structure was required reporting to the programme manager. The programme as a whole was broken down into a number of individual projects; at peak, the number of such projects reached 14. Some of these projects were themselves geographically dispersed: the user interface project, for example, involved SSL, CAP, Strathclyde and Lancaster. To cope with the orthogonal divisions of projects and sites, a matrix management structure was adopted. At each site, there was a site manager responsible, subject to the normal practices of his or her organisation, for the staff at the site and for the financial aspects of the organisation's participation. Each project was under the control of a project manager who was responsible in the usual way for planning, monitoring, reporting and ensuring adherence to the quality plan. A third dimension of management was present in the quality management function.

Such a management structure can only function effectively if the lines of the individual managers' responsibilities are clearly drawn and, most importantly, if the will to make the structure work is present and is supported by good personal relationships. Eclipse was fortunate in having partners who were keen for the collaboration to be successful and staff who usually enjoyed each others' company.

3.2 REQUIREMENTS SPECIFICATION

None of the routine project management tasks can be performed effectively without a definition of the goals of the project, in other words a *requirements specification*. Conventional software engineering practice demands that the requirements specification be detailed, unambiguous, consistent and complete, albeit this ideal is never achieved in practice. The client should be able to validate the specification against his needs. Although the Alvey Directorate acted in many ways as a client, it did not have identifiable needs in this way. It is, anyway, unrealistic to expect the requirements for a research project to be specified so clearly — indeed, if they could be so specified the project would hardly be research. Equally though, one cannot expect to manage even a research project successfully without a clear idea of its goals.

The material in the original proposal was refined to produce an Eclipse 'manifesto'; this was a high level statement of the project goals and was made publically available. From this, a more precise, but still high level, requirements specification was produced, which could be used for planning purposes.

As work progressed, functional specifications of the major components of the system were produced. These were fully detailed and could therefore be used for detailed planning. It was particularly important to produce complete functional specifications of the kernel components because these would be used at many sites in the design and implementation of tools.

In effect, therefore, the requirements specifications were produced much later than they would be in a normal project (and, as it proved, were subject to substantial changes).

3.3 COMMUNICATION

Any large and dispersed programme of work inevitably faces problems of communication. There is a need for information dissemination, for education, for technical discussion between different groups and for reviewing proposals; above all, perhaps, there is a need to generate a spirit of enthusiasm and a feeling for the overall goals of the project.

In addition to the obvious provision for technical meetings and progress reviews, Eclipse tackled the problem of communication in two ways.

Large scale consortium meetings, to which everyone working on the programme was invited, were held every quarter and the average attendance at them was about 45 people; they were also attended by the Alvey project monitoring officers. The agenda for these meetings included a review of progress, educational sessions (describing, for example, how tools were expected to use the database interface), sessions in which new ideas were presented by individual groups and discussed, and demonstrations of early versions of Eclipse software. The social side of these meetings was important for cementing the good relations which were forming among the staff of the different partners and many of us retain happy memories of walking up White Nancy, dancing at the pier disco in Aberystwyth and visiting a night club in Lancaster. It became the custom to hold these meetings in the universities; they have suitable facilities and the costs are much lower than using hotels. The meetings were clearly popular with staff working on the programme; on the single occasion when a consortium meeting was cancelled many complaints were voiced.

The second mechanism adopted to improve communications within the project was the review procedure. Procedures for reviewing all formal documents were, of course, included in the Eclipse Quality Plan. What was unusual was that, for critical documents, senior technical staff from all the partners were encouraged to participate in the reviews and, for all formal documents, a system of postal reviewing was superimposed on the normal reviewing procedure so that all interested parties could comment, without the need to spend excessive time in travelling. While there were times when the project seemed likely to drown in paper, these reviewing mechanisms by and large worked well and achieved their aim of ensuring effective technical communication.

Of great importance during the earlier part of the project was a series of small workshops, attended by one or two senior technical staff from each partner. It was in these workshops that alternative architectures for Eclipse as a whole, and for its major components, were discussed at length and the final decisions arrived at. Inevitably, decisions were not always unanimous but, because of the way that they were reached, all partners were happy to accept them.

At a more physical level the project intended to make extensive use of electronic mail. This was less successful than had been hoped. The universities and SSL were connected to JANET (Joint Academic Network) and were able to obtain a reasonable service, although this took some time to set up and was plagued by hardware and software difficulties at the individual sites. CAP and LBMS were never connected directly to JANET; they used dial-up facilities to read mail from a mailbox at Lancaster but this did not prove very effective.

3.4 PLANNING

The starting point for the planning activity was the list of deliverables and milestones which had been delivered to the Alvey Directorate; this list included some 120 deliverables.

A major weakness in the initial plans was the lack of resources allocated to the central design function. It had been assumed that this activity could be carried out by the Chief Designer but it rapidly became apparent that a team of three or four high calibre staff was required if the design work of the individual projects was to be consistent and effective. This need could only be met by reducing the resources allocated to the less critical areas of the programme. A painful decision had to be made and the result was that the industrial effort was withdrawn from the reuse project, which was therefore left entirely to the universities.

All project plans change and the project manager must allow for this. However, in a project involving so much that is new and uncertain, plans are bound to be very much more volatile than in more normal projects. As described elsewhere in this book (particularly in chapters 2 and 4), there were a number of very large changes to the technical structure of Eclipse, including especially the change to PCTE. The motivation for these changes was primarily technical and sometimes commercial or political but in each case the resource implications of the change had to be assessed and new plans to meet the changed programme produced. This placed a heavy load on the managers of the individual projects and on the programme manager. As a result, it was necessary, for a period, to provide the project with one person occupied full time in planning.

The planning process was subject to some constraints not found in more orthodox projects. Changes to the plans had to remain consistent with the overall resources budgeted for each partner. In this respect, the nature of university research funding is very inflexible. In the event of a major change delaying the start of an activity, A, until another partner has completed activity B which is necessary before A can start, a commercial organisation can usually arrange to deploy elsewhere (on a different project) the staff who were assigned to activity A. Universities do not have this freedom because, in effect, they have to recruit specific staff to work on a project for its whole duration; furthermore, such staff are usually working for a PhD, which imposes further constraints on how far the work assigned to them can be changed. These comments should not be taken as a criticism of the universities, nor indeed of the system of research funding; universities are not software houses and cannot be expected to behave as if they were. Nonetheless, these constraints do complicate the planning process.

3.5 MONITORING

The procedures for progress monitoring were similar to those of any large project. Project managers of the individual projects submitted monthly progress reports to the programme manager; financial and manpower returns were submitted by site managers. Monthly progress meetings were held at each site. The reviewing process provided a valuable check on technical progress.

3.6 QUALITY MANAGEMENT

It was never our intention that the whole of Eclipse should be produced to full production quality. Nevertheless, if the visible parts of the system (i.e. the tool sets) were to be suitable for demonstration and evaluation, the kernel facilities, on which they would depend, would have to be produced to high standards of reliability and would have to provide adequate performance. In addition, some 420 formal documents were produced and the demonstration systems contained a great deal of software, so effective configuration management procedures were essential. In the event, these procedures proved to be very demanding of resources but the quality achieved in the demonstrations amply justified the investment of so much effort.

A substantial quality plan was produced which identified different classes of deliverable and the quality standards appropriate to each class; in particular, this allowed the quality standards applied to research products to be much less stringent than those applied to kernel software. In order to avoid staff on the project having to learn an excessive number of new standards and procedures, the plan was framed in such a way that the existing standards of the industrial partners could be subsumed within it.

3.7 CONTRACTUAL MATTERS

There were two major agreements drawn up between the collaborators. The first, which was a necessary pre-condition for receiving Alvey funding, was the collaboration agreement to cover the work carried out within the programme itself; the second, the exploitation agreement, covers the conditions under which the partners can exploit the work commercially. As should be the case with all commercial agreements, their purpose was to state unambiguously the partners' understanding of what had been agreed, rather than to be used as a stick for beating recalcitrant partners.

Partly perhaps because of the desire to obtain final Alvey approval for the programme, the collaboration agreement was negotiated rapidly and without undue difficulty. The major points covered were the following:

- what developments were to be regarded as part of the programme and the procedure by which these might be modified;

- responsibilities of SSL as leader of the consortium and of the other partners towards SSL;

- ownership of rights in 'background', i.e. products which partners are bringing into the consortium, and the rights of other partners to use such background for the purposes of the project;

- conditions governing the dissemination and disclosure of information stemming from the programme;

- confidentiality of information relating to background or business affairs of other members;

- the obligation of members to exploit their results within three years of the completion of the project or, on request, in collaboration with other members and the Alvey Directorate, to make them available for others to exploit;

- conditions for receiving payments from the Directorate;

- Crown rights in the results.

Not unnaturally, in view of the potential conflict of legitimate commercial interests, the negotiation of the exploitation agreement was much more protracted. The essence of the agreement is that in any sale of the products of the programme, the proceeds are split, in defined proportions, between the organisation which carried out the sale, the organisation responsible for first line support, and the originator of the product (although, of course, in many cases the three organisations may not be distinct). Subject to the agreement, any industrial partner may exploit any of the products. The academic partners do not have the right to exploit the products, except where the industrial partners fail to do so, but, in compensation for this and in recognition of their contribution to the programme as a whole, they each receive a small royalty on all sales, in addition to the sums they receive from sales of products in whose development they have been directly concerned.

Chapter 4

The Evolution of the Eclipse Kernel

Albert Alderson and John Cartmel

Our thinking on the Eclipse kernel has passed through three clearly defined stages. We started with a view of the kernel which was derived from our experience on Foundation and the MCHAPSE. The early work on Eclipse led us to refine and modify these ideas fairly extensively in the area of data representation. The decision, taken about nearly half way through the project, to base our work on PCTE led to further substantial modifications. This chapter presents a largely synoptic view of the way in which our ideas changed and outlines our present thinking about further possible enhancements.

4.1 THE PURPOSE OF THE IPSE KERNEL

In order to justify the term 'integrated', an IPSE needs a set of organising principles around which its tools are produced and in terms of which the tools cooperate and interact in a consistent way with the end-user.

On the one hand, therefore, the IPSE needs principles of user interaction. The end-user does things and sees things: sketches a design, looks at a budget, modifies a program, schedules some activities and is shown end-dates and critical paths. When the end-user does and sees these things then the *manner* of his doing, his detailed actions, and the *appearance* of things to him are determined by the principles of user interaction.

On the other hand there are deeper principles. The things manipulated by the user are as various as project schedules and budgets, design text and diagrams, software items, such as source code, object code and executables and software configurations. These things are represented according to the IPSE's principles of data management. It is important that similar things behave, over time, in similar ways.

If the IPSE is to be easy to extend, then the principles around which it is organised must be encapsulated within a set of interfaces and control mechanisms — a set of *kernel* facilities of the IPSE. To meet the extensibility requirement the kernel facilities must form a well-defined part of the IPSE and must be delivered as part of the IPSE to the end-user. This means that if the IPSE is extended adding new tools which use the kernel facilities, we can be sure that the new tools will be consistent and compatible with the existing tools. To emphasise the way in which the kernel is used, the interface to the procedural kernel facilities is sometimes known as a Public Tools Interface.

What is limiting about a conventional operating system as a development environment is the nature of its kernel. Typically an operating system organises data into files which are sequences of bytes or pages or variable length records. These are the concepts around which tools are made to cooperate and to appear compatible to the end-user. In other words, the kernel only allows stored objects to be classified in a few very simple ways. The users and the tools have a much richer classification of stored objects — programs, schedules, deliverable software items on the one hand, and menus, diaries, flow charts and choice lists, on the other — but these concepts cannot be represented in the database nor can their properties be encapsulated. Rather each individual tool is left to represent the high level concepts in whatever machine oriented concepts the kernel facilities make available. Thus the conventional operating system supports integration, cooperation and compatibility only at the machine level and not at a conceptual level. This is bad for production in three ways. First, it causes unnecessary work to be done by the tool builder or the end user to represent the high-level concepts. Second, the tools produced by different third parties will usually only be compatible at the machine level; they cannot work together because they are logically and conceptually incompatible. Finally, an environment built on such a basis loses many opportunities for error checking.

The nature of the interface between the tools and the kernel and its public availability are major factors influencing how easily and effectively an IPSE can be extended [79].

4.2 INITIAL VIEW OF THE KERNEL

These principles were not at all clear to us when we embarked on the Eclipse programme in August 1984. We had a notion of *core* and *cladding*. The core was defined as design method independent work and the cladding was defined as the design method dependent tool sets.

Within the work on the core we recognised and addressed two aspects of integration. The first aspect was *integration through the user image*. It was clear to us that a strong sense of unity could be given by adopting clear user interaction principles and style, and using these consistently in all interactions with the user. The second aspect was *integration through data*. Here we had the view that for tools to be integrated successfully they should be able to share data easily. This led us to the view that the data should be held in a central database. We had also chosen to consider the problems of distribution of the IPSEs facilities using both local area networks and wide area networks.

At the outset of the programme the kernel was no more definite to us than the need to address the problems of data representation, user interface, and distribution.

The original Alvey call for proposals had however indicated that the IPSE should be based on UNIX. Berkeley UNIX 4.2 bsd was the version chosen as our base and this

4.2. INITIAL VIEW OF THE KERNEL   27

was the version then available on the Sun work stations we had chosen to use. The process model, together with the inter-process communication facilities — including signals — determined the process architecture of Eclipse. The I/O facilities of UNIX were not as influential as those supplied by Sun. It was natural that we wished to use the full power of the sophisticated bit-mapped screens of the Sun work station. Effectively then the UNIX 4.2 bsd kernel, together with the Sun graphics interface, was the basis of the initial kernel of Eclipse.

4.2.1 Initial View of Data Representation

Our first view of data representation was at the time coloured by the work that Software Sciences had undertaken over the previous 12 years, first on SDS [34] and then on the successor SDS-2 [2], upon which Foundation [3] was based. The thinking of SDS and SDS-2 was to use a central database to record details about the products of the life cycle process, to relate them to the recorded plan, and to relate both to details of staff. (The life cycle products themselves were not held.) This approach had been successful but the need to hold the life cycle products and to add configuration management was becoming clear. Foundation was the means by which this was added to SDS-2.

The provision of configuration management facilities meant that Foundation had to capture the derivation history of the life cycle products automatically; this in turn required that Foundation should be the means by which tools were invoked. The implication was that Foundation should be an *open* IPSE.

The notion of an open IPSE has been developed because of the difficulties inherently involved in the development of IPSEs. An open IPSE is expected to be open to the inclusion of foreign tools (tools written without knowledge of the IPSE). Open IPSEs may be open in different degrees of ease and effectiveness — work will usually have to be done in order to install a foreign tool. Nevertheless an IPSE will be considered an open IPSE providing a tool can be integrated without recompiling it. A UNIX based IPSE is expected to inter-work with tools native to UNIX and thus to make use of UNIX documentation tools, compilers, linkers, debuggers and so on.

The original Alvey call for proposals had indicated an open UNIX IPSE as a desired product. It was natural therefore to propose a programme based around SDS-2 and Foundation in a UNIX environment.

SDS-2 and Foundation addressed only the products of the life cycle process such as documents, plans, source code, object code, executable binary, and so on. The content of such products was not of concern. This attitude was reflected in the Eclipse proposal. The only mention of more detailed data was the expressed wish to establish a standard representation for diagrammatic information. This was a necessary outcome of our wish to produce a generic design editor to support the diagram types used by software engineering design methods. We did not see initially any more general need to represent such detailed data.

4.2.2 Initial View of the User Interface

It had always been our intention, as declared in the proposal, "to develop a coherent user interface philosophy" to be used by all tools which interacted with the user. The coherent philosophy that we introduced was the *control panel* [104]. The notion is to have an interface to complex software modelled on the kinds of interface we have to complex hardware as epitomised by an aircraft flight deck. The control panel features lights, buttons, multi-position switches and so. Each of these different kinds of interaction object is given a unique representation by the Eclipse User Interface and this gives Eclipse a very distinctive appearance. This representation of control panel features we call the Eclipse house style. However, a given set of interaction objects, each with standard physical interactions by which the user manipulates them, is no guarantee of a coherent user interface. A consistency of treatment of messages is important, as is the consistent provision and presentation of Help.

Early in our design we determined that the user interface should be implemented "as a communication channel connecting the user and the application software". This communication channel presented an interface in terms of physical interactions to the user, and a procedural interface to the application. The channel itself was to be programmable to allow different physical representations to be adopted.

As a consequence of these ideas we developed the Eclipse User Interface which consisted of a three separate interfaces implementing the control panel interface [113], the message and prompt interface, and the help interface. Each of these interfaces was implemented as a programmable channel interfacing the user and the application. The user interface philosophy and these interfaces are discussed in Chapters 6 and 7.

4.2.3 Initial View of Distribution

The SDS-2 database was designed to run on a single machine and it did not make sense either technically or financially to attempt to produce a distributed SDS-2, within the context of the Eclipse programme. Neither did we consider this necessary. It was also clear to us that SDS-2 and Foundation were too large to run on the Sun work station. We therefore decided to consider a network with a central VAX running SDS-2 and Foundation, and Sun work stations connected to the VAX using Ethernet. Logically this formed a star architecture. The processing was distributed statically across the network [56].

It was envisaged that a distributed version of Eclipse would be implemented in a number of phases of increasing sophistication. In the first, any file to be processed would be extracted from Foundation and exported to the work station for processing. Following processing, the file would be imported from the work station and entered into Foundation together with appropriate derivation network data. The exporting and importing of files would be under the control of the user at the work station. File transfers would be carried out using the Berkeley remote file copy mechanism. Direct user access to the query facilities of SDS-2 executing on the VAX would be through the Berkeley remote login mechanism. This phase was never implemented.

The second phase was intended to give integrated access to all data in Foundation from tools executing on the work station. Here all access to data in Foundation was to be through a remote procedure call mechanism operating between the work stations and the VAX. A file access facility was to be included. Files would still be exported, operated upon and then imported again, but transparently under the control of the Eclipse core. The interface of remote procedure calls was defined. It was named the Integrated Tools Interface, since tools which were integrated (not foreign) could call it directly to manipulate the derivation network. This scheme left the representation of detailed data as an independent concern.

4.3 REFINED VIEW OF DATA REPRESENTATION

4.3.1 Representing Detailed Data

Early in the programme the representation problem was described as "concerned with the storage of information within the IPSE. It is concerned with the distribution of data between database item records, database version records and file store version files. It is not concerned with the detailed data structures needed for any particular method or tool; those data structures are the province of individual projects."

In this context we had conceived the idea of *participation*. An entity participates in different views of the world in different ways. For example, a computer is an entity in its own right and we would represent it by an item. It may also have detailed information recorded about it which may change over time; this we may represent using versions. The computer may participate in a floor plan of the computer room and it may also participate in a wiring diagram of the computer room. In each of these contexts detailed information may be recorded about the computer's participation. This information belongs to the context of the participation; it is not directly information about the computer itself. The distinction to be made is a generalisation of the distinction made between types and instances of types in a programming language. A programming language usually has only one kind of instantiation; our representation allows for many different kinds.

Where versions are being represented the participation relationship can take one of three forms.

- There may be a direct relationship from one item to another. This represents the fact that every version of the first item participates in every version of the second.

- There may be a relationship from a version of one item to some other item. This indicates that the particular version of the first item participates in every version of the second.

- There may be a relationship from a version of one item to a version of some other item.

We considered the idea of participation to be important to the representation of derivation networks.

We had also begun to explore the representation of diagrammatic information and to consider IDL [90]. IDL was known to us through an implementation, called MIDL, which was used to store detailed data between phases of the Ada Group Limited Ada compiler. The MIDL implementation was available to us and so provided a readily available means of storing data produced by the generic design editor.

We soon realised that MIDL could be used to interface tools in the same way that the phases of the Ada compiler had been interfaced. A feature of MIDL that assisted in this was that either transient or permanent storage of the data was supported. We saw that such an implementation of IDL could be the means for representing and storing detailed data.

4.3.2 IDL and IDLE

IDL describes data structures by means of a type hierarchy. Each type may be defined as a subtype of some other type. Each type may have attributes associated with it and every type inherits the attributes of its parent types. Attributes may have types such as string, integer or any type defined in the type hierarchy. These latter attributes are interpreted as references to instances of the quoted type. Complex types such as set are also available. The MIDL representation added other attribute types, such as enumeration, and other complex types, such as table.

A MIDL data structure definition was compiled to produce an Ada package which allowed instances of the types to be created or deleted, and the attributes of such instances to be manipulated. This had two drawbacks. First the packages were very large and taxed the abilities of the Ada compilers then available. Second it was not possible to create generic tools capable of operating on a variety of data structures; every relevant Ada package had to be linked with such a tool.

We therefore determined to implement our own IDL system. In this the data structure definition was compiled into a table which was interpreted by a single package; facilities were provided for creating and deleting instances of types described in the table and for assigning values to their attributes. In this formulation, the relationship of an IDL description of a data structure to an instance of that data structure is seen to be the same as the relationship of a database schema to the data stored in the database. This view was to be of importance later in allowing us to unify the data modelling within Eclipse.

A revised language, IDLE — IDL for Eclipse — was defined. The major addition to IDL was the notion of external links. We had recognised, as described earlier, the importance of representing participation relationships. Such relationships can be represented as relationships between database records for items and versions. However where versions of items occur, the relationships should be allowed to emanate from within the detailed data of such versions. For just as the content of a version is the refinement of the version, so the external links are refinements of participation links.

4.3.3 The Granularity Problem

We needed to represent data in two different ways. Foreign tools would be integrated down to the level of a single file. The structure represented would be *coarse grain*. This data would model items and versions of items and be the basis of configuration control and impact analysis. It would relate data to its producers and consumers or to its specifications and refinements.

Yet the files which would be held as versions of items would themselves be objects with contents which were very often structured: documents have paragraphs and paragraphs have sections. Object code files have lists of entry points and unresolved references.

4.3. REFINED VIEW OF DATA REPRESENTATION

The central database would give a way of integrating and controlling different stages in the software life cycle but would not provide any way of representing the structured contents of the versions of items, i.e. the products of the individual steps, such as:

- requirements documents
- diagrams and designs
- program structure.

The internal structures of documents, designs and programs are examples of *fine structure*. The grain of detail goes down to the individual sentence (in a requirements document, for example), to nodes and arcs within diagrams, and to nodes in an abstract syntax tree of a program. We came to represent these structures in IDLE.

The question of whether a single database that integrates and controls the life cycle can also represent fine grain structure has become known as the granularity problem. The fineness of grain relevant to the software engineering process at any time depends upon the smallest grain of interest to the software engineering tools we wish to implement. The finer this grain is the more difficult the granularity problem becomes.

4.3.4 The Integrated Tools Interface

Two different interfaces were considered. One was to be used to manipulate derivation network data in the central database and had been called the Integrated Tools Interface. The second interface to manipulate detailed data was called the Intimate Integrated Tools Interface.

It was clear that we should combine these two interfaces into a single interface for use by applications programs. The interface itself would determine whether the central database or the detailed data was to be amended and initiate the appropriate action. The combined interface, named the Integrated Tools Interface was designed, but only the access to detailed data was successfully implemented. The Integrated Tools Interface was our first attempt at solving the granularity problem.

This interface provided 178 functions to applications programs such as the design editor. It was approximately 1.2Mb of compiled code and had to be linked with every application. This size in itself caused difficulties since we were using Sun work stations with only 2Mb of random access memory.

A rather greater problem was that the Ada compiler available to us had difficulty compiling Ada source making heavy use of generics. Having persuaded the compiler to compile the source, the linker took more than 48 hours to link the code. This made the interface virtually unmaintainable.

The pressure of the approaching Alvey Software Engineering Conference at Lancaster in April 1986 at which we were committed to demonstrate Eclipse, forced us to shelve this implementation. We produced an implementation in PROLOG in 26 man days and used that instead! This PROLOG interface implemented only the Intimate Integrated Tools Interface aspects and omitted the remote access to Foundation. Although much of the full Ada implementation was produced and tested, it was never used. Version 1 of Eclipse ran as a stand-alone system on single work stations. Consequently the SDS-2 and Foundation aspects of Eclipse were not used as part of Version 1 of Eclipse and subsequent events ensured that they were never used as part of Eclipse.

4.4 REVISED VIEW OF THE KERNEL

We had been aware of PCTE for some time but had never considered it seriously prior to October 1986 because no suitable implementation existed. In that month, we were invited to a meeting coordinated by the Alvey and Esprit Directorates and attended by GIE Emeraude, the producers of the Emeraude PCTE implementation. The Alvey Directorate was seeking a base on which all Alvey products could be developed. Esprit wished to spread the use of the PCTE base which they had commissioned.

As a result of the meeting and an immediate technical reappraisal of PCTE by the Eclipse programme, we decided to develop the second version of Eclipse on PCTE. The necessary PCTE implementations on the Sun were to be the products of the Esprit Sapphire project [121], in which three of the Eclipse collaborators, SSL, CAP and UCW were to be partners with GIE Emeraude. In order to avoid halting the Eclipse programme an immediate Sun version of PCTE was produced. This was done by GIE Emeraude, Sun and Software Sciences porting the then partial Emeraude implementation in 12 man weeks. The resulting implementation became known as Dirty Garnet, because it was a rough and ready implementation of a semi-precious object. The alternative name for a Garnet, a Carbuncle, was often felt to be more appropriate, but the desired effect was achieved.

4.4.1 PCTE

The PCTE specification [96] is probably the most comprehensive definition yet of an IPSE kernel. PCTE is conceived as a kernel which provides for all of a tool's requirements with respect to execution, inter-process communication, input-output, database access including concurrency control, distribution and user interface. The interface to the kernel provides a machine independent interface between the tools and the underlying system. Providing that tools use only this PCTE interface, then they will be portable to other implementations of the same interface.

In a sense there is nothing new in the concept. It is typically the way in which operating systems provide facilities to tools. The UNIX operating system shows the extent to which such an interface provides machine independence. What is new is the extent of the services offered, and in particular, the database facilities.

The Object Management System

PCTE presents a data model in which objects are typed, and have attributes and relationships according to their type. Objects may also have a *content* which behaves like the content of a file. PCTE provides facilities for defining objects types, and for manipulating objects. This capability is called the Object Management System (OMS). One of its most striking features is that, whilst its object management system (OMS) is a database in its own right, nevertheless the Emeraude implementation of PCTE is binary-compatible with existing UNIX tools. This is possible because the

4.4. REVISED VIEW OF THE KERNEL

PCTE data model subtly generalises the capabilities of the UNIX file store. Thus Emeraude is open to the easy inclusion of native UNIX tools.

The object types form a hierarchy with a single predefined root type and there are predefined object types which relate to the basic kinds of data operated on by PCTE. Every object type inherits the properties of its ancestors. The root type has a predefined set of attributes such as owner and date of last modification which every other object type inherits.

PCTE offers a limited set of attribute types all of which are scalar. These are integer, date (which is a date and time), string and Boolean. Links implement relationships in PCTE. They give the data model great power. Links are unidirectional but are maintained in bi-directional pairs. The attributes and relationships of object types have to be declared to the system. This is done by defining Schema Definition Sets (SDS). An SDS may define some new object types, and add attributes and relationships to those new types and to existing types. The root type and its attributes, and the other basic types are defined in a special SDS called **sys** (system), which is built into PCTE. SDSs themselves may be added, modified or deleted provided that they are not currently in use. The system does not need to be stopped.

When a tool is executing, PCTE must be informed of the SDSs which the tool is using. This is done by setting the *working schema* to be a named set of SDSs. When a tool is executing the data it may access is limited by its working schema.

The Basic Mechanisms

The basic mechanisms of PCTE are concerned with functions to manipulate programs and processes.

A program is a set of instructions that may be executed as a process. However a program may have attributes other than its code. Thus a program may be executed or it may be interpreted. If it is executed then the class of processor required to execute its instructions must be recorded. If it is interpreted then it will require the program which is to be used to interpret it to be recorded. The *static context* allows such details of a program to be recorded. The static context is a predefined type which records such information. The content of a static context contains the binary to be executed or the instructions to be interpreted.

A process is an instance of the execution of some program. A process is brought into existence by some parent process invoking execution of some program. A process executes within a dynamic context which is initialised by the parent process. Effectively the process inherits various attributes from its parent such as a working schema. Once it begins executing the process may change its dynamic context. However the process model in PCTE is effectively block structured giving scope to the dynamic context. Thus the child can have no effect upon the parent's dynamic context and the parent can have no effect on the child's once invocation has occurred.

PCTE provides a number of mechanisms for inter-process communication. The most important is the ability for processes to send and receive messages. Messages are sent to and read from message queues which act as post boxes.

In a multi-process environment such as PCTE control of concurrent access to the database is vital if its integrity is to be preserved. In PCTE concurrency control is based upon the locking of resources in the context of an activity; an activity is classified as unprotected, protected or transaction. The class of the activity determines the strength with which the resources are locked. A transaction activity is such that if it is abandoned it will be as if no modifications had occurred to the resources it has locked. Activities may be nested.

Distribution

A PCTE network is a community of closely cooperating work stations, possibly of differing types, communicating via an Ethernet LAN. A PCTE network is viewed as a single distributed system, not a collection of separate work stations. The user has access to all resources of all stations on the network and the means by which PCTE achieves this are totally invisible to the user. Processes can be started on both the local machine and on other machines in the system. Interaction with remote processes is transparent. Activities can be made up of collections of distributed processes.

User Interface

The PCTE user interface is aimed at software engineering tool developments which, whilst expecting adequate response times, have a need for standardisation, ease of development and a broad interface capability. The PCTE user interface is a genuine attempt to abstract the end-user interaction style from the application interface definition and thereby force tool developers to think in a device independent manner, thus contributing to tool portability. The basic model is the familiar WIMP (Windows, Icons, Menus and Pointers), and this in itself assumes certain device capabilities. In particular a bit mapped screen and a pointer with at least three buttons with up/down transition notifications are assumed.

The User Concept

One interesting aspect of the PCTE specification is that it addresses the concept of user very sketchily. In fact the **sys** SDS has no data definitions addressing the concept of user. As a result it is not possible to implement a user-based login procedure without further data definitions. Emeraude has chosen to address this problem by defining a second SDS called **env** (environment). The **env** SDS must be included in all working schemas just as **sys** must be. This has consequences for portability of applications using PCTE. Theoretically it is possible to port any application which uses only the PCTE Interface to any implementation of PCTE simply by recompiling. Unfortunately many applications need to be aware of the definitions in the **env** SDS. Clearly any Emeraude-based implementation of PCTE will have the **env** SDS but it is not clear that other implementations will address the user concept in this way. Thus application code may need modification when it is ported.

4.4.2 The Revised View of Data Representation

The influence of PCTE on the Eclipse programme has been profound. The major consequence was the replacement of SDS-2 and Foundation by the PCTE OMS. This generally provided the similar data modelling facilities to SDS-2, but also integrated access to files. One of the achievements of Foundation was to unify access to the SDS-2

4.4. REVISED VIEW OF THE KERNEL

database and to files, but it was clear that the PCTE approach was far superior. The replacement of SDS-2 and Foundation had many beneficial consequences.

It was very fortunate that PCTE and IDLE had similar data modelling concepts; this allowed us to unify the modelling of the two levels of data even more successfully than we had in the first version of Eclipse. The data modelling aspects of PCTE, as expressed by the PCTE SDS definition capabilities, and of IDLE, as expressed by the IDLE language, were unified in the Eclipse DDL (Data Definition Language).

It also proved possible to unify the data access aspects of PCTE, as expressed by the PCTE OMS facilities, and of IDLE, as expressed by the Intimate Integrated Tools Interface. PCTE OMS was used for maintaining the first, coarse structure, tier of data, and a new implementation of Intimate Integrated Tools Interface, now named the IDLE-FSD (Fine Structure Database) was used for maintaining the second, fine structure, tier of data. The unified interface was named the Eclipse Database Interface (DBI).

A more detailed description of these unified interfaces is given in chapter 5.

The DBI and IDLE-FSD were implemented in C, which had finally become the programme's chosen implementation language due to the Ada compiler problems. Only the Eclipse Ada tool set (Chapter 8) is now written in Ada.

Items, Versions and Configurations

With the loss of Foundation it was important to re-establish a single Eclipse way of modelling items and versions and the relationship 'has_versions' between them. We had the following principles and constraints:

- the behaviour of foreign tools placed tight constraints on the names we might use to identify versions;

- we had to ensure that the discretionary access controls in PCTE could be used to protect configurations from misuse;

- we did not want a model in which entire environments were copied to build a new configuration i.e. we wished to ensure that versions could be shared between configurations.

Using the facilities of PCTE we were able to provide the concepts of item, version and of configuration. The latter we were able to provide in a far more effective form than had been possible in Foundation. On the debit side, however, we lost the ability to capture the derivation network automatically; for such capture to be effective it would need to be achieved within the PCTE kernel.

The UNIX tool Make [35] illustrates an effective alternative approach to automatic capture of derivation information; here the user specifies the process of derivation and the system then interprets this specification. Recapitulation of the development process then involves re-interpreting the specification and, where changed or new versions exist (say because of editing), generating new versions of the derived products. We have undertaken research into such derivation descriptions which we have shown can be derived from descriptions of desired system structure. The SySL work described in Chapter 11 explores system structure descriptions and their use as derivation descriptions. The configuration control interface is described in Chapter 5.

4.4.3 Revised View of the User Interface

The PCTE User Interface did not cause us to revise our view of the user interface. There were two reasons for this. First, at the time that we decided to base version 2 of Eclipse on PCTE, there was no implementation of the PCTE user interface in existence. Second, the Eclipse user interface, which is currently implemented using the Sun graphics facilities, has developed through continual enhancement of our original ideas and provides direct support for our user interface philosophy. The PCTE user interface is at a lower level than the Eclipse user interface and is much closer to the level of the Sun graphics facilities. In the interests of portability, a re-implementation of the Eclipse user interface, using PCTE user interface facilities, is being undertaken by the Sapphire project. No significant changes will be made to the facilities provided.

4.4.4 Revised View of Distribution

The decision to dispense with SDS-2 and Foundation and to use the PCTE OMS in their place had a profound effect upon our view of distribution. Since PCTE provided transparent distribution of data and transparent distributed access to data over the local area network, we no longer needed to consider these problems. The PCTE distribution facilities allowed us to move away from our original star architecture to a fully distributed network. The Sapphire project will produce implementations of PCTE for the VAX and the VAXstation 2000, as well as for the Sun. It is intended that all of these implementations should interwork by virtue of the implementation of the PCTE distribution facilities. Networks of work stations and minis from different manufacturers will therefore be supported.

As a result of introducing PCTE the Eclipse Distribution project became entirely research orientated. The results of that research are described in chapters 14 and 15.

4.5 SUMMARY

The Eclipse kernel has evolved considerably both conceptually and structurally during the Eclipse programme. It now consists of two elements — the PCTE kernel and the Eclipse database interface, configuration control interface and user interface supplementing it. These supplementary interfaces form a service layer on top of PCTE, specialising it to meet the requirements of a particular kind of tool set. This service layer also has the benefit of insulating the tools from change in the underlying PCTE kernel. This may be important given the possibilities of direct evolution of the PCTE interfaces (particularly the user interface [51]), the work within NATO to define PCTE+ [32] and the possible merging of PCTE and CAIS [81].

Some aspects of the service layer may also be viewed as candidate facilities for inclusion in an expanded PCTE kernel. This is certainly the case with the Eclipse database interface and configuration control interface.

The PCTE kernel together with the database interface, configuration control interface, and Eclipse user interface defines the Eclipse Public Tools Interface [28]. The Public Tools Interface is delivered to users who wish to build their own tools for integration into Eclipse. However the Public Tools Interface is not sufficient for this purpose. Tool builders need further facilities such as the DDL compiler. These further

4.5. SUMMARY

facilities are not part of the kernel but support the use of the kernel. The Eclipse kernel together with these support tools is called the Eclipse Tool Builders Kit and is available to third party tool builders wishing to utilise Eclipse.

We consider the current Eclipse kernel to be stable and unlikely to undergo the extensive remodelling of earlier versions. Its implementation however will be refined and improvements to the DDL processor, the IDLE compiler, and to the storage allocation policy of IDLE-FSD are in hand. The most interesting potential addition is an intelligent front-end to the Eclipse DBI. The DBI presents the conceptual schema (in standard ANSI-SPARC terminology). We envisage an interface offering the same functions as the DBI but provided external views of the conceptual schema, applying checks to the data entered through it, and providing query evaluation. This interface would be programmable in the way that the Eclipse User interface is.

Although the adoption of PCTE by the Eclipse programme was central to the successful outcome of the programme, it was not without its drawbacks. A major side effect of replacing SDS-2 was the loss of the query facilities for the first tier of data. These have not been replaced. A major side effect of replacing Foundation was the loss of the configuration management facilities. These were extensive and it was not possible to replace all of them during the remainder of the Eclipse programme although the configuration control interface provides the basic facilities for doing so.

The adoption of PCTE solved many implementation problems but created a few of its own. In general these problems have been caused by our use of the Emeraude implementation at such an early stage. The first Garnet implementation was a partial implementation of the OMS and the basic mechanisms. It had many missing facilities, including activities and static contexts, and was unstable. Subsequent versions of Emeraude have been of much higher quality but each new release has extended the range of implemented facilities. Early versions of Emeraude did not implement the **sys** SDS as defined in the PCTE specification, and the **env** SDS was introduced in April 1987. The PCTE distribution facilities have not yet been implemented by Emeraude, and the implementation of the PCTE user interface became available after the demonstration of Eclipse at the Alvey Conference in July 1987.

Tracking the changing releases in the implementation of the Eclipse kernel has been a major difficulty. An associated problem has been the move from the Berkeley 4.2 UNIX to a kernel using UNIX System V concepts. This has caused particular architectural problems due to the differences in signals.

As a consequence, Eclipse still needs further development before it can fully exploit the PCTE facilities, it is still a stand-alone system, and its user interface is still implemented using the Sun facilities directly. These defects are being rectified. When the reimplementation of the Eclipse user interface using the PCTE facilities has been completed, Eclipse will be portable to any Emeraude based implementation of PCTE simply by recompilation, as will all of the applications which are based on the Eclipse kernel.

Chapter 5

The Eclipse Two-Tier Database

John Cartmell and Albert Alderson

5.1 TWO-TIER DATABASE

The chapter addresses the two aspects of the unification of the two tiers of the Eclipse Two-Tier Database - the unification of the PCTE [96] and IDLE data models, addressed in Part 1, and the unification of the interface to data stored at both tiers, addressed in Part 2.

As discussed in Chapter 4, the two tiers of data represent the integration of the whole life-cycle and the individual stages within it. The first tier of data represents the integration and control of the different stages in the software life-cycle. This involves the version control and configuration management of data and the maintenance of relationships such as those between specification and refinement and between compiled code and its source. Versions may be associated with reason of change, author of change and so on and configurations of versions may be maintained.

This first tier is based upon PCTE. In PCTE data is held as objects in an object management system (OMS) which is at once both a filestore and a database. Both *files* and *directories* on the one hand and *records* on the other are modelled by the single unifying concept of an *object*.

Second tier data refines first tier data. It represents the details of individual stages within the life-cycle. The grain of structural detail may be down to the individual sentence (in a requirements document, for example), to nodes and arcs within diagrams, and to nodes in an abstract syntax tree of a program. Second tier data is held in the contents of PCTE files and is described using the IDLE language. The things modelled in IDLE, the sentences, nodes, arcs and so on are represented as *entities*. Those files that have known internal structure are represented as objects of type *fine structure object* in the OMS.

According to the Eclipse data model the world, being a world of designs, specifications and programs and so on, is modelled by a database which is a collection of entities. Entities are typed and, according to their types, entities have attributes. Attributes may be String, Integer, Date or Boolean valued attributes in which case they are said to be *printable attributes* or they may have values which are links to other entities, in which case they are said to be *entity-valued attributes* which are also known as *links*. Attributes are defined to be single-valued or many-valued. Many-valued attributes are defined to have their values organised into *sequences* or *keyed bags*.

Sequences may be printable or entity valued sequences. A sequence of values has order and may have multiple occurrences of the same value. *Bags*, like sequences, are collections of values but they are not ordered. Finally, *keyed bags* are bags in which each value has a key and can be selected by its key. Further, keyed bags in Eclipse are always keyed bags of entities. PCTE cardinality-many linktypes are examples of keyed bag attributes.

There is a root entity which always exists. Otherwise an entity only exists so long as it is the destination of a distinguished kind of link called a composition link [1]. The schema determines those links which are composition links. An entity is created in relation to another as the destination of a composition link. Subsequently it may become related via composition links to other entities. An entity ceases to exist when it is no longer the destination of any composition link.

The Eclipse two-tier database is a solution to the representation and granularity problems discussed in chapter 4. When the database is viewed as a functional whole it has the following important features each of which is an element in solving the *granularity problem*:

- A fine structure object is treated as a single grain to the access control, version control and configuration management systems. There is no locking of individual elements of the fine structure.

- Only one user at a time may update an object or its fine structure.

- When an object is copied or deleted or distributed (moved across volumes) then its fine structure is copied or deleted or moved across volumes too.

These three points characterise the differences between first and second tier data.

5.2 THE FUNCTIONAL DATA MODEL

The design of the Eclipse data model and database interface has been greatly influenced by the approaches of Shipman [110] and of Buneman [13] and their development of a functional data model. Shipman and Buneman describe different aspects of a functional approach to data modelling. Shipman's approach emphasises the connection between many-valued functions, sets and types. For him many-valued functions are set-valued and sets are types. For Buneman on the other hand, types are distinct from functions and many-valued functions are sequence-valued. Buneman is concerned most of all with functional programming languages as interfaces to databases. Both Shipman and Buneman see the functional model as a way of unifying the application interfaces to different databases such as network and relational databases.

The functional approach is characterised by

---

[1] Just as Bishop Berkley believed that things only exist when they are being looked at.

5.3. TYPES

- the way it models data - in terms of types and functions. Data is represented as typed entities and the type of an entity determines what attributes it has. Attributes are typed and may be String or Integer valued, or the like, or may be entity-valued in which case they are typed by an entity type. In either case they are understood as functions. For example an entity-valued attribute f, say, is understood as a function with a signature

    $f : A \to B$

    where A and B are entity types. A string-valued attribute g of the entity type B, say, is understood as a function with the signature

    $g : B \to String.$

- providing attributes which may be single-valued or many-valued. For example, many-valued attributes in IDLE may be sequence valued. A sequence-of-string attribute h of entity type B is shown as having the signature

    $h : B \to Seq\ Of\ String.$

- the manner in which data may be accessed through the use of functional expressions representing derived data.

Having taken this basic approach then the functional model is further characterised by the following:

- database navigation is just functional composition - thus database navigation can be fitted into the functional framework of computation. Following the PCTE and UNIX convention, the composition of f with g is written f/g. For example, if f and g have the signatures shown in (a) above, then the composition f/g is a derived attribute of A. It has the signature

    $f/g : A \to String.$

- database iteration through entities of a given type can be seen as iteration through the values of a many-valued function. The iteration through all entities of a type A is seen as iteration through the values of an attribute $!A$ with the signature

    $!A : () \to Seq\ Of\ A.$

For Buneman, at least, it is also true that all data is typed and that derived data may be typed by a derived type.

5.3 TYPES

Both PCTE and IDLE support notions of subtyping of entity types. We shall use the notation

$A \leq B$

to mean that type A is a subtype of type B. The subtype relation $\leq$ is a relation between types. The meaning of subtyping is that the subtype has all of the attributes of the supertype and maybe more beside:

if $A \leq B$ and $f : B \to C$ then $f : A \to C$.

The subtyping relation is a transitive relation:

if $A \leq B$ and $B \leq C$ then $A \leq C$.

In section 5.2 we have seen an example of the use of the type expression *Seq Of A* — the type of sequences of A's. We shall also need

$A * B$ — meaning the product of types A and B. An instance of $A * B$ is a pair consisting of an A and a B.

$A \mid B$ — the join of types A and B. An instance of $A \mid B$ is either an instance of A or an instance of B (in fact, it may be an instance of both). The attributes of $A \mid B$ coincide with those attributes common to A and to B.

The components of a join are subtypes of the join:

if $B_1, \ldots B_m$ are entity types then $B_j \leq B_1 \mid \cdots \mid B_m$ for each j, $1 \leq j \leq m$.

If each of the components of a join is a subtype of some type C then so is the join[2].

if $B_j \leq C$, for each j, $1 \leq j \leq m$, then $B_1 \mid \cdots \mid B_m \leq C$.

The type hierarchies in the PCTE and IDLE data models are conceptually different. In the terminology of Abiteboul and Hull [1] the difference is that PCTE supports definition of types by *specialisation* whereas IDLE supports definition by *generalisation*. IDLE type hierarchies are exactly generalisation hierarchies in the sense of Smith and Smith [113][3]. *Specialisation* is the act of defining a new entity type A as a subtype of an existing entity type B. *Generalisation* is the act of defining a new entity type A as a join of existing types $B_1, \ldots B_m$.

5.4 IDLE

In IDLE, data is organised into entities. An entity is something which has attributes. Entities are typed. The type of an entity determines what attributes it has (what can be attributed to such an entity). Each attribute is defined to be single-valued or many-valued. Many-valued attributes are defined to have their values organised into sequences. Attributes are typed either by one of the printable types — these are Integer, Date, Boolean and String — or by being entity-valued and being typed by some entity type. Instances of entity-valued attributes are known as links because

---

[2] the relation $\leq$ is a partial order and the operation $\mid$ is a join operation with respect to this partial order. Note that $A \mid A = A$ and that this distinguishes join from coproduct or disjoint union.

[3] This is the terminology used even though they need not form a tree. In general they form a directed acyclic graph. Having generalisation in the data model circumvents, to an extent, the need for supporting specialisation lattices.

5.4. IDLE

they link entities together. In Figure 5.1 there is an example of a diagrammatic representation of an IDLE schema and of the data it might describe. The range of possible signatures of user definable attributes in IDLE are shown in Figure 5.2.

The IDLE language enables many attributes of an entity type to be described in a single statement such as:

    top_left_x : Integer,

    top_left_y : Integer,

    height : Integer,

    width : Integer;

Functionally this is equivalent to defining:

    top_left_x : box$\rightarrow$Integer

    top_left_y : box$\rightarrow$Integer

    height : box$\rightarrow$Integer

    width : box$\rightarrow$Integer

In the IDLE language, entity types are defined by generalisation(see 5.3 above). For example an entity type *shape* may be defined by

    shape ::= box | circle | triangle

The user may define attributes which are common to boxes, circles and triangles as attributes of shape. Types defined by generalisation do not have instances other than the instances of their subtypes.

Every IDLE fine structure schema supports predefined types ENTITY and UNIT. ENTITY is the most general of entity types and UNIT $\leq$ ENTITY.

Every fine structure object has a local root entity of type UNIT. The local root is the value of a predefined attribute % that leads from the fine structure object. Every fine structure object has within it exactly one entity of type UNIT. Within the fine structure object, UNIT has the role of the SYSTEM object within CODASYL systems (for further discussion of this see [17]). Entity attributes of UNIT may be understood as access paths into the second tier data from the first tier. In general an attribute with the signature $f : UNIT \rightarrow A$, also written as $f : () \rightarrow A$, can only be evaluated at the one entity - the local root.

5.4.1 Virtual Attributes

A number of virtual attributes are supported by IDLE in order that entities can be searched for by giving the values of one or more of their attributes or by giving patterns which are to match against these values. The reason that IDLE supports such attributes is for the convenience of the user but also so that the way entities are searched for is an implementation issue which does not affect the user. In particular the existence of indexes supporting the lookups is hidden.

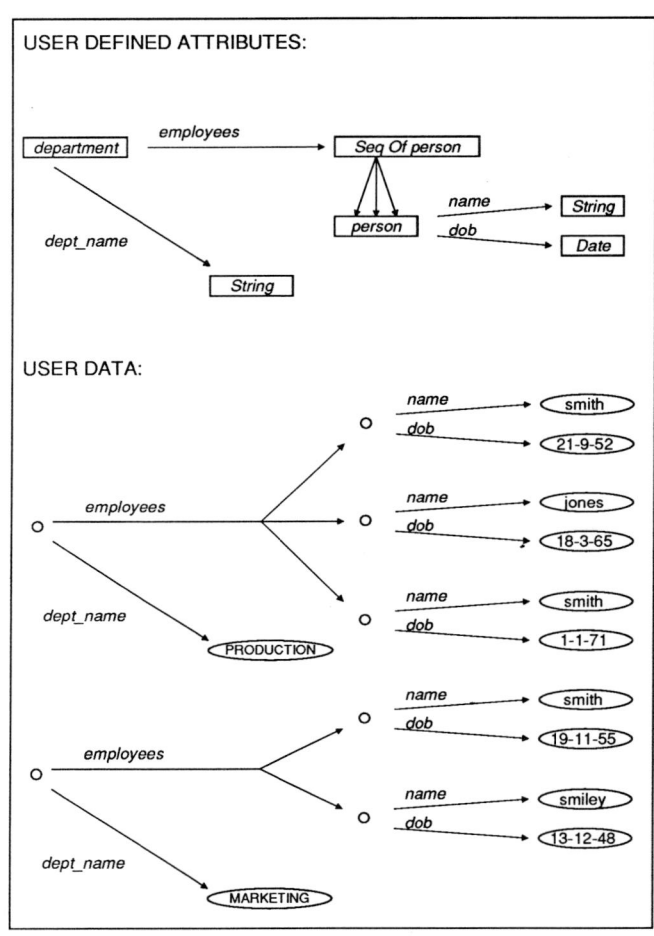

Figure 5.1: An example of IDLE attributes and data

5.4. IDLE

attributes	$f : A \to String$
	$f : A \to Boolean$
	$f : A \to Integer$
	$f : A \to Date$
	where $A \leq ENTITY$
entity attributes	$f : A \to B$
	where $A \leq ENTITY$ and $B \leq ENTITY$
many-valued attributes	$f : A \to$ Seq Of String
	$f : A \to$ Seq Of Boolean
	$f : A \to$ Seq Of Integer
	$f : A \to$ Seq Of Date
	where $A \leq ENTITY$
many-valued entity attributes	$f : A \to$ Seq Of B
	where $A \leq ENTITY$ and $B \leq ENTITY$

Figure 5.2: The possible signatures of IDLE User Defined Attributes

5.4.2 Predefined Attributes

After the manner of Buneman [12], every IDLE structure supports virtual attributes, !A, for every entity type A, whose meaning is *all 'A's* i.e. all entities of type A. This is defined to be an attribute of the type UNIT and so it is an attribute only of the local root entity. !A is of type $Seq\ Of\ A$. !A is a composition link attribute. These are the only composition links supported at the second tier. Entities of type A are created by creating them in relation !A to the local root.

5.4.3 Derived Attributes

This section describes the derived attributes that support searches of IDLE structures enabling entities to be identified from the values of their attributes by exact matches and by pattern matching. The patterns that are recognised in IDLE include string patterns involving wild card characters (? and * to match one and many characters, respectively), and integer and date patterns involving comparison operators and specifying ranges. Patterns can be put together disjunctively. The general principles of pattern matching are expressed by the signatures given for patterns as predefined attributes in Figure 5.3 and the selection rules given in Figure 5.4.

In Figure 5.4 we give the different forms of derived attributes are given and rules are given to show in what circumstances they are meaningful and what their signatures are. The rules are of the form:
$$\frac{Premise}{Conclusion}.$$
These rules correspond to the type-checking rules of typed programming languages.

In Figure 5.4, the rule IL2 for virtual keyed attributes expresses the following. If f is an IDLE entity-valued sequence attribute having the signature

```
!A  : UNIT → Seq Of A                    - all entities of type A

ip : () → Seq Of Integer
       whenever ip is an integer pattern  - for example 1..20 is the sequence
                                            of all integers in the range 1..20
sp : () → Seq Of String
       whenever sp is a string pattern    - for example fred* is the sequence
                                            of all strings beginning "fred"
dp : () → Seq Of Date
       whenever dp is a date pattern      - for example < 1960 is the sequence
                                            of all dates earlier than 1960
```

Figure 5.3: IDLE Predefined Attributes

$f : A \to Seq\ Of\ B$

and if $n : B \to X$ is a printable-valued attribute (i.e. if X is String, or Integer, or Boolean or Date), then the attribute $f \uparrow n$ is an attribute with the signature

$f \uparrow n : A * X \to Seq\ Of\ B$

$f \uparrow n$ is said to be a virtual keyed attribute. The ordering of the sequence of values of $f \uparrow n$ is undefined and its set of values at a particular instance $< a, x >$ of $A * X$ is given by:

$$< a, x > \quad \stackrel{f \uparrow n}{\mapsto} \quad \{f(a) | n(f(a)) = x\}$$

The rules IS1 and IS3 show how particular values may be selected from many by supplying a particular key. The reason for the particular notation $k.f$ for selecting values with key k is for compatibility with PCTE (see 5.5). IDLE has only virtual keyed attributes. The value of $!k.f \uparrow n$ for some A and some value k of the key type X, is the sequence of all Bs from the sequence f for which the value of n is x. The order is undefined and the set of values for some instance a of A is given by:

$$a \quad \stackrel{!k.f \uparrow n}{\mapsto} \quad \{f(a) | n(f(a)) = k\}$$

Whereas $!k.f \uparrow n$ selects *all* matching values, $k.f \uparrow n$ selects just one. The value of $k.f \uparrow n$, for some A, is the first value from the sequence of values of $!k.f \uparrow n$.

Rules IS2 and IS4, in conjunction with Figure 5.3, show how selections may be made by matching patterns. When k is a pattern, i.e. a sequence of values of the key type X then the set of values of $!k.f \uparrow n$ at an instance a of A is given by

$$a \quad \stackrel{!k.f \uparrow n}{\mapsto} \{f(a) | n(f(a))\ matches\ k\}$$

5.4. IDLE

$$
\begin{array}{ll}
\textbf{Tuple Rule.} & \\
(IT_n) & \dfrac{f_1:A \to X_1 \quad f_2:A \to X_1 \;\cdots\; f_n:A \to X_n}{[f_1;f_2;\cdots f_n]:A \to X_1 * X_2 .. * X_n} \\
& \text{where } X_i \text{ is String or Integer or Date or Boolean}
\end{array}
$$

Virtual Key Rule.

$$
(IL1) \quad \dfrac{f:A \to B \quad n:B \to X}{f\hat{\,}n:A*X \to Seq\ Of\ B}
$$

$$
(IL2) \quad \dfrac{f:A \to Seq\ Of\ B \quad n:B \to X}{f\hat{\,}n:A*X \to Seq\ Of\ B}
$$

Selection Rules.

$$
(IS1) \quad \dfrac{f:A*X \to Seq\ Of\ B \quad k:() \to X}{k.f:A \to B}
$$

$$
(IS2) \quad \dfrac{f:A*X \to Seq\ Of\ B \quad k:() \to Seq\ Of\ X}{k.f:A \to B}
$$

$$
(IS3) \quad \dfrac{f:A*X \to Seq\ Of\ B \quad k:() \to X}{!k.f:A \to Seq\ Of\ B}
$$

$$
(IS4) \quad \dfrac{f:A*X \to Seq\ Of\ B \quad k:() \to Seq\ Of\ X}{!k.f:A \to Seq\ Of\ B}
$$

where X is String or Integer or Date or Boolean.

Figure 5.4: IDLE Derived Attributes

In Figure 5.5 we give examples of attributes that may be derived from the attributes and data given in Figure 5.1.

The selection of a particular employee from the many employees in a department:

> smith *from* employees *by* name.

is written as a derived attribute smith.employees↑name which has the signature:

> *smith.employees* ↑ *name* : *department* → *person*

A similar form is used to select all entities matching a given value or pattern. The selection

> *all* smith *from* employees *by* name

is written as the derived attribute !smith.employees↑name which has the signature

> !*smith.employees* ↑ *name* : *department* → *Seq Of person*

Also in Figure 5.5, examples are given of combinations of patterns and tuples of patterns and the use of the predefined attributes of the form !*A*. For example:

> !*sm* ∗ .*person* ↑ *name*

finds *all* persons whose names begin with the letters "sm", while:

> *smith*.!*person* ↑ *name*

finds *some* person whose name is smith. Finally:

> [*sm*∗; < 1950].!*person* ↑ [*name*; *dob*]

may be used to find some person whose name begins with the characters "sm" and whose date of birth is earlier than 1950.

5.5 FUNCTIONAL ANALYSIS OF PCTE

PCTE has a data model of objects and binary relationships. Relationships are bi-directional links. Both objects and links are typed and may have attributes. Attributes are typed and may be Integer, Boolean, Date or String.

Navigation around the PCTE OMS is expressed in terms of *pathnames*. PCTE pathnames generalise the pathnames of UNIX. The syntax for pathnames given in [95] shows them built from *reference objects* (of which the UNIX home directory and the UNIX current directory are special cases) and from *relative pathnames*.

The syntax shows that relative pathnames are built from *linknames* and that the possible linknames are:

- the predefined linkname

    . : *object* → *object*

    which is a (pseudo) link linking every object to itself

5.5. FUNCTIONAL ANALYSIS OF PCTE

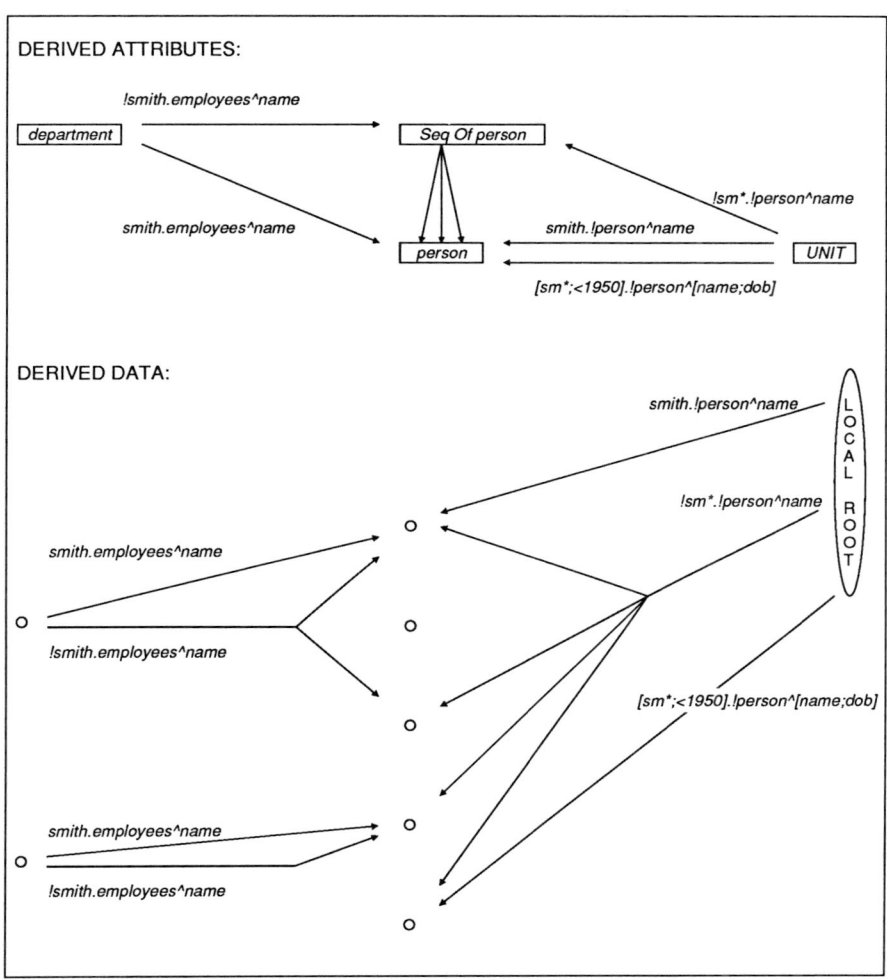

Figure 5.5: Example of derived attributes and data (derived from figure 1)

- cardinality_one link_names

   $.f : A \to B$

   whenever f is a cardinality_one linktype

- cardinality_many link_names

   $k.f : A \to B$

   whenever f is a cardinality_many linktype and k is a key of the appropriate type.

The functional categorisation of PCTE that follows is based on an analysis of these pathnames as virtual attributes. According to this analysis a pathname is a derived attribute with the signature

   $: () \to object$.

Each pathname is built by functional composition from reference objects, which have the signature

   $: () \to object$

and from relative pathnames which have the signature

   $: object \to object$

or, more specifically,

   $: A \to B$

for some subtypes A and B of object.

Relative pathnames are functional compositions of linknames and each linkname is a virtual attribute derived from cardinality_one and cardinality_many linktypes by the *selection rules* shown in figure 5.8.

5.5.1 Type Hierarchy

Some object types are predefined and others are defined by the user. A user defined object type is defined (in the schema or SDS defined by the user) as a subtype of a previously defined type i.e. by specialisation. The predefined type *object* is the root of the type hierarchy and the ancestor to all types.

5.5.2 Predefined Attributes

The predefined functional attributes of PCTE are the attributes and linktypes defined in the *sys* SDS, the reference objects (excluding the reference object ! which escapes from the data model) and the pseudo-link '.'. The predefined attributes other than those in *sys* are shown in figure 5.6.

5.5. FUNCTIONAL ANALYSIS OF PCTE

Attribute	Signature
.1 $\cdots$ .n	:()$\rightarrow$object
_	:()$\rightarrow$object
/	:()$\rightarrow$object
~	:()$\rightarrow$object
#	:()$\rightarrow$object
%1 $\cdots$ %n	:()$\rightarrow$object
.	:()$\rightarrow$object
.	:object$\rightarrow$object
.	:object*Integer$\rightarrow$object

Figure 5.6: PCTE Predefined Attributes

attributes	$f:A \rightarrow String$
	$f:A \rightarrow Boolean$
	$f:A \rightarrow Integer$
	$f:A \rightarrow Date$
	where $A \leq object$
cardinality-one linktypes	$f:A*() \rightarrow B*X_1 \cdots *X_n$
	where $A \leq object$ and $B \leq object$
	and $n \geq 0$ and X_i is Integer, Date, Boolean or String.
cardinality-many linktypes	$f:A*T_1 \rightarrow B*X_1 \cdots *X_n$
	$f:A*T_1*T_2 \rightarrow B*X_1 \cdots *X_n$
	$f:A*T_1*T_2*T_3 \rightarrow B*X_1 \cdots *X_n$
	$f:A*T_1*T_2*T_3*T_4 \rightarrow B*X_1 \cdots *X_n$
	where $A \leq object$ and $B \leq object$
	and $n \geq 0$ and X_i is Integer, Date, Boolean or String
	and T_j is Integer or String

Figure 5.7: PCTE User Defined Attributes

5.5.3 USER DEFINED ATTRIBUTES

In figure 5.7 we show the possible signatures that user defined attributes can have in PCTE. These general forms are complicated by the fact that attributes and linktypes can be applied to many different object types, linktypes may have many valid destination types and cardinality-many links may have up to four keys. Keys can be typed as Integer or String.

To give the forms for signatures as we have presented them in figure 5.7 we have made the following observations:

- If an attribute or linktype has been applied to many different object types, to $A_1, \ldots A_n$, say, then its source type, in functional notation, is $A_1 | \cdots | A_n$.

- Similarly a linktype may have many destination types, $B_1, \ldots B_m$, say, in which case its destination can be expressed as the type expression $B_1 | \cdots | B_m$.

- If a linktype f with source type A and destination type B has attributes $a_1 : X_1, \ldots a_n : X_n$ applied to it, then its functionality is:

	Selection Rules.	
	(PS0)	$$\dfrac{f : A * () \to B}{.f : A \to B}$$
	(PS1)	$$\dfrac{f : A * T \to B \quad k_1 : () \to T_1}{k.f : A \to B}$$
	(PS2)	$$\dfrac{f : A * T_1 * T_2 \to B \quad k_1 : () \to T_1 \quad k_2 : () \to T_2}{k_1.k_2.f : A \to B}$$
	(PS3) and (PS4)	similar to the above, defining $k_1.k_2.k_3.f$ and $k_1.k_2.k_3.k_4.f$
		where T_i is Integer or String
	Composition Rule.	
	(PC)	$$\dfrac{f_1 : A_1 \to A_2 \; \cdots \; f_{n-1} : A_{n-1} \to A_n \quad f_n : A_n \to A_{n+1}}{f_1/f_2/...f_{n-1}/f_n : A_1 \to A_{n+1}}$$
		where $A_i \leq object$

Figure 5.8: PCTE Derived Attributes

$f : A \to B * X_1 * \cdots * X_n$.

5.5.4 Derived Attributes

The rules given in figure 5.8 express the rules for building meaningful pathnames from reference objects and linktypes.

5.6 THE ECLIPSE DATA MODEL

5.6.1 Type Hierarchy

The two tiers, PCTE and IDLE are joined as follows. There is an Eclipse predefined object type *fine_structure_object* which is defined along with other predefined Eclipse types and attributes in a PCTE SDS called *eclipse*.

When the user defines a new type of fine structure object, A, he does so, in the Eclipse DDL, by defining it as a subtype of *fine_structure_object*:

$A \leq fine\_structure\_object$

and by associating with this subtype an IDLE schema which describes the fine structure of this type of object. The complete data definition encompassing the first tier, including fine structure objects, and the second tier fine structure is a *two_tier_sds*.

5.6. THE ECLIPSE DATA MODEL

```
diagram ≤ fine_structure_object ;

diagram ⇒
[
    ENTITY ::= box | arrow;

    arrow ⇒
        source : box,
        destination : box;

    box ⇒
        top_left_x : Integer,
        top_left_y : Integer,
        height : Integer,
        width : Integer;
];
```

Figure 5.9: Example of Eclipse DDL

$$entity ::= object \mid \sum_{A \leq fine\_structure\_object} \sum_{a:A} ENTITY(a)$$

Figure 5.10: The Eclipse Type Hierarchy - where $\sum$ represents the join operation | applied to a family of types

In Eclipse DDL, fine structure is shown in square brackets associated with a subtype of fine structure object as shown in figure 5.9. In this example, a diagram is shown as having fine structure consisting of entities of types *arrow* and *box* where arrows are linked to boxes by virtue of having *source* and *destination* as entity-valued attributes. A box in a diagram also has attributes representing coordinate position and size and other attributes.

An IDLE type B that is local to the fine structure of some object type A is in the sense of [13] [96] a *dependent type*. Considered in the database as a whole it is a different type $B(a)$ at each instance a of A. These considerations lead us to summarise the type structure of the two-tier database as a whole by the equation shown in figure 10.

5.6.2 Predefined Attributes

The predefined attributes of Eclipse are those of PCTE and of IDLE and the attributes defined in the *eclipse* SDS. The two-tier database supports a number of other predefined attributes. These attributes and their signatures are summarised in figure 5.11.

To connect the two tiers of data a predefined attribute fine structure objects into their fine structure. The value of is the local root of the fine structure object. Since the root of an IDLE structure is of type UNIT the signature of given by

$$\% : (a : A) \to UNIT(a), \text{ whenever } A \leq fine\_structure\_object$$

%	:$(a{:}A) \rightarrow UNIT(a)$ whenever $A \leq fine\_structure\_object$
$TEXT	:$(Integer\ |Boolean\ |Date\ |String) \rightarrow String$
$DAY	:$Date \rightarrow Date$
$TYPE	:$entity \rightarrow String$
$READ_ONLY	:$entity \rightarrow Boolean$

Figure 5.11: Eclipse Predefined Attributes

The two-tier database also supports attributes derived by type conversion. The basic type conversion operations supported are conversion to text form and conversion of a date and time to be an exact day date. These are represented by predefined attributes $TEXT and $DAY. $TYPE represents the type of an entity and $READ_ONLY represents its access permissions.

5.6.3 User Defined Attributes

The user definable attributes in Eclipse are those definable in PCTE and those that can be defined in IDLE. Each fine structure object type has a set of IDLE definitions associated with it. The signatures of these are, in the context of the two-tier database, dependent on instances of the fine structure. For example, an IDLE entity attribute

$$f : B \rightarrow B'$$

associated with some fine structure object type A is, in the context of the two-tier database as a whole, an attribute with signature given by:

$$f : B(a : A) \rightarrow B'(a).$$

The signature expresses that f is an entity attribute whose value is local to a particular fine structure. In this sense the type of f expresses its *scope*. It is forbidden to insert a value in f from an entity of type $B(a_1)$ to an entity of type $B'(a_2)$ if a_1 and a_2 are distinct objects . This is a type error in Eclipse.

An example of the use of this modelling facility is in the fine structure representation of diagrams such as is shown in figure 9. A type *diagram* is modelled as a subtype of fine structure object. An IDLE schema describes the contents of diagrams in terms of the types *box* and *arrow* and entity-valued attributes *source* and *destination*. It is a type error to attempt to draw an *arrow* from a *box* on one diagram to a *box* of a distinct diagram because *source* and *destination* may not span different fine structure objects. They are said to be local.

Non-local links may also be defined. These may be 1st-to-2nd-tier, 2nd-to-1st-tier or 2nd-to-2nd-tier. It is a part of the notion of fine structure that these links refine links that exist solely at the first tier — just as fine grain structures refine objects at the first tier. The first tier links which have refinements at the second tier are called summary links. When a non-local link is inserted or deleted then the database manages the insertion or deletion of an appropriate summary link. The link into which the summary is inserted is defined as part of the type of the non-local link. The

5.6. THE ECLIPSE DATA MODEL

	Signature of Summary	Signatures of Refinements
1st to 2nd	$g:A*X \rightarrow A'$	$\%g:(a:A,x:X) \rightarrow ENTITY(g(a,x))$
	where $A \leq object$ and $A' \leq fine\_structure\_object$ and for some m, $0 \leq m \leq 4$, X is $T_1* \cdots *T_m$ where T_j is Integer or String	
2nd to 1st	$g:A*Integer \rightarrow A'$	$f:B(A)*Integer \rightarrow A'$
	where $A \leq fine\_structure\_object$ and $A' \leq object$	where $B \leq ENTITY(A)$ f is subject to the constraint: for all $a:A$, for all $b:B(a)$ $f(b,i) = g(a,i)$.
2nd to 2nd	$g:A*Integer \rightarrow A'$,	$f:B(a:A)*(i:Integer) \rightarrow B'(g(a,i))$ $f:B(a:A)*(i:Integer) \rightarrow Seq\ Of\ B'(g(a,i))$
	where $A, A' \leq fine\_structure\_object$	where $B \leq ENTITY(A)$ and $B' \leq ENTITY(A')$

Figure 5.12: Eclipse User Defined Attributes

summary link of a non-local link whose source is at the second tier is many-valued. It is modelled as a cardinality-many linktype keyed by Integer, the key is managed by the database. The only non-locals having a first tier source are those with a name $\%g$, where g is a linktype whose destination is a subtype of $fine\_structure\_object$.

The different kinds of non-local link, their signatures and the signatures of the summary links they refine are given in figure 12.

The possible signatures of user definable attributes in Eclipse are therefore those of PCTE, those of IDLE (local to some fine structure object) and those non-local link signatures given in figure 5.12. The way of defining 2nd to 1st and 2nd to 2nd tier links in the DDL is shown in figure 5.13.

As an example of the use of 2nd to 1st tier link consider the representation of the hierarchical design of a system. Each component in the design is represented at least twice. First it has a representation as a node within the system structure of some higher level component. Second, there is a representation of its own system structure. Typically a 2nd to 1st tier link is used to connect the first representation to the second. This is the participation concept discussed in chapter 4.

The two-tier schemas used by the MASCOT tool set are described in Chapter 9.

5.6.4 Derived Attributes

The derived attributes supported by the two-tier database are those supported by its components PCTE and IDLE. Functional composition in the two-tier database is

```
A ≤ fine_structure_object ;

A ⇒ g(summary_key: Integer): A';        -- the summary link

A ⇒
  [
    .
    B ⇒ f 1: Object (Summarised By g),   -- f1 : B*Integer → A'
                                         -- in this case every B is
                                         -- linked to at most one A'
        f 2: Seq Of Object
             (Summarised By g),          -- f2 : B*Integer → A'
        f 3: B' From A'
             (Summarised By g),          -- f3 : B*Integer → B'
                                         -- in this case every B is
                                         -- linked to at most one B'
        f 4: Seq Of B' From A'
             (Summarised By g);          -- f4 : B*Integer → Seq Of B'
    .
  ];

A' ≤ fine_structure_object ;

A' ⇒
  [
    .
    B' ⇒
         .
         .

         .
  ]
```

Figure 5.13: Associating Summary Links and Refinements in the DDL

5.7. THE DATABASE INTERFACE

$$\text{(EC1)} \quad \frac{f:A \to B_1 \quad g:B_1 \to B_2}{g'f:A \to B_2}$$
whenever $A \leq$ *entity* and each B_i is String, Integer, Boolean or Date

$$\text{(EC2)} \quad \frac{f_1:A_1 \to A_2 \quad \cdots \quad f_{n-1}:A_{n-1} \to A_n \quad f_n:A_n \to B}{f_1/f_2/...f_{n-1}/f_n:A_1 \to B}$$
whenever each $A_i \leq$ *entity* and B is String, Integer, Boolean or Date

Figure 5.14: Eclipse Derived Attributes

more general than in the components and may cross the tiers using the cross tier links and/or the predefined attribute %. For implementation efficiency reasons there are two different notations for functional composition. Both notations and the circumstances in which they apply are shown in figure 5.14. Rule EC1 relates to the use of the predefined attributes shown in figure 5.11 (% excepted). Rule EC2 relates to the pathname notation.

5.7 THE DATABASE INTERFACE

The Eclipse Database Interface is the procedural interface used to access data stored in the Two-Tier Database. As discussed in section 4.4.2, it unifies the PCTE OMS interface and the IDLE-FSD interface. This interface is based on the functional approach described earlier.

After our experience with the first version of the interface (see 4.3.4), we were aware of the importance of the architecture of the Two Tier Database implementation to performance. Our first attempt, written in Ada, had produced a 178 function ITI interface and was implemented by a single piece of code of 1.2 Mb. This interface had to be bound in with every tool using the database. The size had been an enormous problem given the random access memory and disk space limitations on our SUN workstations and had caused a great deal of unnecessary process swapping.

There was clearly a need to reduce the size of the code to be bound in with each tool and we resolved this by moving that code dealing with the second tier of the database into a separate process and using inter-process communication. To further reduce the size of the bound-in code which effectively implements remote procedure call for second tier data we needed to reduce the number of functions. To minimise the performance overhead of having a separate process for second tier data we had to minimise the inter-process communication rate and this implied reducing the number of function calls required on the DBI. The only way to achieve both objectives was to increase the functionality of individual DBI functions.

A particular feature of our architecture is that the same functions are supported by each component of the two tier database, the Switch, the Kernel[4]. which uses PCTE functions to access first tier data, and the FSD which accesses second tier

---
[4]This refers not to the Eclipse kernel but to an internal component of the database.

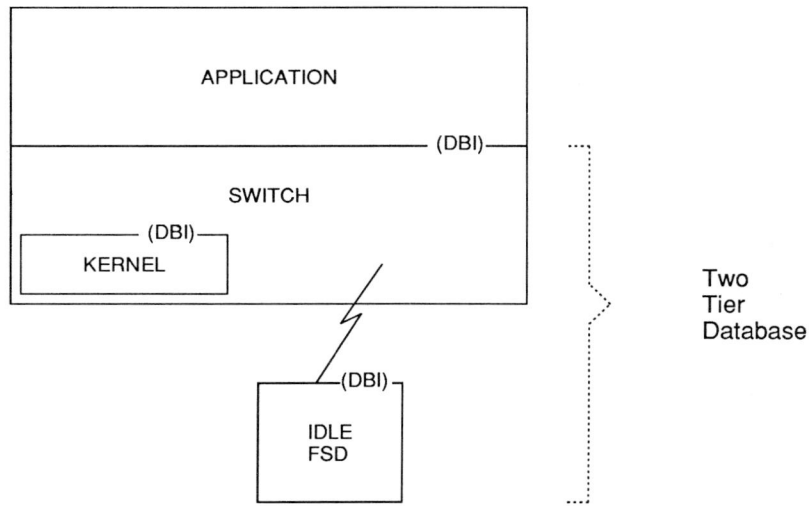

Figure 5.15: The DBI Architecture

data. (See figure 5.15). This allows us to substitute the whole functionality of the two-tier database for just second tier access. This is appropriate where the application accesses only one object and is concerned only with the second tier data. Performance is improved by avoiding the inter-process communication.

The twin principles of reduced number of functions and increased functionality fitted well with two other aims. Firstly, we wished to provide database searches some of which would be fast searches implemented by indexes. The searches were to be invoked in the same way no matter what the implementation — because we wanted tools to be independent of data representation. Secondly we wished pattern matching to be implemented beneath the database interface and not above it. This was because we had the criticism of tools written in UNIX that the end-user does not as a matter of course get the benefit of pattern matching — it depends on how the tools are written.

The principles also fitted well with the UNIX style navigations supported by PCTE. The functionality of a navigation "a/b/c" is that it can be applied to a starting point — an entity — and it yields another entity. So, a navigation can be seen as an entity-valued attribution (see 5.6.4). In particular it is a *derived attribute* since its value is one derived from the values of others. We also realised that searches and pattern matching could be expressed in terms of many-valued derived attributes (see 5.4.3).

To reduce the number of functions we looked at the way we had strongly typed the interface. In the first version there were many functions to read the value of an attribute each one corresponding to a different attribute type: entity-valued, integer-valued, string-valued and so on. We replaced these by a single function whose value had a discriminated union as its type (see 5.9.3). We rationalised the rest of the interface in the same way. We also made the major decision to represent the database schema within the database and thus to rid ourselves of the necessity of providing schema interrogation facilities.

The decision to represent attribute values by a discriminated union made it possible to conceive of derived attributes whose values were themselves tuples of values (see 5.9.3). Thus a single DBI function call could access a number of attributes and not just one.

The course that has been followed has been to design a database interface that consists of a basic set of functions for the manipulation of the concepts defined by the user (using DDL) and also providing composite manipulations by supporting a system of predefined and derived attributes. This basic set of functions is described in 5.9 below.

For performance reasons some extra functions have been added to this basic set but only when the desired functionality could not be achieved by extending the language of predefined and virtual attributes or when this was deemed unsuitable. These functions are described in section 5.10.

5.8 NOTATION

The Eclipse project has used the functional signature notation for designing and describing programming language interfaces. It is used in the description of the Eclipse Public Tools Interface given in [27].

When the notation is used in the role of describing interfaces, then the signature of a function expresses the types of its *in* parameters and *out* parameters but not what the formal parameter names are. Often the formal parameter names are of no concern to the designer.

Here are two examples of the notation. The function to negate an integer has the signature

> negation : Integer → Integer.

The function to add two integers has the signature

> addition : Integer * Integer → Integer.

The absence of *in* parameters or the absence of *out* parameters is shown by empty parentheses. Thus we might have

> todays_date : () → Date

or

> print : string → ().

Notice that in these two examples a hidden state is involved and in the second case the function has a side-effect. The functions in the DBI have the database as a state which they side-effect.

5.9 BASIC DBI FUNCTIONS

This set of functions has been chosen as a minimal set giving expression to the concepts within the database of typed entities and attributes and providing facilities for navigation around the database (starting at the root entity) and for the manipulation of entities — for creating them and deleting them and for reading and writing single-valued and many-valued attributes.

5.9.1 Root

The DBI function 'root' returns an entity token as a reference to the root of the entire two-tier database:

root : () $\rightarrow$ entity.

This is the starting point for navigations around the database.

5.9.2 Creating Entities

Entities are created in relation to other entities as the destinations of composition links (see section 5.1 above). The function 'create-entity' takes the type of the entity to be created and the entity and attribute in relation to which it is being created, as parameters. The signature is:

create_entity : entity * entity_type * attribute $\rightarrow$ entity

where entity types and attributes are represented by their names which are strings.

5.9.3 Reading and Writing Attribute Values

The values of attributes are obtained using the function:

value_of_attribute : entity * attribute $\rightarrow$ attribute_value

and attributes are updated by using the function :

attribute_becomes : entity * attribute * attribute_value $\rightarrow$ ()

The result returned by 'value_of_attribute' is of type attribute_value. This is implemented as a discriminated union with the cases shown here. (This notation is a variant of ML [84] where upper case identifiers represent the values of the discriminant and lower case identifiers are the names of data types.)

```
attribute_value ::= INTEGER integer
                  | BOOLEAN boolean
                  | DATE date
                  | STRING string
                  | ENTITY entity
                  | UNDEFINED
                  | TUPLE attribute_value_tuple
                  | ITERATOR iterator
```

5.9. BASIC DBI FUNCTIONS

```
where attribute_value_tuple ::=    attribute_value
                              |    attribute_value * attribute_value_tuple
```

In line with the general principles, the attributes read by 'value_of_attribute' may be user defined attributes (5.6.3) or they may be predefined (5.6.2) or derived attributes (5.6.4). The derived attributes that are evaluated by this function include UNIX pathnames, attributes such as "fred.c" which selects a value (keyed by "fred") from a keyed bag attribute "c", and attributes that enable entities to be selected by patterns over values of their attributes.

Similarly, the attributes that may be updated by 'attribute_becomes' include derived attributes of the form "k.b", where "b" is a keyed bag attribute.

5.9.4 Deleting Links

The function delete_link is for removing the values of attributes of type entity i.e. for removing links:

  delete_link : entity * attribute → ()

In designing the interface, we considered subsuming the functionality of 'delete_link' into the function 'attribute_becomes' by interpreting the overwriting of a link by the UNDEFINED value as effectively removing the link. This was in line with the principle of reducing the number of functions in the interface and was to an extent natural because 'value_of_attribute' returns UNDEFINED if the value of a link attribute has not been set. However, the deletion of a composition link may cause the destination of the link to be deleted (see section 5.1 above). In this case the removal of a link is the inverse to 'create_entity'. For this reason 'delete_link' was kept a separate function and its name was chosen carefully with this detail of its functionality in mind. We had also learned from earlier experience which showed that it was unwise to treat UNDEFINED as a value of type entity because it weakened the type and therefore increased the amount of precondition checking throughout the implementation of both the database and the tools.

5.9.5 Many-Valued Attributes and Iterators

At both tiers of the database there are many-valued attributes. It is not practical to return all the values of a many-valued attribute at one go. Rather the DBI has facilities which enable the many values to be iterated through by the tool. To this end, there is the notion of an iterator. An iterator is a token which is maintained by the DBI and which represents the many values of a many-valued attribute and a current iteration position within the values.

Iterators are returned by the DBI when the 'value_of_attribute' function is called to read a many-valued attribute. Other functions involving iterators have a side-effect on the iterator (for example, stepping it forwards).

The functions for iterating through values are:

next : iterator → attribute_value

next_value_and_key : iterator → attribute_value

The 'next' function is straightforward. It steps forward and returns the next value. If it reaches the end of the many values then it returns an exception.

The 'next_value_and_key' function is only valid on iterators through keyed attributes. The function returns the next value and the key to the next value. This pair of attribute values is returned as a tuple.

Note that to reduce the number of functions and function calls, both these functions combine the functionalities of testing for the end condition, stepping forward and returning a value. In the first version we had made the mistake of supporting these with separate functions. In the context of the layering of the implementation of both the interface and the tools, having 'test' and 'step forward' as separate functions proved to be inefficient. This was because it was natural for each layer to implement 'step forward' so that it tested its precondition before moving forward. In the integrated whole a single end-user action of stepping forward could generate an explosion of procedure calls[5] and many tests of the end condition as the different layers checked the precondition.

Sequence-valued attributes are manipulated using functions:

add_to_tail : entity * attribute * attribute_value → ()

and

insert_before : iterator * attribute_value → ()

to add values to the sequence of values and

remove_current_value : iterator → ()

to remove values from them.

5.10 OTHER DBI FUNCTIONS

These functions are DBI functions whose rationale is not solely in terms of the functionality they offer but also in terms of performance. The actions of these functions can be specified in terms of the actions of the basic functions given in section 5.9 above.

5.10.1 Manipulating Sequences

There is a clear need for the end-user to be able to scroll back through the lists of values of a many-valued attribute as well as being able to scroll forward through them. Implementing such functionality in terms of the basic functions described in 5.9 is expensive. Therefore to reduce the number of calls made on the interface the following function is provided:

previous : iterator → attribute_value

---

[5] As many as $n(n + 1)/2$, where n is the number of layers!

5.10. OTHER DBI FUNCTIONS

The end-user may also want to append to a sequence of values at the head rather than the tail. Using the basic functions this can be achieved but to reduce the number of calls and for reasons of symmetry and convenience to the tool writer, the following function is a part of the interface:

add_to_head : entity * attribute * attribute_value → ()

5.10.2 Supporting Sets

Set-valued attributes are not provided by the data model, they were removed as a part of the rationalisation of the first version of the database. However, functions that enable the tools to maintain sequences of values to be sets have been provided. They are:

attribute_gets_value : entity * attribute * attribute_value → ()

attribute_loses_value : entity * attribute * attribute_value → ()

attribute_becomes_empty : entity * attribute → ()

These functions have simple functionalities which would otherwise cost more than n calls of the database, where n is the number of values of the sequence attribute. The function 'attribute_gets_value' adds a value to the end of a sequence of values unless it is already in the sequence in which case no action is taken. The function 'attribute_loses_value' is inverse to 'attribute_gets_value', it removes the first occurrence of a given value from a sequence of values. Finally, the function 'attribute_becomes_empty' removes every value from a sequence of values.

The function 'attribute_becomes_empty' allows a simple illustration of the power of derived attributes. Using the data definitions of section 5.4.3, we may remove every entity of type person by:

attribute_becomes_empty(LR, "!person"),

where LR is a token representing the local root.

We can however be more selective and delete only entities of type person relating to persons named smith by:

attribute_becomes_empty(LR, "!smith.!person↑name")

5.10.3 Copying Fine Structure

It is one of the characteristics of the two-tier database that it is possible to copy fine structure data *en masse*. Though it is a crucial concept it is nonetheless a performance issue and so the function that provides copying has been included in this general section. Having this function in the interface gives an enormous reduction in the number of calls made of the database in copying an entity such as a diagram. The signature of the function is as follows:

create_copy_of_entity : entity{given} * attribute{1} * attribute{2} → entity{result}

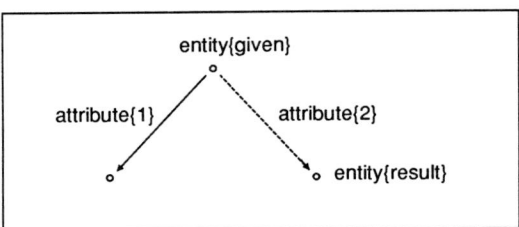

Figure 5.16: Copying Entities

The behaviour of the function is to create a new entity as a copy of an old one as shown in figure 5.16.

The new entity is created as a partial copy of the destination of attribute{1} of entity{given}. It becomes the destination of the composition link attribute{2}. A token identifying the entity{result}is returned.

If the entity that is copied is a file (i.e. if it is first tier and its type is a subtype of the type file) then the contents of the file are copied into the contents of the newly created entity. If the entity that is copied has fine structure then the fine structure of the entity is copied.

A copy link is one that is copied when the object is copied and a duplicate link is one that is copied by copying its destination object. Any first tier link can be nominated to be a copy link and any first tier composition link can be nominated to be a duplicate link.

5.10.4 Access to Type Information

In principle, information in the schema is accessed by interrogating the schema as data using the basic DBI functions. For the accesses that are most commonly required a small number of additional functionalities have been explicitly provided. Some of these are represented by predefined attributes for example there is a one that returns the type of an entity as a string (see 5.6.2 above). In addition to these there are the two explicit functions which could not be expressed by way of predefined attributes because their signatures are not of an appropriate form.

The first function is important because it enables a tool to offer to an end-user a menu of actions on an attribute. In this way it supports, to a degree, an object oriented user interface.

$$\text{type\_of\_attribute} : \text{entity} * \text{attribute} \rightarrow \text{attribute\_type} * \text{action\_set}$$

The data type action_set represents which DBI functions may be applied to the given entity-attribute pair.

When entities are passed between tools or indicated by the end-user then the following function enables the type to be checked by the tool:

$$\text{is\_classified\_by} : \text{entity} * \text{entity\_type} \rightarrow \text{boolean}$$

It determines whether the given entity is an instance of the given entity type. The existence of the function in the interface ensures there is no performance overhead for this kind of type checking.

5.11 CONFIGURATION CONTROL

To provide a configuration control scheme, we need to represent that which is versioned. To do this we introduced the *item*. The versions belong to the item. The versions will be PCTE objects, frequently of subtype file or fine structure object (see 4.4.2).

With foreign tools, it is frequently of importance that the correct file extension is used. (In PCTE terms, that particular linktypes exist.) For instance, the C compiler makes assumptions about the content of files which have .c, .o and certain other file extensions.

Ideally we would model item and versions so that all objects related to the item had the same file extension (i.e. that the item represented all versions of a particular source file or of a particular executable binary, and nothing else). This however is not possible because of the action of existing foreign tools. The C compiler is a sufficient example. If some file fred.c is compiled, the output is automatically directed to fred.o. This requires that the same object provides both the 'c' and 'o' linktypes.

Therefore we define that objects accessed through a particular linktype are the *primary objects* of the item. When the Database Interface selects a preferred version, it always selects one of the primary objects of the item. Any object related to the item may be accessed by naming it specifically but only primary objects may be accessed by the preferred version mechanism. Further the CCI functions can only be applied to primary objects of an item. We say that the primary objects of an item are its versions.

Eclipse Configuration Control has the concept of configurations. A configuration delimits the set of versions of items currently in scope (i.e. visible and available to be operated on). New versions are created in the scope of only one configuration. Versions may be published from the configuration within which they were created and subsequently acquired into the scope of other configurations.

Configurations may be created and deleted. At any time one configuration may be the current configuration for a process. Any processes started by this process will inherit the current configuration at the time of invocation. (Note that a process may subsequently change its current configuration. However this will have no effect on the current configuration of the parent process or on the current configuration of any child process which has already been invoked.)

Configurations only affect the visibility of versions; for example, they do not affect the visibility of items. However the objects accessible by a user depend not just on the current configuration but also on the SDSs in use; this is the function of the PCTE working schema. Since Eclipse uses two_tier_sdss rather than just SDSs a function is required to add a two_tier_sds into the working schema.

Configuration Control functions operating on versions (see below) require some configuration to be current. Five functions are provided to manipulate configurations:

- to create a configuration in a directory of configurations, create : configuration_name * configuration_directory → ()

- to delete a configuration from a directory of configurations,

    delete : configuration_name * configuration_directory → ()

- to make current a configuration,

    make_current : configuration_name * configuration_directory → ()

- to add a two_tier_sds to the working schema,

    load_tts : seq of tts → ()

- to obtain the name of the current configuration.

    name_of : () → string

The configuration control mechanism is based on a developer creating a version in some configuration and then publishing it so that access may be acquired to it from any configurations. Until it has been published it will not be accessible from any other configuration. Four functions are provided to manage versions of items:

- Publish a version. This can only be performed by the owner of the version. (In applications this function is usually associated with the version reaching some quality status.) Once published, a version cannot be modified until the owner withdraws it.

    publish : pcte_pathname → ()

- Withdraw a version. This can only be done by the owner of the published version. A version cannot be withdrawn if it is still acquired.

    withdraw : pcte_pathname → ()

- Acquire access to a version. Access to a published version may be acquired into a configuration so that the version may be used and may be prevented from being withdrawn. (Note that write access cannot be acquired.)

    acquire : pcte_pathname → ()

- Release access to a version. Access to a version may be released from a configuration into which it has been acquired. When access to a particular version has been released by all configurations into which it has been acquired, the owner may withdraw it.

    release : pcte_pathname → ()

There is no copying of versions implied. All users of a version use the only instance of that version.

The versions of an item are distinguished by a single integer version number. The version numbers used to distinguish a version in any particular configuration are private to that configuration. However when versions are published they are given an issue number (again a single integer), by the publish function, which is the same in all configurations. A further function, issue_number_of, issue_number_of : pcte_pathname → integer

is provided which given a version returns the issue number of that version. Note that if the version has not been published then it will have no issue number.

5.12 CONCLUSION

A two-tier database has been built to support the life-cycle as a whole and the individual stages within it. The two-tier database has been built from PCTE and IDLE. By considering the two data models functionally we have reached the underlying concepts and this has led to a meaningful union of the data models in which IDLE structures refine the structure of PCTE objects and relationships.

The database interface in Eclipse has a small number of functions in it because a great amount of the functionality is carried by the virtual attributes. We have found this to work very well. This style of interface has led to a greater ease of extensibility. During development, the extension of the functionality of the interface has been possible by extending the virtual attributes supported. This has caused less work than supporting new types and new functions and has led to new insight.

This implementation satisfies the requirements we set ourselves in terms of reducing the code size to be bound with each tool; it is now 150Kb. The related FSD process is also 150Kb.

The implementation also satisfies our aim to limit interprocess communication within the DBI and provide acceptable efficiency for tools accessing the database. This is apparent from the response provided to the end user by the tools we have produced.

Recent benchmarks indicate that functions operating on the second tier of data are 2 times faster for reading an attribute, 5 times faster for updating an attribute and 25 times faster for creation of entities and for navigation via relationships than when operating at the first tier. Generally we achieve around 100 function calls per second at the second tier.

Of course the small speed difference for reading an attribute, two times faster in the second tier, is because the operation is so simple in both cases, and is dominated by the inter-process communication for second tier access. Note however that we can also read many attributes in a single function call. For the first tier access the time taken increases linearly with the number of attributes. For second tier access the time taken for each extra attribute is not noticable, since it is very small compared to the inter-process communication time. We are studying the benchmark results and are already aware of potential performance improvements in the DBI. We have also indicated areas of Emeraude where performance should be investigated.

In conclusion we claim that the Eclipse Database demonstrates that two-tier databases can be implemented which give very natural way of modelling software engineering data and provide acceptable performance.

Chapter 6

Interaction with Eclipse

Stuart Potter, John Smart, Ian Sommerville and Ray Welland

One of the principal tasks of the MMI group was to design an integrated user interface for Eclipse. The integration of tools via the database was obviously essential but it was considered equally important to provide a fully integrated end-user interface and support for the construction of such an interface. Thus an end-user would not be presented with a completely different interface for each different tool used (or worse still, a subtly inconsistent interface for each tool).

An early task undertaken by members of the MMI group was the evaluation of suitable work stations for Eclipse. The original choice was the Sun 2 series of work stations with a medium resolution 19" landscape screen and a three button mouse. The Sun window manager (SunTools) provided a means of manipulating multiple windows, closing windows down to icons, designing icons, etc. It was decided that, since it was not a primary aim of Eclipse to develop a new window manager, the integrated user interface should be built on top of the Sun window manager.

It was decided that the Eclipse user interface required a unifying *metaphor* which could be used consistently across all tools. The best known such metaphor is the 'desk top' metaphor, typified by the Apple Macintosh. However, it was felt that this was not the most appropriate metaphor for a software engineer carrying out a variety of system development tasks. The Eclipse 'house style' which evolved was based on the *control panel* metaphor and this is described in the next section of this chapter.

Although a particular work station had been chosen for the development of the prototype of Eclipse it was undesirable to tie the user interface to the Sun window manager. An interface definition layer was used to isolate the user interface from the underlying system architecture. This layer allowed the user interface structure to be described in a definition language which could be translated into the appropriate representation for the underlying window manager. Therefore, it is possible to port the Eclipse User Interface between different machines and operating systems by redefining the translation.

The other important areas of interaction which the MMI group considered were message handling and the provision of help facilities. An end-user interface cannot be considered well integrated if each tool makes an arbitrary decision about where and how messages are displayed. Therefore, the message handling procedures were designed to provide a unifying mechanism for all messages passing between tools and the end-user.

In many systems help is added as an afterthought and consists of a few pages of poorly structured text or possibly just on-line copies of the user manual. In Eclipse, the objective was to design a context sensitive help system which would be related to the tasks currently being undertaken by the end-user and allow browsing of the help frames. Supporting software was developed to allow tool builders to build the necessary help structures.

6.1 CONTROL PANELS

Eclipse is an *open* environment and therefore it was not possible to support the tight integration which can be provided in single language environments such as Interlisp [123] and Smalltalk [44]. The most general environment is that pioneered in the Xerox Star system and now widely known through the Apple Macintosh. In this system all tools have a common interface style and make use of standard routines to create their own user interface. These principles should obviously be applied to the Eclipse UI.

We rejected a simple desk top metaphor because the objects which it represents are office documents with a limited set of allowed operations such as move, delete, etc. Software engineers are concerned with programs, designs, and specifications which have different sets of allowed operations (such as compile, link, check, etc.). The number of possible operations applied to software is, typically, much larger than those allowed using the desk top metaphor. Furthermore, it is difficult to devise appropriate iconic representations for many of the abstract objects which are involved in the software process.

A further motivation for our work was the terse and inconsistent command language syntax of UNIX and, as we discovered, the even less consistent PCTE command language. Inexperienced and occasional users find this difficult and even expert users regularly make mistakes using UNIX commands. We wished to conceal this completely from the Eclipse user. Therefore, we looked for some compromise between the easy to understand but simplistic desk top metaphor and the terse command language offered by systems such as UNIX. In short, we sought to develop a graphical interface with sufficient functionality for the more experienced user.

In seeking a suitable metaphor for Eclipse, we considered the control panel used to control complex engineering systems. Obviously, some aspects of such interfaces were inappropriate for us to adopt - we were not in the business of designing revolutionary interfaces which incorporated foot pedals or new types of hand controls! Some other aspects of physical interfaces were also rejected because it was felt they were inappropriate in the Eclipse environment. For example, the use of analogue dials is computationally expensive and there seemed to be few sensible uses for them. Similarly, the slider type of control did not seem very useful within the control panel although it proved very useful for scroll bars where windows were being moved over a larger underlying area.

Control panels are built using five basic types of object (Figure 6.1).

Having identified these basic control panel objects we then designed their graphical

6.1. CONTROL PANELS

Object type	Description
1. Button	A button is an object which, when picked ('pressed'), always initiates a single action, such as quitting a tool. The same action is initiated each time the button is pressed. Its effect is not context dependent.
2. Menu	A menu displays a list of objects one of which may be chosen by the user to initiate some action. Menu elements are not necessarily static. Their entries may depend on the context in which the user is working.
3. State Selector	A state selector is a composite symbol consisting of a menu and a value. The value displays the current state which may be changed by selection from the menu. For example, in the Design Editor, a state selector is used to display and change the current entity type.
4. Sign	A sign is a two part object with a fixed title and a value. The value part may be static, dynamic (changed by the system) or user-changeable. In the Design Editor, a static sign is used to display the name of the current design method. A user-changeable sign is used to display the name of the entity being edited. To change from one entity to another, the user overtypes the old name in the sign with the new.
5. Light	A light is a binary status indicator. Lights may be used to indicate the active window, whether a process is busy or any other on/off state. Tools may arrange for a light to 'flash' during time consuming operations to assure the user that the system is still active.

Figure 6.1: Control Panel Object Types

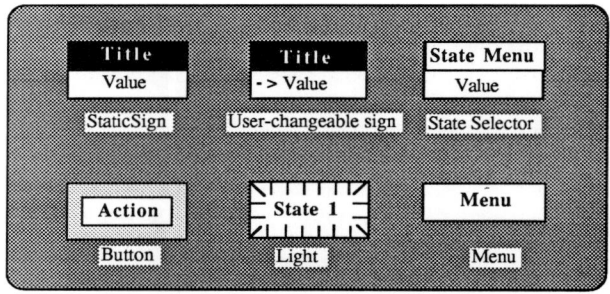

Figure 6.2: Control Panel Object Representations

representations. We carried out some experiments with different images and recommended an initial set of symbols. These then evolved during the project after feedback from users. The basic principle we used was that the representations should be visually distinct so that the user could not confuse them. However, we quickly recognised a second, pragmatic constraint; that symbols must be regular shapes which could easily be fitted into a rectangular control panel. If irregular, possibly more meaningful, images were used then they caused the control panels to become over-large and dominate the screen.

The final set of symbols used is shown in Figure 6.2 and examples of the use of control panels are shown in Figures 6.3 and 6.11. Note that a user-changeable sign includes the visual cue → to indicate that input is allowed.

Control panels have been used throughout Eclipse to provide interfaces to a wide variety of tools. However, they are not a universal panacea. One widely recognised problem in designing user interfaces is that providing mechanisms, such as control panels, does not guarantee good interface design. A control panel with fifty buttons would be horrendous to use! The tool builder has to design the control panel with care, deciding which options can sensibly be grouped into menus, which values need to be displayed via signs, etc. This process of design should be iterative using feedback from users of the tool.

A control panel is not suitable for providing low-level commands such as those used when editing a piece of text. The interface to a text editor would be unusable if each simple character editing command required the user to select from a menu or use a button. Therefore, these low-level commands should be provided via special key sequences or function keys. The higher level commands, such as identifying the file to be edited or saving the current version of the text, are sensible candidates for the control panel.

In addition to the work on control panels we also carried out some experiments on designing an Eclipse house style for the positioning of windows and the use of icons, etc. These ideas are discussed in [104] but no generally accepted standards were agreed for use within Eclipse.

6.1. CONTROL PANELS

6.1.1 Control Panel Construction

Control Panels appear to be a useful metaphor but we know that the 'look and feel' of specific user interfaces can only be discovered by building a prototype interface. The manual creation of control panels using FDL (see later) is a tedious and error-prone business and not a means of fast prototyping. Accordingly, we have developed an interactive system for control panel construction [30].

The user is presented with a menu of the basic control panel elements (buttons, signs, lights, etc.) and picks items from this menu for inclusion on a control panel (Figure 6.3). The interface builder may then position these on the control panel and move them around at will until he or she is satisfied with the look of the display.

The advantages offered by this approach are:

- The designer is given assistance in laying out the interface because the tool can ensure alignments, etc.

- End-users can become involved in interface design because they get instant feedback on the appearance of the interface.

- Interfaces can be produced and modified very quickly thus allowing experiments with specific interfaces to be carried out.

Work in this area is continuing with the development of a complete user interface prototyping tool set [30]. As well as being able to construct control panels interactively, the designer may also specify action sequences using augmented transition diagrams.

6.1.2 Control Panel Implementation

The initial implementation of control panels was accomplished using a set of C routines interacting with the work station window management system. This worked well but was a non-portable solution. We sought a solution which could be implemented using either the SunWindows package or the PCTE UI primitives.

The solution which was discovered was based on the development of an existing product developed by CAP. This was called MMIMS (Man-Machine Interface management System) and, in its initial implementation provided a terminal-independent set of facilities to support user interface creation. This product was extended and developed to support the Control Panel metaphor and to add facilities allowing it to interact with different window management systems. This extended system is discussed in the following section.

Figure 6.4 shows how are control panels are implemented using this system.

A description of a tool interface is produced using a notation called FDL (Frame Description Language). This includes a control panel description and also a description of the windows and sub-windows used by the tool. At run-time, this FDL is interpreted to provide control panels and control panel actions.

For each interface object, the FDL description may specify the following attributes:

- its position and extent;

- its visibility (is it actually displayed on the terminal?);

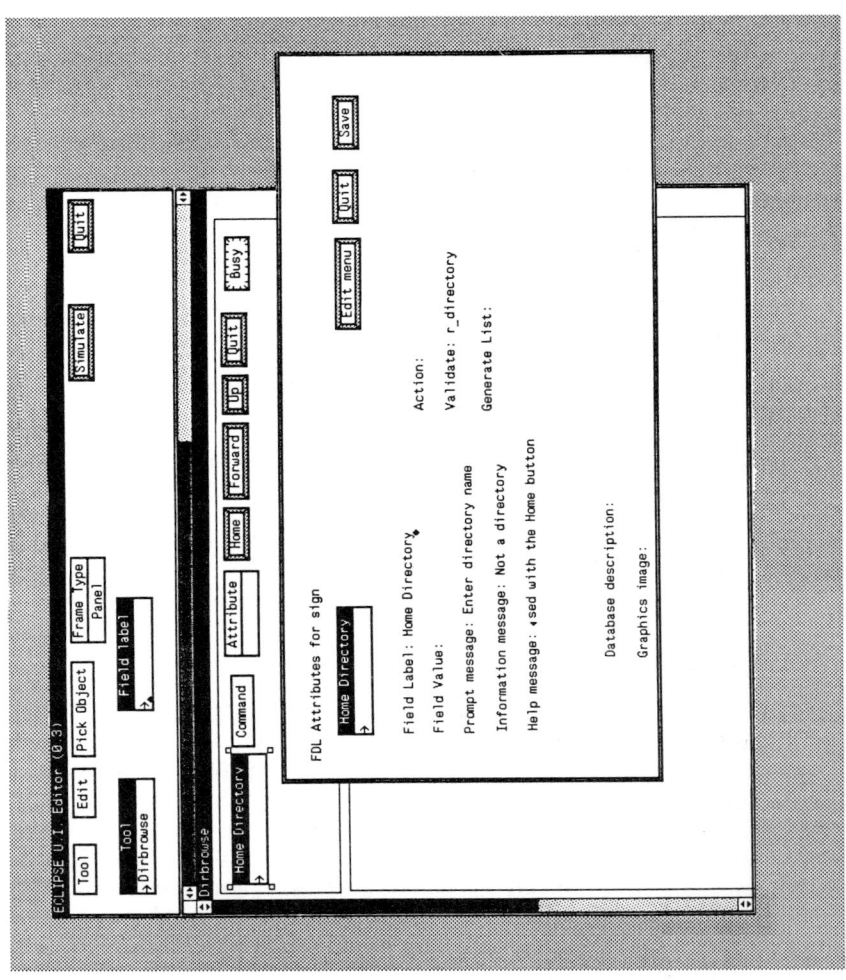

Figure 6.3: The Control Panel Creation Tool

6.1. CONTROL PANELS

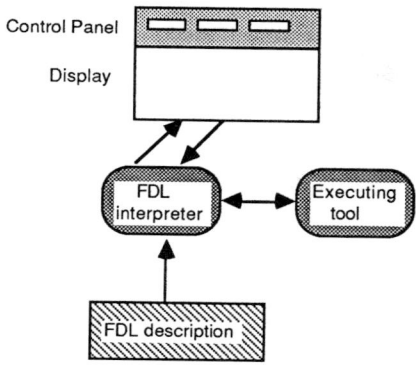

Figure 6.4: FDL and Tool Interaction

- its selectability (can it be picked by the end-user?);
- the text labels associated with the object;
- for each type of field, the actions to be carried out when that field is selected by the end-user or activated by a tool.

FDL is used to define the hierarchy of tool user interface objects and their relative positions and extents. The positions and sizes of the objects are concealed from the tool using the interface and objects are simply referenced by name. This has the consequence that the layout of a Control Panel or the window organisation of a tool may be changed without requiring changes to the tool code.

Similarly, the text associated with an object may be changed in the FDL without any effect on the tool. The textual values of the choices in a fixed list (a menu) have integer values associated with them in the FDL definition. Tools use this reference to specify a choice which means that the order and textual values of a choice list may be changed without requiring changes to the code of the tool.

At any single time in a system interaction, only a subset of all possible interface operations are valid. If the user attempts an invalid operation, the conventional response is to generate an error message and allow the user to retry. However, the interpretative implementation of FDL makes an alternative approach possible. The interface may be modified dynamically so that only valid operations are presented to the user. Thus, it is impossible for the user to select an invalid operation and cause an error report to be generated.

An example of where this facility is used is in the Eclipse MASCOT design editor. Once an entity has been registered in a design database, its semantics may not be changed although its position on a design diagram may be modified. Thus, once registered, destructive operations are simply not presented in the editor operations menu.

For user inputs, the FDL description may specify one or more prompts and a procedure which generates a list of data values from which a choice may be made.

For example, say an interface offers access to the design editor initiated by picking a 'DE' button. Picking this button may activate a sign where the name of the design to be edited is input. The FDL description of this sign may include a procedure which searches the user's workspace and presents a list of entities of type 'Graphical design'. Selecting one of these entities causes that name to be filled in the sign.

In other circumstances where the user provides input information, the FDL description may also include details of a syntactic pattern which the input value must match, a procedure to check the input value, an error message which is displayed if validation fails and actions setting out what to do when valid input has been made.

The FDL defining a button may specify the procedure that provides the required operation, a message to be displayed before the command is obeyed, whether the end-user is to confirm the action before the command is obeyed, the context in which to obey the command and an error message to be displayed if the command fails.

6.2 THE APPLICATIONS INTERFACE

We have already alluded to the fact that the mechanism used to implement control panels is actually a very general user interface management facility. Not only does it support the Eclipse metaphor, it also allows window and sub-window layouts to be specified. The tool builder is presented with a set of high-level, abstract primitives which are used to construct the tool interface. This is called the *Applications Interface*.

The basis of the high level abstract user interface supported by the Applications Interface is a hierarchy of objects representing the various classes of images that a tool may use to construct its user interface (Figure 6.5). There are five levels to the hierarchy, denoted as the Screen, Windows, Frames, Panes and Fields.

The root user interface object is called the Screen and represents the whole output area available on a work station. Within the Screen, any number of Window objects can be defined although only one of these can be completely visible at any one time. This is an artificial restriction but it has been introduced to enhance system portability. It means that the user interface is not dependent on a system supporting multiple windows.

User interface objects are also objects in the Smalltalk sense. They have a set of associated operations and they are always referenced and accessed by tools via these operations. All underlying representation information is concealed from the tool so that any representations may be changed without change to the tool using these objects.

Each object is associated with two rectangular areas which are always contained within the object's parent in the hierarchy. Each rectangular area has a position and extent relative to its parent which determines where each object will appear on the work station display. This is set out in character units to avoid dependence upon the pixel resolution of any actual work station.

Windows may be subdivided into a set of areas called Frames. There are four different classes of frame as shown in Figure 6.6.

A window showing each of these frame classes is shown in Figure 6.7. The large frame shows the FDL text which is used to generate the interface.

With the exception of formatted frames, frames may not be subdivided. Thus, all

6.2. THE APPLICATIONS INTERFACE

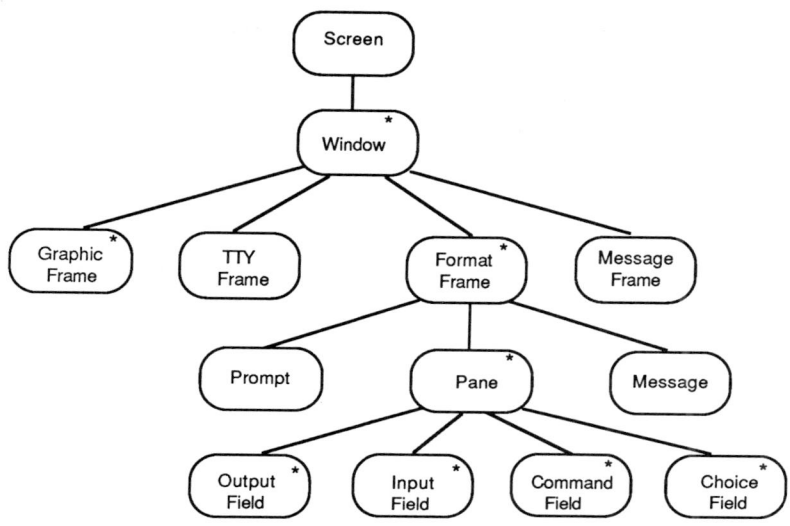

Figure 6.5: The User Interface Object Hierarchy

Frame Class	Description
1. Graphic Frame	This class of frame supports simple object-oriented graphical primitives for diagram drawing.
2. TTY Frame	This class of frame emulates a character terminal (standard I/O in Unix terminology). Tools which use such a device for I/O can run unchanged on a workstation.
3. Formatted Frame	This class of frame is used to represent frames which have sub-divisions. One of its most important roles is to represent Control Panels.
4. Message Frame	This class of frame is used to display text messages generated by the message system as discussed later in the paper.

Figure 6.6: Applications Interface Frame Classes

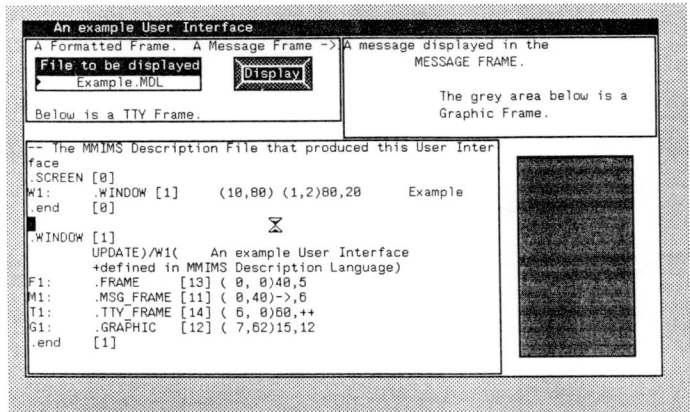

Figure 6.7: Frame Classes Supported by the Applications Interface

window partitioning must be implemented using formatted frames. Frame subdivisions are called Panes and consist of a set of Fields which a tool wishes to manage as a group.

Fields are the lowest level objects in the hierarchy and are generalisations of the elements of a control panel through which a tool can interact with an end-user. There are four classes of Fields, some of which can have different styles of presentation when visible on the user interface (Figure 6.8).

As discussed above in the FDL description, selecting a user interface object is not the responsibility of the executing tool but is handled by the Applications Interface. Tools have no knowledge of the mechanisms used and are not concerned with the input devices available to the end-user.

Control Panel entities are represented using Fields as shown in Figure 6.9. Notice that there are two types of menu represented by different fields. menus which have a fixed set of options may be represented by Choice fields; menus which have a variable set of options may be represented by Command fields.

6.3 THE USER GUIDANCE SYSTEM

The user guidance facilities of Eclipse have two major components namely the help system and the message passing system. At the beginning of the project a survey of existing user guidance systems was carried out and from this we extracted the following pragmatic principles:

- on-line help and the provision of messages to the user should be *integrated*;

- the help system should provide context-dependent help, related to what tool is being used and any message just received by the user;

- the help system should *not* provide an on-line tutorial and should definitely not just be an on-line copy of the printed user manual;

6.3. THE USER GUIDANCE SYSTEM

Field Class	Description
1. Input	This class of field is used for capturing user input. Its data value may be selected from a dynamically generated list of values presented to the end user as a menu or may be input directly by the end user.
2. Command	When selected, a field of this class initiates command execution. The action may be defined as a tool procedure or as a separate process using a TTY frame as its I/O device.
3. Choice	Fields of this class have a fixed list of possible values (usually presented as a menu) and set out in the FDL description. One of these is chosen by the end user.
4. Output	Output class fields are used to display fixed text or graphical images. These may not be modified by the end user.

Figure 6.8: Field Classes Supported by the Applications Interface

Control Panel element	Frame Class
1. Button	Command
2. Menu	Input or Choice
3. State Selector	Choice
4. Sign	Input
5. Light	Output

Figure 6.9: Frame Representations of Control Panel Elements

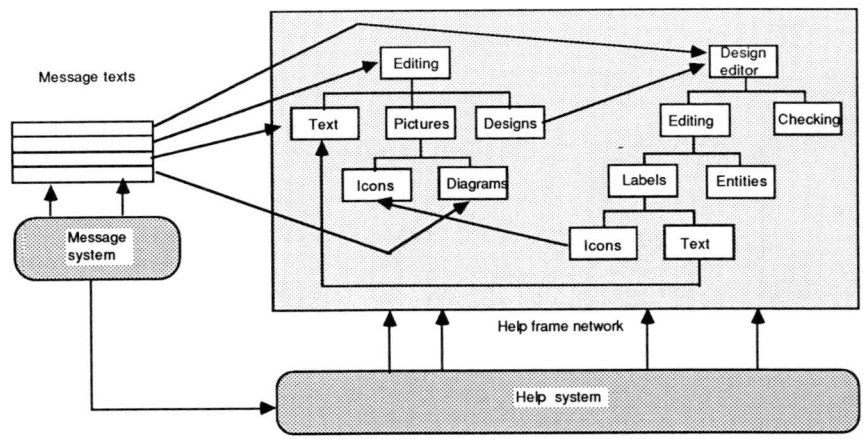

Figure 6.10: An Integrated User Guidance System

- the help information should be designed in suitable 'chunks' for the interactive user; these help frames should be connected into a *network* of frames which can be browsed by the user;

- all messages from tools to the user should pass through some common interface so that all tools present a consistent interface to the user;

- the user should have some control over where messages are displayed and whether and where they are logged for further inspection;

- messages should be linked at run-time to allow flexibility in modifying messages without recompilation.

The architecture of the integrated user guidance system which was implemented for Eclipse is illustrated in Figure 6.10.

6.3.1 The Help System

The prime objective of the Eclipse help system is to give users the information they need quickly and to assist them to relate that information to the task in hand.

We assume that users are familiar with the tool they are using and require a quick 'memory jog', not a comprehensive tutorial on using the tool. To achieve this, help frames are kept short in the hope that the user will find the desired information at the first attempt without having to scroll through pages of data seeking what they need. (This is, of course, a common problem with on-line manuals which were not designed for interactive use.) However, if the user fails to find what is required then the help system provides a mechanism for browsing through the network of help frames seeking more detailed information on a topic or looking at related topics.

6.3. THE USER GUIDANCE SYSTEM 81

The relationship between help and the task in hand is achieved in two ways. The context sensitive approach and the link to message handling mean that the user should enter the help system at an appropriate node rather than having to traverse a hierarchy from its root, for example. The multi-windowing environment allows the help tool to run asynchronously so that the user can switch between the current task and the help system, keeping his or her place in both. Thus, the user may get a message from the current tool invocation, use help for clarification of the problem, switch back to the tool and take some action, switch back to help for further information, etc.

It has been recognised that Eclipse will include a growing number of tools which may be developed explicitly or may be brought in as foreign tools. The foreign tools may have their own help systems and the Eclipse help system is designed to enable these 'alien' systems to be, at least partly, integrated. As an example, Eclipse includes tools which are documented by UNIX Manual pages and the help system provides a hook facility by which the relevant manual pages can be collected and displayed.

For each Eclipse tool, a help frame-set is produced to describe that tool. The unit of help is the frame and each frame has a name and title plus a page of information. The frame-set is tree-structured with more detail provided as the user moves from the root to the leaves. However, links across branches to related frames may be established. The help system provides a means to navigate this network (see Figure 6.10).

As a software tool is used, the user's context within that tool changes as different phases or levels of processing are accessed. In order to provide the most effective user assistance, it is a convention for Eclipse tool builders that these context changes are recorded on a 'context stack'. When a user selects the tools 'Help' button, the context stack is transferred to the help system which retrieves and displays the topmost frame referenced by the stack and stores the other frame references for subsequent viewing.

An example of the use of the Help tool is shown in Figure 6.11. There are two control panels at the top of the help window, a frame of help information and a panel containing the navigation facilities for browsing the help database.

The first frame of information displayed can be replaced by one showing more detail by the user selecting one of the entries under the title 'Further Information'. A new frame is displayed and the navigation panel is changed to reflect any further breakdown of information available. Links from the current frame to other frames of interest are listed under 'Related Topics' and can be selected in the same way using the mouse.

A list of help frames which have been examined is kept under 'Previous Frames' enabling users to retrace their steps. This helps to avoid the problem of users losing their way in the help network and being unable to return to their original entry point. To assist users in returning to frames which they found useful, the system provides a marking facility whereby users can tag those frames. This list which is displayed in the navigation panel under 'Marked Frames'.

Select and search facilities on the help network are available through the lower of the two control panels. If the name of a frame is known, this is typed into the Sign entitled Frame Reference and 'Select' is invoked. That frame is retrieved and displayed. Alternatively, a topic keyword may be typed into the sign and the 'Search' button pressed. Each help frame name and title is compared with the input string and those containing the keyword are recorded. If a single match is found, that frame is displayed. If multiple matches are discovered, their names and titles are displayed for

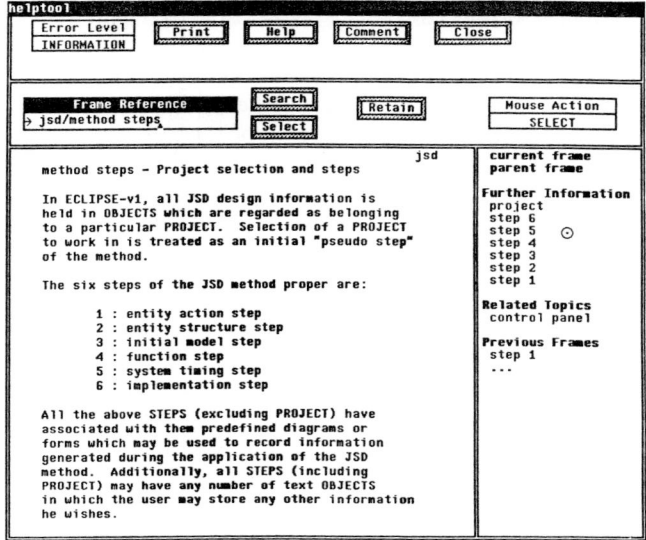

Figure 6.11: The Eclipse Help Tool

the user to select one for display or mark a number of them for subsequent viewing.

The top control panel enables users to suppress certain types of message if they wish ('Error Level'). 'Print' allows a hard copy of the currently displayed frame to be made and, 'Help' allows the user to get help on the help system. The comment facility ('Comment') allows user remarks to be passed to tool builders as discussed in the next section and 'Close' closes the window to an icon.

6.3.2 Message Handling

One of the characteristics of a project support environment, like Eclipse, is the wide variety of potential users and their knowledge and skills. A design objective was to provide a support system which would give tools a consistent means of displaying messages about the user's interaction to these diverse users.

Approaches to this problem include the classification of user skill level (novice, experienced, expert, etc.) or message layering where the user can repeatedly ask for more levels of detail. The problem with this approach is that users are dynamic rather than static. their skill levels vary from tool to tool and change with time as they gain experience or forget about system facilities. Furthermore, individuals vary in their tolerance for verbosity and may rapidly tire of long, explanatory messages.

The Eclipse message system does not impose such a scheme on the tool builder but provides a framework with which a number of different levels of user message may be provided. Significantly, this is under the control of the tool builder and is not imposed by the system. The key characteristics which allow tailorability are:

6.3. THE USER GUIDANCE SYSTEM

Message Class	Message type	Description
1. Interaction messages	Information, error, warning, fatal.	Interaction messages provide details of the status of an ECLIPSE interaction. Messages of this type are generated by tools for user information.
2. Input messages	Comment	These messages allow users to provide feedback to tool builders.
3. System messages	Metric, diagnostic, tracking, console, security, system.	System messages provide system status information and are generated by tools for tool builders rather than users.

Figure 6.12: Classes Supported by the Eclipse Message System

Message text and code separation. This means that different messages can be created for different user populations and can be represented in different languages (French, German, etc.). These message sets are read at run time so can be changed without software rebuilding.

Structured message texts. All messages are typed and fall into three classes namely interaction messages, input messages and system messages (Figure 6.12). A message is structured into a type, a text, a parameter list where the parameters normally represent the user's context and a link to the help system. For example, the message below might represent that produced if a user tries to open a file which has already been opened. The message is preceded by its type and the parameters are represented using the UNIX convention of dollar numbering.

warning: File $1 has already been opened. Command ignored.

Help → File manipulation ;

Help system integration. Each message is linked to a help system frame. To display the associated frame the user selects the 'Help' button which is standard on every Eclipse tool. The user then has access to all the help frames relevant to the current context.

Interaction messages are those which are generated to provide user information. Users may also send messages to tools using the comment type of message. These are a means of capturing user's observations about Eclipse and any of its tools. During any session, a user is able to record comments about problems encountered or system facilities. Comment messages are logged for subsequent analysis by tool builders. System messages are used to record tool diagnostic information and are normally transparent to tool users.

As well as being useful to the tool builder in formulating messages, the fact that messages are typed allows the message system to provide facilities allowing the user and the tool builder control over the destination and display of messages.

Each Eclipse user has an associated message log where all generated messages may be retained. Messages may be directed to the log as well as or instead of the user's display and logged messages are automatically time stamped by the system. In addition, messages may also be routed to a system console window.

Messages are routed according to their type. A routing table is used to specify the destinations for each message type and the user may modify message destinations for different tools or different interaction sessions. If a user wishes to ignore messages, he or she simply leaves out any destination specification in the routing table. For example, a user might wish to suppress all information and warning messages but see errors. He or she might choose to display fatal messages (messages which result from an unrecoverable error) in the current window and on the console as well as recording them in the message log. All other types might be routed to the message log for later analysis.

6.4 CONCLUSIONS

The work on the development of the Eclipse user interface and the MMI project in general was an epitome of a successful Alvey collaboration. It integrated work from two universities and two industrial collaborators and it took ideas generated in the universities and successfully used these in an innovative product. The interaction facilities of Eclipse set the system apart from its competitors and are a key component in the success of the system.

Chapter 7

The Design Editor

Stephen Beer, Ian Sommerville and Ray Welland

7.1 INTRODUCTION

Although they have been criticised for lack of formality, graphical approaches to software design such as Structured Design/indexStructured Design [22] and JSD/indexJSD [60] are widely used and reportedly successful. Thus, it was a requirement of Eclipse that it should be possible to incorporate support tools for such methods and to allow designs produced with such tools to be stored and manipulated in the Eclipse database. Eclipse is an open IPSE so the methods to be supported could not be predefined — indeed as the system construction progressed we changed our mind on which methods should be supported in Eclipse. A further requirement on Eclipse was an integrated approach to the user interface so we came to the conclusion that the most effective way to provide a design support tool for graphical design methods was to produce a generic tool which could be tailored by the system builder for whatever methods were supported in any single release of Eclipse.

However, we did not simply want a graphical editing system which allowed us to produce neat diagrams. We also wished to provide as much design checking as possible as the design was created — in essence we wanted to provide a syntax-driven editing system to support whatever graphical method was in use. Thus, we decided that we should define a notation for defining the method to be supported and use this to generate tables to drive the design editor. Furthermore, as we wished to support notations with arbitrary symbolism we also needed a tool with which we could define symbols and relate them to their names used in the design definition language.

The design definition language which we developed is called GDL [117] and is a notation for defining the syntax and partial semantics of software designs which are expressed as directed graphs. This means that most graphical design methods may be supported. The relationship between GDL, the symbol editing system, the design editor and the database is shown in Figure 1.

The mode of use is as follows:

1. The Eclipse tool builder defines the syntax and the semantics of the design method to be supported using GDL.

2. The GDL compiler generates tables for input to the design editor.

3. The symbols associated with a method are defined by the Eclipse tool builder and tables are generated for the design editor.

4. The design editor uses these generated tables to provide an interface which is tailored to whatever design method is in use.

5. The generated designs are stored in the Eclipse database.

Notice that we have defined a canonical form for all software designs (as a directed graph) so that generic design processing tools may be produced.

In the remainder of this chapter, we describe the notations for defining software design methods, briefly introduce the symbol editing system, illustrate the user interface and facilities of the design editor, paying particular attention to its design checking facilities and, finally, discuss how the editor was developed incrementally.

7.2 GRAPHIC DESCRIPTION LANGUAGE

Our basic premise is that a design diagram is a directed graph. Therefore, our design description notation (GDL) must be able to define the general structure of a graph, the symbolism and naming of each entity type, and other rules associated with the method.

The initial version of Eclipse was tested using the JSD method and the examples in this section are drawn from the GDL definitions for JSD. In particular, the main example is of the synchronisation process node of the System Structure Diagram (SSD). A synchronisation process takes a single system input ('time stamp') and produces many data streams ('time grain markers').

Representing a directed graph, suggests that there should be two basic types of entity: *node* and *link*. From these two basic types a hierarchy of user-defined types can be specified with each level in the hierarchy inheriting properties from its predecessors.

To declare a node the first thing we consider is its interface to other nodes in the diagram, that is what directed links come into the node and what directed links leave the node. A link is always assumed to have a single source node and a single destination node. For example:

```
type SSD_SYNC   is NODE (time_in  :  in SSD_LINK;
                         times_out :  out set of SSD_LINK)
type SSD_LINK   is LINK (start : in NODE; finish :  out NODE)
```

This GDL fragment indicates that a synchronisation process, SSD_SYNC, has a single input of type SSD_LINK and a set of outputs, also of type SSD_LINK. The type SSD_LINK is a simple link between two entities of the base type node.

Having established the 'shape' of the network we can now turn our attention to the symbolism of the entities and any annotation associated with the entities. Any type declaration may have an associated representation expression which gives these

7.2. GRAPHIC DESCRIPTION LANGUAGE

details. A representation expression contains a list of entity annotations, which are represented as *labels* in the Design Editor. Continuing the previous example:

```
for SSD_SYNC use SYMBOL(JSD_ssd.synchronisation)
                            ++ NAME(STRING)
for SSD_LINK use SYMBOL(JSD_ssd.arrow)
```

The SYMBOL part references a component in a shape library (see next section). Thus JSD_ssd is a shape library and 'synchronisation' and 'arrow' are components defined within it. A synchronisation process also has a name of type STRING. A SSD_LINK is an unannotated arrow. Provision is also made in GDL for optional annotations, which are indicated by enclosing the label definition in square brackets.

The type declaration and associated representation expression establish the basic framework for a design diagram but there are other rules which need to be associated with a design diagram. In GDL these rules are expressed as *assertions* which are written as predicates. Assertions can be roughly divided into two categories, those which express further syntactic or semantic constraints and those which express spatial relationships.

Continuing the example of the synchronisation process, we find that input must come from a system input node, SSD_SYS_IN, and all outputs must be connected to nodes of type data stream, SSD_DATA_STREAM. These constraints can be expressed using the following assertions:

```
assertion Input (SSD_SYNC) :
        GetType (Source(time_in)) = SSD_SYS_IN
assertion Outputs (SSD_SYNC) :
        forall i ; Member(times_out, i) :
        GetType (Destination(i)) = SSD_DATA_STREAM
```

In these assertions GetType, Source, Destination and Member are examples of built-in functions. GetType is a generic function which takes an entity reference and returns its type. Source and Destination both take parameters of type link and return a reference to the node at the relevant end of the link. The function Member(X, i) is true if i is a member of the set X and so we can use this in combination with the iterator **forall** to scan all members of a set.

We also note the need for a simple spatial constraint that the name of any instance of a SSD_SYNC should appear within the symbol for the node. This can be expressed as follows:

```
assertion Name_enclosed (SSD_SYNC) :
        inst i :
        Encloses (Getlabel(i,SYMBOL),Getlabel(i,NAME))
```

Getlabel and Encloses are further examples of built-in functions. Getlabel (A,B) returns a reference to the label named B associated with entity A. One of the attributes of a label is the area which surrounds the label. Encloses (X, Y) is true if the area surrounding Y is enclosed by the area surrounding X. Thus the above assertion is true if the NAME annotation is enclosed by the SYMBOL defined for SSD_SYNC.

```
type SSD_SYNC is NODE (time_in : in SSD_LINK;
                       times_out : out set of SSD_LINK)
for SSD_SYNC use SYMBOL(JSD_ssd.synchronisation)
                 ++ NAME(STRING)
assertion Input (SSD_SYNC) :
          GetType (Source(time_in)) = SSD_SYS_IN
assertion Outputs (SSD_SYNC) :
          forall i ; Member(times_out, i) :
          GetType (Destination(i)) = SSD_DATA_STREAM
assertion  Name_enclosed (SSD_SYNC) :
           inst i : Name_inside(i)

type SSD_LINK is LINK(start:in NODE;finish:out NODE)
for SSD_LINK use SYMBOL(JSD_ssd.arrow)
```

Figure 7.1: Example 1

In addition to the Encloses function there are a number of other positional functions such as: Above, Below, Left_of, Right_of, Vertically_aligned and Horizontally_aligned. These are useful in enforcing diagramming conventions such as parent above child in a hierarchy, alignment of nodes in a tree, temporal ordering of nodes, etc.

A facility for including user defined functions is available in GDL and the above spatial constraint occurs so frequently that it is likely to be defined as a named function, as follows:

```
-- the name of the node must be enclosed by the
-- node's symbol
#define Name_inside (X : NODE) \\
Encloses (Getlabel(X,SYMBOL),Getlabel(X,NAME))
```

and the above assertion then becomes:

```
assertion Name_enclosed (SSD_SYNC) :
          inst i : Name_inside(i)
```

We can combine all the above fragments of GDL into a definition for a synchronisation node as shown in Example 1.

There is a trade-off between the strength of typing in the type declaration and the use of assertions. For example, the declaration of the type SSD_SYNC could be changed to:

```
type SSD_SYNC is NODE (time_in : in SSD_TIME_IN;
                       time_out : out set of SSD_TIME_OUT)
```

and the corresponding link type declarations would be:

```
type SSD_TIME_IN is LINK (start  : in SSD_SYS_IN;
                          finish : out SSD_SYNC)
type SSD_TIME_OUT is LINK (start  : in SSD_SYNC;
                           finish : out SSD_DATA_STREAM)
```

In general, stronger typing implies more entities in the GDL and consequently in the entities menu of the design editor. This means that the end-user is faced with a lot of artificial types which are not part of the method. The writer of the GDL must decide where to strike the balance between the number of entities and the strength of typing.

The description of MASCOT 3 diagrams gave us some problems because of the concept of *junctions* (ports and windows) which are used as the connecting points of links with nodes. In fact a MASCOT 3 diagram is not a simple connected graph! This problem was solved by extending the type definition to include *dependent nodes*, that is nodes which are owned by other nodes, rather than linked to other nodes. For example:

```
type SUBSYSTEM is NODE (junctions : owner of set of JUNCTION)

type JUNCTION is NODE  (parent_node : owned by NODE;
                        in_links  : in set of PATH;
                        out_links : out set of PATH)
```

This simplified piece of MASCOT 3 GDL shows that the principal node type SUBSYSTEM owns a set of junctions but has no direct links, whereas the dependent node JUNCTION is owned by some other node type and has a set of links into and out of it. The number of paths allowed for a particular junction type is specified via assertions. In general, a node may own any number of dependent nodes but a given dependent node must have a unique parent node.

There are also some design methods which allow composite nodes on a single level diagram, for example the Systems Implementation Diagram of JSD. These composite nodes are represented by using the dependent node approach, if necessary allowing a node to own dependent nodes of its own type.

The GDL definitions for a method are compiled into tables for input to the design editor. The compiler was constructed using the lex and yacc tools available under UNIX [64]. The user-defined functions were implemented using the C preprocessor.

7.3 THE SHAPES EDITOR

The SHAPES editor provides a drawing tool tailored for the production of symbols which appear on design diagrams. The symbols which the user creates are stored as components in a method-specific library which is used as input to the design editor and referenced in the SYMBOL label of the GDL representation expression (for ... use).

The SHAPES editor is *not* a general-purpose drawing tool, it is designed specifically for constructing the stylised symbols which appear on design diagrams. The user is provided with a set of basic shapes including: rectangle (square), ellipse(circle), triangle, diamond and line (single-headed and double-headed arrow). These basic shapes are provided in a graphical menu which is positioned at the left-hand side of the editor's drawing area, see Figure 2.

The user can select a shape from the menu and instantiate it in the drawing area at any required size. Shapes in the drawing area may subsequently be modified by stretching or shrinking in any planar dimension and other shapes may be selected from the menu and added to the existing shape to form composite shapes.

Some shapes are treated as special cases of others, a rectangle is constrained to be a square by holding down the shift key while drawing, similarly a circle is a constrained ellipse. Arrows, single-headed and double-headed, are treated as special cases of line, the user selects the appropriate line style from a menu. If a shape is to be used for a link, rather than a node, this is indicated via an option in the shape list pull-down menu.

When the user is satisfied with a new symbol, constructed in the drawing area, it can be named and added to the graphical menu of shapes. The user can then continue shape development building further symbols from basic shapes or by modifying the additional shapes already added to the menu.

At the end of a SHAPES editor session the user can store the new shapes, currently displayed in the graphical menu, in a shape library for use by the design editor. Shapes are stored in a shape library geometrically rather than as bit-map images. Any shape library can be reloaded into the SHAPES editor to allow further development of the symbols.

7.4 THE DESIGN EDITOR (DE)

The envisaged user of the DE is a software designer having knowledge of the particular design method being used within the DE. Rather than interacting in terms of graphical drafting terminology (e.g. box, circle) the DE uses the same terminology as the designer. A designer selects a SSD_SYNC or a SSD_LINK, for example, and adds it to a design as opposed to selecting a box or a line and drawing on a diagram. Therefore the designer interacts in terms of the design entities of a method, namely nodes, links and their annotations.

The major facilities offered by the DE allow the user to:

- add images representing design entities, move and delete such images;

- add, move or delete labels (textual or symbolic) associated with a design entity;

- create a design diagram larger than the designer's work station window;

- view the total diagram; it is necessary to be able to 'step back and look at' large areas of a design. This cuts out the 'noise' of detail in order to view the overall structure,

- annotate the diagram only, not the underlying design, with text, boxes or lines.

7.4. THE DESIGN EDITOR (DE)

The DE assumes that the diagram is based on a directed annotated graph containing nodes, links and labels. The objects which may be manipulated within the graph structure are:

node denotes a software component or state;

link denotes flow of control or data, etc;

label denotes the textual and graphical descriptions for labelling a design.

The object oriented approach to user interaction has been pursued throughout development of the DE. The functions available to the designer in constructing a design are applied to a currently selected object from the design. The current selection may consist of a node, link, label or collection thereof. Functions are applied consistently across all objects wherever it is sensible to do so. It is nonsense to edit the graphical symbol of a node but sensible to edit its labels.

The implication here is that the designer points at an object to make it the current selection and then applies some editing function, such as delete or move. The converse to this philosophy is the function oriented approach where a function is first selected followed by the objects to which the function is to be applied. The choice of interface essentially depends on whether user interaction is more natural with the object or the function. For a design editing tool we believe that the best interface is via the object oriented approach.

The DE has been implemented on Sun work stations running under the Suntools window environment. The user interface, see Figure 3, consists of a tool window subdivided into four subwindows:

- a drafting area where a design is constructed;

- a control panel giving access to the editing functions and entity types;

- two subwindows containing scroll bars which allow the drafting area to be moved around the total diagram. (Remember a diagram can be larger than the drafting area).

The interface makes full advantage of the mouse pointing device in that all user interaction is via the mouse, except for textual input. The user interface to the DE follows the WYSIWYG ('what you see is what you get') approach where text is input at the position of display rather than a point remote from the actual display.

Editing functions are selected from a control panel (discussed in chapter 6) containing pull down menus and 'soft' buttons. The entities menu displays the types of entity available for the supported method. The designer selects an entity type from the menu and then adds this to a design by fixing the position for its graphical image on the diagram.

The concept of a label is used within the DE to associate either a name or a graphical symbol with a node or link. Therefore, the label is a generic object for capturing textual and graphical descriptions. Labels have a defined enclosing boundary, contain a value and may be manipulated in the same fashion as other objects of the design.

A design entity (node or link) may have an associated set of labels. The type and number of labels is specified in the representation expression of the entity type in the

GDL description of the method. For example, Example 1 shows that the node entity type SSD_SYNC has an associated label type NAME. To associate a NAME label with an SSD_SYNC instance in the design, the designer first selects the instance, making it the currently selected object. At this point the labels menu in the control panel dynamically changes to show the available types for the current object. The designer can select the label type NAME and type in the name of the SSD_SYNC instance.

The user has complete control over where and when a label should be placed. There is no notion of the editor being syntax directed — it is syntax driven but not syntax directed. The use of a syntax-directed editor would force the user into specific ways of design creation, such as always labelling a node immediately after drawing its symbol. We feel it more natural that the designer should create a design as he pleases, and that most design checking should be initiated when required rather than imposed at each step of the editing session.

As mentioned previously, the DE has built-in knowledge that the design must be in the form of a graph. Therefore, the DE enforces the restriction that a link must originate from a node and end at a different node. This prevents designs being created where dataflow links, for example, lead to or originate from nowhere. This restriction is enforced implicitly within the DE when the designer attempts to add a link. The DE prevents a source point for a link from being fixed unless it lies within a node boundary, similarly for the destination point.

This graph knowledge is used in other situations. For example, each node can have an associated set of input and output links and labels. When a node is made the currently selected object then its links and labels are also automatically selected. Subsequent functions applied to a node are also applied to its links and labels, for example, if a node is deleted then all its associated links and labels are also deleted — it makes no sense for them to be left hanging in mid-air. In the same way a move operation automatically moves all links and labels associated with a node.

7.5 DESIGN CHECKING

In a software design editing system the provision of drafting facilities for automating diagram production is important. What is even more important, from the point of view of Eclipse, is that the underlying design is captured in the project database. A beautiful looking diagram is of no use, and indeed may be be harmful, if it is incorrect. Design checking therefore is a major function of the DE and is one of the ways in which it differs from a straightforward drafting tool.

Other design support tools have demonstrated the need for method-specific checking of a design [120] but the novel feature of the DE is that checking is enforced at three levels and at various times throughout an editing session. These checks are all closely integrated with the GDL description of the method being supported and the three levels can be defined as :

- parameter list checking;

- assertion checking;

- completeness checking.

7.5. DESIGN CHECKING

In the case of a node the strong typing of parameters can be used to enforce correct design automatically. This is so because each node has associated links defined as being either in or out. Subsequently, in the DE, at the time when a link is added to a design the parameter lists of both the source and destination nodes can be checked. This check ensures that the link type is consistent with the legal types of the source node's out links and also with the destination node's in links.

For example, referring to the GDL in Example 1, the designer is allowed to use only links of type SSD_LINK to connect a node of type SSD_SYNC to any other node. This restriction can be enforced by checking that if an SSD_SYNC instance is selected as the source or destination node when drawing a link then the current link type, selected from the entities menu, must be SSD_LINK. If an attempt is made to draw an illegal link then no link is added to the design, the design image remains unchanged and a suitable message indicating a wrong connection is displayed in the control panel.

The rules of any particular method to be enforced in the DE are called assertions. These are compiled by the GDL compiler into rule tables which drive the DE. In Example 1 there are three assertions on a node of type SSD_SYNC. They concern the types of the connected input and output nodes, and the placing of the name label. These assertions could be enforced at different times in an editing session, as described later, but we believe that the best approach is to allow the user to specify when checking should take place. At this time any entity in error is highlighted and made the current selection. An appropriate message is displayed in the control panel and the designer can then apply functions to the erroneous entity to correct the design.

The DE evaluates assertions using an interpreter which operates on a reverse-Polish form of the assertion. This interpreter uses three-valued logic so that an assertion can be evaluated as *not applicable* when all components referenced in the assertion do not exist at the time of checking. This prevents the user from receiving spurious error messages.

The GDL trade-off between the number of entities and the strength of typing affects not only the size of the entities menu in the control panel. Type checking can be enforced mainly through assertions if the link parameters are specified as the generic type NODE and appropriate assertions on connections are written. Alternatively, a strongly typed description removes the need for such assertions but increases the number of checks each time a link is added to the design. This effectively means striking a balance between continuous checking (closer to syntax-directed editing) and user-initiated checking.

In a GDL representation expression a label can be specified as being compulsory or optional (by using square brackets). This information on the optionality, or otherwise, of a label is transmitted to the DE through the GDL generated tables and the presence of mandatory labels is checked at an appropriate time. This is an example of a completeness check which can only be carried out under the control of the user. Again, looking at Example 1, a node of type SSD_SYNC must have a name. The DE therefore has to check each instance of an SSD_SYNC node and if no name exists then an appropriate message is displayed and the offending node highlighted.

The specific timing of checks is a contentious subject. The basic philosophy behind the DE is that the designer should be given as much freedom as possible to construct a design diagram is his or her own way. This is achieved by provided an object-oriented, modeless interface with most of the design checking initiated at user specified times.

Checking in the DE can be classified on its timing during an editing session as follows:

Implicit/Restrictive There is implicit continuous checking throughout an editing session because certain editing operations are restricted at certain times. For example, at the point when a node is selected only certain label types are made available to the designer. This ensures that, by restriction, the designer cannot associate a label of incorrect type with a particular node.

Immediate As soon as an editing operation alters a design certain checks will be executed immediately. These include checking that a link has source and destination nodes of the correct type.

User-Initiated Rather than providing a syntax directed editor where the user is forced to construct a design in a certain manner the DE allows the designer the freedom to construct a design in whatever manner favoured. Checking can be called at the designer's convenience and such checking might include:

- assertions concerning completeness and consistency;
- assertions about spatial arrangement of objects;
- completeness of label sets.

7.6 DEVELOPMENT

The design editing system was developed in a number of stages. The first prototype system was developed at the University of Strathclyde and included the first version of the GDL compiler, the SHAPES editor and a DE with drawing facilities but no checking. This system was used in Eclipse version one to provide basic support for JSD diagram production. The system was interfaced to standard UNIX files via an Abstract Data Interface (ADI), the intention being that the DE would be interfaced to the database, when it became available, via a new mapping of the ADI.

The second prototype system, also developed at the University of Strathclyde, included an enhanced GDL compiler and a DE which included checking of assertions. The major changes in the second prototype system were concerned with the addition of dependent nodes, an improved type hierarchy in GDL and the compilation of assertions into rule tables which were then interpreted in the DE. This version was tested for both MASCOT 3 and some LSDM design diagrams.

In parallel with the development of this second prototype system the first 'industrialised' version of the DE was developed by SSL. The production of this version of the DE involved a re- implementation of the ADI in order to ensure efficient mapping of the DE operations onto the database interface. Some aspects of the user-interface were also modified to improve the operation of the DE. The two versions of the DE use the same GDL compiler and SHAPES editor, and much of the code is shared.

The industrialised DE allows nodes or links on a diagram to be refined into more detailed diagrams, or other representations, via a simple extension to GDL. Each component in the GDL representation expression has an associated *attribute string* which was originally provided to allow specification of font style and sizes, perhaps colour, etc. for labels. The GDL compiler simply passes the unparsed attribute strings

7.6. DEVELOPMENT

to the DE where they can be interpreted as required. Thus different versions of the DE can use these attribute strings in different ways.

In the industrialised DE the attribute string associated with the SYMBOL of a design entity can include the attribute 'open' which indicates that the the object may be opened into another representation. Therefore, the control of movement through a hierarchy of design representations is not embedded in the DE but provided externally via the tool controlling the current invocation of the DE. We are not locked into a hierarchy of diagrams, a design entity on a diagram can be opened into any valid representation using appropriate tools. Attribute strings are also used in the industrialised DE to provide straightforward information about linkage between GDL labels and database entities, fonts, sizes of text boxes, etc. They are also used to specify replication of symbols in the DFD diagrams of LSDM.

Chapter 8
Eclipse as an APSE

Ron Pierce and Mike Pickett

8.1 INTRODUCTION

Eclipse has facilities for developing and maintaining Ada programs, very much in the spirit of the Stoneman document [15] which appeared in 1980 but which still provides a good description of the requirements for an Ada support environment. Stoneman first gave wide currency to the term APSE (Ada Programming Support Environment) and it can reasonably be claimed that Eclipse meets all the requirements of Stoneman, in addition to addressing wider issues of software engineering.

Clearly the central component of any APSE is the Ada compiler (or compilers, because host-target working will typically be needed for the development of real-time systems). In the case of Eclipse the Ada compiler has been produced by CAP Industry Ltd, and is based upon the 'second generation' of Ada compiler technology developed by TeleSoft Inc. CAP was already the UK agent of TeleSoft when the Eclipse project was started, and it was clearly natural to base the Eclipse Ada system on the TeleGen 2 root compiler. Recognising the need for host-target working in many Ada applications and the relative scarcity of good cross-development environments, the decision was made to develop a compiler for the Intel 80286 microprocessor and use this cross-compiler as the basis of the Ada support facilities in Eclipse. The necessary cross-development tools were also developed, and the whole system is described in more detail in section 8.3.

The availability of a cross-development system for Ada programs is not in itself sufficient to produce an APSE in the Stoneman sense; the compilation system must be integrated with the support environment as a whole, and in particular must provide adequate configuration management facilities for Ada programs. How this is achieved in Eclipse will be described in the following sections, starting with the concept of integration itself.

8.2 INTEGRATION

There are two possible scenarios for integrating an Ada development facility into Eclipse. The first and easier would have been simply to use the Eclipse MMI system with its distinctive control panel style of user interface to provide user access to the various tools in the cross-development system. This would have had the advantage that the common MMI system would be used for both Ada and the other Eclipse tool sets, thus making it easier for the user to come to grips with the Ada environment. However, it would not have achieved the goal of data integration, by which we mean the ability of different tool sets to interact via shared data structures. Integration at this level is achieved by using the Eclipse database to store both the inputs to and outputs from the Ada compilation and program building process, and in particular to represent the Ada program library as an Eclipse database structure.

The program library concept is of central importance to an Ada compilation system. Ada programs can consist of many modules called compilation units, and the distinctive feature of Ada in this respect is that these modules are not compiled in isolation from one another, as they are in for example the FORTRAN or C languages. In the Ada separate compilation system, each compilation unit must explicitly name all the other compilation units to which it requires access. Before a compilation unit can be compiled, all the other units which it requires must previously have been compiled into the program library, from which the Ada compiler can extract the necessary symbol table information about the entities accessible from the unit being compiled. This feature of Ada allows the same level of semantic checking to be applied to a program consisting of many compilation units as that applied to a single unit.

The program library in Ada thus serves several functions. Firstly, it provides a context in which the name of a compilation unit can be interpreted; secondly it stores the compiler output information for all the compilation units of a program; and thirdly it records the *dependencies* between compilation units in the library. When an Ada program is built, all the necessary units must be present in the library, and the dependency information stored therein replaces the linker steering file which is needed to build complete programs written in languages which have independent compilation of modules. Moreover, if a compilation unit which exists in the program library is recompiled, all the other compilation units which depend on it must also be recompiled to keep the program library consistent; it is not possible to build an Ada program from a program library which is inconsistent in this sense. The program library is thus a natural starting point for the configuration management of Ada programs, and this aspect of the Ada support system is described in section 8.6 below.

The program library and its dependency structure is stored using Eclipse database objects and relationships. This not only allows Eclipse version and configuration management facilities to be applied to program libraries, but it achieves the goal of data integration by allowing other tool sets to examine the compilation unit dependency structure represented by the Ada program library and, indeed, the MASCOT tool set (see chapter 9) takes advantage of this facility.

8.3 THE CROSS-DEVELOPMENT SYSTEM

The basic Ada cross-development system consists of the following tools.

The Ada cross-compiler As noted above this is a version of the TeleSoft Inc. Tele-Gen2 portable Ada compiler generating code for the Intel 80286 processor, with the 80287 floating-point co-processor.

A cross-assembler This allows assembler language modules to be prepared for inclusion in an Ada program. (Ada has an INTERFACE pragma which allows subroutines to be given an Ada specification but an implementation in another language.) Both the Ada compiler and the cross-assembler produce object modules in a target-independent object module format, which is accepted by the target-independent linker and image builder components described below.

An Ada linker This is a tool which uses the dependency information stored in the program library to determine which compilation units are needed to form a complete Ada program, given the name of the 'main program' in the Ada sense. The Ada linker does not actually carry out the linking process but simply provides a steering file for the target-independent linker.

The target-independent linker This component performs the classical linking function, combining a number of object modules into a single module (again in target independent format). Where an Ada program requires some assembly language modules to be included, the linker steering file produced by the Ada linker can be edited to direct the target independent linker to include those modules.

An Intel 80286 image builder This tool accepts a module or modules in target independent format and builds a program image file which can be down-loaded into an appropriate Intel 80286 processor. The image builder allows the user to control the layout of the program image and the size of various memory areas; this is not a straightforward operation in the segmented architecture of the 80286 and an extensive set of directives is provided to steer the building operation. For users who are not concerned with the details of program layout, a standard file of image builder directives is supplied.

A test controller This is a tool which down-loads a program image into an Intel 80286 single-board computer attached to the host system by a serial link. It allows the Ada program to be started and stopped, and provides a method of communication between the Ada program running on the target and the host. Machine-level debugging of the Ada program is also provided by the test controller.

The run-time system This is not a tool, but consists of the support routines which provide the Ada tasking and storage management system and the Ada predefined library units. The packages TEXT_IO and SEQUENTIAL_IO for character data are provided, and input and output is provided for both host-target communication and for local devices connected to the 80286. The run-time support system also includes the monitor which runs in the 80286 and which communicates with the test controller tool to support loading and interactive execution of the Ada program.

The PROM formatter While host-target working is ideal for testing an embedded system application, the production system will usually be stored in PROM. The cross-development tools therefore include a PROM formatter tool which will convert a program image into a suitable format and send the resulting image to a PROM programmer attached to the host by a serial link.

The cross development tools described above are largely host-independent, and of course have no knowledge of the Eclipse system. The first version of the tool set was developed for VAX machines running under the VMS operating system, and indeed the VAX-VMS cross-compilation system was first validated by the UK Ada Validation Centre in December 1986. (Validation is the official process of certifying that an Ada compiler conforms to the Ada language standard.) Subsequently the entire cross-development system was re-hosted to run under UNIX on the Sun 3, the work station used for Eclipse, thus providing the basis for the Eclipse Ada system. The process of rehosting the cross-development system was quite straightforward since all the tools are written in Ada.

One notable omission from the tool set as described above is a symbolic debugger for Ada programs. An Intel 80286 version of the TeleSoft symbolic debugger is available under VMS; this provides powerful source-level debugging facilities for the host user for programs executing on the target 80286. However, at the time of writing, this tool has not been ported to Eclipse.

In addition to the cross-compiler, TeleSoft compilers are also available for both VAX-VMS and Sun 3, allowing Ada program to be developed on the host before target development is undertaken.

8.4 A COMMON PROGRAM LIBRARY SYSTEM

While all Ada compilers use their own proprietary representations for an Ada program library , the Ada language imposes some mandatory requirements due to its rules on consistency. We therefore concluded that it should be possible to develop a general Eclipse program library storage mechanism which could, at least potentially, be used with different compilers, and more particularly with compilers from different suppliers. This would allow the development of a comprehensive program library and configuration management system which could be used with a variety of Ada compilers. The benefits of this approach from the user's point of view would be considerable, because he could use different Ada compilers for different aspects of a project while using only one set of program library and configuration management tools. The use of different Ada compilers will be relatively common, since in host-target working the host compiler and the target compiler may well be produced by different suppliers, and would be chosen on the quality and characteristics of the compilers available for the various machines involved. There may also be more than one target computer used for a project.

8.4. A COMMON PROGRAM LIBRARY SYSTEM

It would moreover be worth spending considerable effort in developing good quality program library management tools if this effort were to be re-usable for different Ada compilation systems.

The actual implementation of the common Eclipse program library system for any given compiler is of course not necessarily straightforward. The Eclipse system requires that compilation units should be shareable between different program libraries, as discussed in section 8.6. This may not be possible to implement (for technical reasons which need not be discussed here) given the program library representations assumed by some compilers. Even if it is possible, an Ada compiler produced by some independent supplier will have its own particular program library system different from that of Eclipse. To integrate such a compiler into Eclipse can therefore be done in two ways.

- The compiler may be modified so that its program library management component uses the Eclipse program library scheme rather than its own. This would be more or less easy depending on how well the details of the program library system were isolated from the rest of the compiler into one or a small number of modules. Apart from technical difficulty, modifying the source text of a proprietary software system would require the cooperation of the compiler supplier. Moreover, maintenance of the composite system may present difficulties since the compiler supplier may not be able to guarantee that upgrades of the program library will remain compatible with Eclipse.

- A tool might be written to convert between the Eclipse representation of the program library and the supplier's own representation. This would avoid the problem of having to modify the compiler itself, but would inevitably incur an overhead in changing the library representations. The extent of this overhead will vary with different compilers. In general, the bulk compiler outputs such as object code files and symbol table information need not in principle be affected; if the compiler chooses to store these as individual files then only the program library structural and dependency information would need to be modified when converting between program library representations.

In practice, the TeleSoft-based cross-compiler discussed previously has been integrated into Eclipse by the second of these methods. A tool called the compiler manager is responsible for converting between the TeleSoft representation of a program library and the Eclipse representation. This tool can be briefly summarised as follows. Given an existing Eclipse program library, it examines the dependency structure of the compilation units in the library and converts this into a form which the TeleSoft compilation system will accept. It then calls the cross-compiler to perform the compilation, and upon the successful completion of the compilation it examines the TeleSoft program library structure and modifies the Eclipse representation to reflect the changes which have occurred due to the compilation. Unfortunately, some file copying is necessary in this process, largely due to a restriction on the number of separate file descriptors which a UNIX process may have open at any one time. This restriction means that a program consisting of a large number of compilation units would cause the compiler to run out of file descriptors. Consequently the internal representations of compilation units, which are stored as individual files in the Eclipse representation, must be concatenated to form an manageable number of 'sub-libraries' before being presented to the TeleSoft compilation system. This does impose a certain overhead on compilations and would be undesirable for production use, but the integration of the compiler has nonetheless been successful and has proved the feasibility of the concepts involved.

If other compilers were to be integrated into Eclipse, each one would be likely to need some modifications to the standard program library schema. Provided however that those parts of the schema assumed by the program library management tool remained constant, that tool would not be have to be modified. The program library management system is described after the user's view of the Ada development system has been described.

8.5 THE IADS TOOL

The Integrated Ada Development System or IADS is the tool through which the Eclipse user invokes the various facilities of the cross-development system. IADS offers the usual Eclipse house style interface, using a window which is split into several areas or frames. The topmost frame has a fixed content and is used for the overall control of the tool. A state selector called 'Step' allows the user to select the current development step (such as compilation, linking, execution and so on). The second frame allows parameters and options relevant to that step to be entered, displaying only items relevant to that particular step. In each case, a button is provided to cause the action associated with that development step to be performed, usually the invocation of one of the cross-development system tools. The third frame is a 'teletype' frame used for interaction with the cross development tool while it is in operation (bearing in mind that the cross development tools are written without any knowledge of Eclipse, they interact with the user by means of standard UNIX input and output channels). The fourth frame is the message area in which Eclipse messages from the IADS are displayed. The development steps available are as follows.

CREATE PL This step allows the creation of a new program library to allow compilations to begin.

COMPILE This step allows the Ada cross-compiler to be called to compile one or more source files.

ADA LINK performs an Ada link operation by calling the Ada linker tool.

CROSS ASSEMBLE invokes the Intel 80286 cross-assembler tool.

LINK This step allows the target independent linker to be invoked.

IMAGE BUILD This step allows the Intel 80286 image builder tool to be invoked to generate an executable image file.

RUN This step allows Ada programs to be down-line loaded into the target Intel 80286 processor attached to the host Eclipse system. When the program has been loaded, it may be started up and run, with machine-level debugging facilities provided. The teletype window is used both for controlling the execution of the Ada program, and for interaction with it via one of its input and one of its output streams. An Eclipse-hosted version of the symbolic debugger would be invoked

8.6. CONFIGURATION MANAGEMENT 103

by means of a SYMBOLIC DEBUG step which would be provided in addition to this RUN step.

PROM FORMAT This step provides for the loading of a program image into PROM, as discussed in section 8.3 above.

The various program development steps are expected to be carried out approximately in the order in which they are listed above. Where appropriate, IADS carries forward information entered or generated in one step to the next. For example, the name of the linker steering file entered by the user in the Ada link step is used as the default value for the steering file in the link step which normally follows it, thus avoiding the need for the user to re-type information which can be deduced by the system. Naturally this default can be modified by the user before the link operation is performed.

IADS also provides the means of creating and editing Ada source files. This is not quite straightforward, since the Ada source must be an item with versions and this requires objects of the correct PCTE type to be created. IADS isolates the user from the details of this system by creating objects of the correct type and then invoking the 'vitool' text editor in a separate window. The user may either create a new Ada item and its first version, or may edit a version of an existing item, possibly creating a new version. In addition, the user may elect to enter the editor automatically whenever an Ada compilation fails; in this case two editor windows are created, one to view the error message listing and one to allow the source to be modified.

There is also a facility to summon up the program library maintenance tool, which is described in section 8.7 below. A useful feature of the IADS is that the identity of the compiler and target computer are stored in the program library. When a new program library is created, the user nominates the compiler and target to be used, and thereafter the IADS system extracts these details from the library whenever a compilation or other operation is to be performed. The user therefore never specifies the tool to be used in any development step, since the system determines this from the current program library.

Figure 8.1 shows an example of an IADS control panel with the COMPILE step selected.

8.6 CONFIGURATION MANAGEMENT

Configuration management implies the ability to define a set of entities which have internal consistency relationships, to record those relationships in some way, and to protect the entities from accidental or malicious modification or deletion. Since an Ada program library defines the relationships between the compilation units of a program and ensures the consistency of these units, it is the natural starting point for any configuration management system for Ada programs. Eclipse has configuration management facilities built around the program library mechanism. This section discusses these facilities in general terms, while the following section reviews the program library management tool which provides access to the program library and configuration management system.

8.6.1 Derivations

The Eclipse system maintains derivation relationships between Ada source text objects and the compiled forms of compilation units in the program library. Using bi-directional links, this allows units in the program library to be traced back to their original source text objects, and conversely a source object to be traced to the program libraries into which it has been compiled. It is possible to compile a given source object into many different program libraries, which is a useful feature when re-using Ada components. The semantics of the PCTE link types ensures that whenever a source text object has been compiled into a program library it cannot be deleted, thus providing one of the basic mechanisms for configuration management. The impact analysis facilities described below make use of this derivation information. In addition, a link is established between the executable image of an Ada program and the program library from which it was created; thus it is possible to determine all the Ada sources (in their correct versions) which go to form an executable item.

8.6.2 Versions of program libraries

In Eclipse, Ada program libraries are items which may exist in a number of different versions. This feature is unique to Eclipse (as far as is known) and offers considerable operational advantages. For program developers, it allows modifications to be made to a program library in the knowledge that the previous state of the program library need not be lost, and can be reverted to if the modifications prove unsuccessful. For configuration management purposes, it allows successive releases of Ada programs or subsystems to be represented as successive versions of a program library, and as noted above this preserves the record of which source text versions appear in each release. Moreover, by acquiring a program library into an Eclipse configuration (chapter 5) it can be frozen against any further modification.

Creating versions of program libraries is efficient, since compilation units which are unchanged between versions are only represented once and are linked into the various versions in which they appear.

8.6.3 Sharing compilation units

In a project of any size, it is desirable to be able to develop parts of an Ada program in parallel, using different program libraries for the different subsystems. At some stage, these various subsystems will have to be integrated, which in Ada terms means that they will all have to appear in a single program library. Rather than recompiling the source text of each Ada compilation unit into the integration library, which is a time consuming process, it is preferable to be able to form a single (conceptual) program library by merging a number of existing libraries. Thus it is important to be able to share the compiled forms of compilation units between libraries. Almost all Ada compilation systems have some provision for this. In Eclipse, the scheme used is to explicitly enter or 'acquire' an existing compilation unit from one program library into another. There is no restriction on the number of different program libraries from which compilation units can be acquired, allowing very flexible sharing and integration strategies. As far as the user is concerned, there is no difference between a compilation unit which has been compiled directly into a program library and one which has been acquired.

When a compilation unit which has been compiled into one library, say for example A, is shared by another (say B), and is subsequently compiled again into A, the library B does not see this change but continues to use the original form of the compilation unit. This feature isolates sharing libraries from changes made to the original libraries, and is provided to ease problems of configuration management using shared libraries. If users wish to move to the new versions of such shared compilation units, they must re-acquire them. This operation is manual at present, but could be made automatic in future versions of Eclipse.

8.7 THE PROGRAM LIBRARY TOOL

The program library tool provides the user with the program library and configuration management functions. It has a control panel interface for interactive use, but may also be invoked through a command line so that it can be used in command scripts. The functions of the program library tool can be divided into two groups — those which provide information, and those which modify program libraries in some way.

8.7.1 Information Output

The following functions are provided.

UNITS This command allows a program library to be inspected for the presence of named compilation units, and optionally allows information on the structure of selected compilation units to be displayed. Compilation unit names can be entered as patterns, and all units matching the pattern will be found. The names of selected units appear as the pick-list associated with the CURRENT_CUs sign, and further selection of compilation units can be made using the pick list, in this command and in others which require compilation units to be selected.

LIB_DETAILS This command simply allows details such as the name and creation date of the current program library to be displayed.

HISTORY This command displays the history of state-changing operations performed on the current program library.

IMPACT This is a powerful command which performs a source impact analysis using the derivation information discussed in section 8.6.1 above. Given a source text object, it reports all the program libraries into which it has been compiled (and all libraries which share its compiled form) and further reports all the other compilation units which depend on it and which would be potentially affected by a change to the given source object. This allows the ramifications of change proposals to be assessed.

CHECK_PROGRAM This command checks that all the compilation units necessary to form an Ada program are present in the library and in a consistent state. It can be used prior to attempting an Ada link using the IADS tool to ensure that the link operation will not fail.

REBUILD This command produces a UNIX 'make' file which will rebuild the current program library (or more probably, a new version of it with the most recent versions of its constituent source objects).

8.7.2 Modification functions

These functions are provided to create program libraries and perform operations upon them.

CREATE_LIBRARY This command creates a new program library and initialises it with the predefined Ada language environment appropriate to the target machine. The newly-created library becomes the first version of this specified name.

COPY_LIBRARY This command is used to create a copy of an existing program library, or to create a new version of such a library. A new version can also be created on request when a compilation is performed via the IADS tool.

DELETE This command is used to delete selected compilation units from a program library. Its use is not expected to be very frequent, but it can be useful in rare circumstances.

INVALIDATE This command allows selected compilation units to be marked as obsolete without the need to recompile any units upon which they depend. It can be used to force recompilation of selected units in conjunction with the RECOMPILE command, or when it is necessary to re-acquire compilation units from another library.

ACQUIRE This is the command which allows existing compilation units from other libraries to be shared by the current library, as discussed in the previous section. The library from which the units are to be acquired is first nominated, then units from it are selected, and finally an ACQUIRE button is used to action the acquisition of the selected units.

RECOMPILE This command is used to force the recompilation (from source) of any units which are present in a program library but which are 'invalid', due to the fact that they depend on other units which have already been recompiled, or due to the use of the INVALIDATE command. This command is useful in that it can restore a program library to a fully consistent state by means of a single request. At a later stage, further options may be added to this command, notably ones to force recompilation of any compilation unit whose source text has been modified or up-versioned since it was last compiled.

Figure 8.2 shows a typical window for the program library tool. In the upper frame, the current program library and currently selected compilation units are displayed by means of signs, together with the state selectors which set the current display or update function. The next area is a multi-line output field which is used to display the output from the tool, although there is an option to direct this to a named file since some reports from the tool may be lengthy. The second frame is used for information pertinent to the currently selected function, which in the example given is the UNITS command, while the third frame is the standard message area.

8.8 FUTURE EXTENSIONS

The most obvious extension to the Ada facilities of Eclipse would be to integrate other compilers, to achieve a wider spread of target machines and compiler characteristics. Further facilities for configuration management of Ada programs would also be useful.

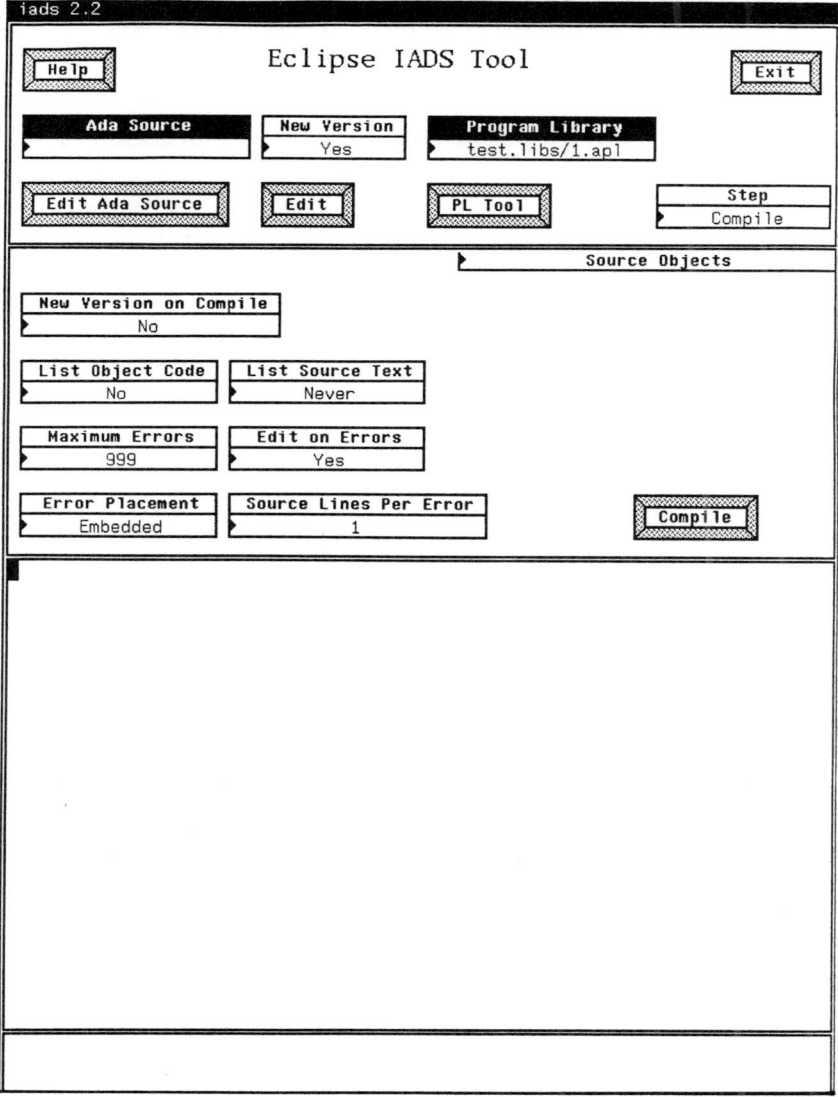

Figure 8.1

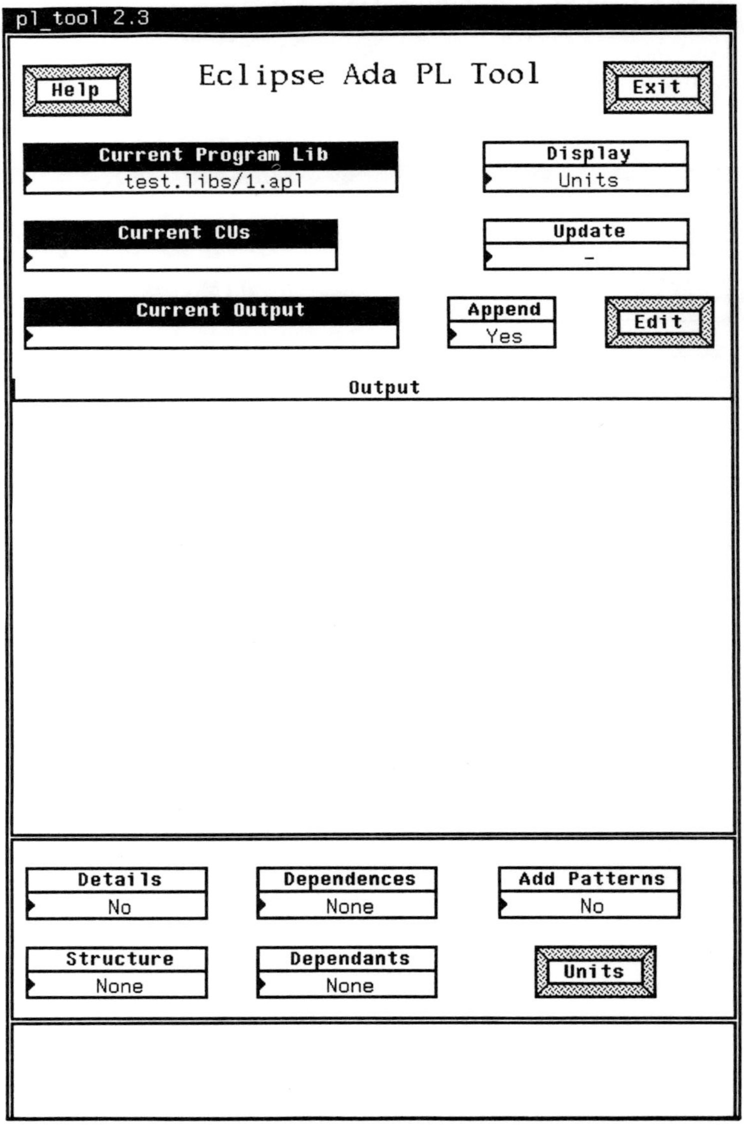
pl_tool 2.3
Help
Eclipse Ada PL Tool
Exit
Current Program Lib
test.libs/1.apl
Display
Units
Current CUs
Update
-
Current Output
Append
Yes
Edit
Output
Details
No
Dependences
None
Add Patterns
No
Structure
None
Dependants
None
Units

Figure 8.2

Chapter 9

Development of the MASCOT 3 Tool Set

Tony Elliott

9.1 INTRODUCTION

The major tool set development during the Eclipse Programme was to support the MASCOT 3 design method in conjunction with Ada. MASCOT 3 had been identified as an important forthcoming method in the original proposal to the Alvey Directorate.

The objectives identified in the Alvey proposal were fairly modest. They were to design a database representation of MASCOT designs, to develop tools for interactive editing of MASCOT designs, and for construction of complete Ada programs corresponding to MASCOT systems. This covered both first-level support (i.e. parameterisation of generic tools for the method) and second-level support (i.e. development of method-specific tools). A number of areas of further investigation were identified, but not put forward as part of the proposal. These were tools in support of prototyping, performance analysis, test harness production, and analysis of system behaviour.

The choice of MASCOT 3 with Ada was, in many ways, an ideal combination to exploit and demonstrate features of Eclipse.

- MASCOT 2, and its successor MASCOT 3, are more than 'pencil and paper' methods; they require some form of automated support.

- MASCOT is a predominantly graphical method. Although MASCOT 2 was a widely used and accepted design method, typical MASCOT 2 support systems were text-based, with diagrams being produced a posteriori. The emerging MASCOT 3, given its graphical improvements, would enable designs to be captured directly in graphical form.

- Software Sciences was assisting the MOD with the definition of MASCOT 3. Eclipse therefore had in-house advance knowledge of the emerging definition.

- The use of Ada as the implementation language made possible an integration of the MASCOT 3 tools and Ada tools. This would further promote Eclipse as an APSE.

The development of tool sets was an important part of the overall Eclipse programme. Whilst the Eclipse kernel, on which the tools were built, was of fundamental and central importance, it was not in itself a demonstrable piece of software. The tool sets were the visible means by which Eclipse could be demonstrated, and hence judged. The design and development of the tool sets were also the means by which the kernel software could be evaluated and its evolution directed.

This chapter describes the development of the MASCOT 3 tool set. First an historical account of the project is given followed by a brief overview of MASCOT. The main body of the chapter is devoted to a description of the tool set and the design of the underlying data structures. In conclusion we examine the extent to which the original objectives were met, and lessons learnt from the project.

9.2 HISTORY OF THE PROJECT

The development of the tool set was not, in any sense, a straightforward or continuous process. On the contrary it suffered from numerous discontinuities. There were a number of different project teams set up during the lifetime of Eclipse to develop some form of MASCOT support. Each of these teams had different objectives and sometimes radically different ideas as to what form the support should take. The specification of the kernel software, on which the tools would be built, was often in a state of flux. Thus initial efforts at tool design and development were being attempted on moving targets.

There were four distinct phases to the MASCOT project. Chronologically the first three phases occupied just over half of the three year Eclipse programme. The final phase, leading to the Alvey conference in July 1987, took the remainder.

The first phase was characterised by the view that to do anything less than a production quality 'full' MASCOT 3 support system was, from a commercial viewpoint, a waste of time. Such a system it was estimated would take at least 12 man-years, i.e. twice the effort allocated in the Alvey proposal. Since the necessary resources were not available, this approach was rejected.

The second phase was rather more modest. Given the uncertainty over the Eclipse design editor, and given the limited resources available, it was felt that a text-based approach would be a low risk and low cost alternative. Due to staff changes this approach did not proceed far.

The third phase again recognised the folly of trying to develop tools on still fluid specifications. Although the design editor was more of a known quantity, the Integrated Tools Interface (ITI) was still being developed. It was therefore decided to prototype some tools using SDS-2. The work was completed at about the same time as the decision to transfer to PCTE was made. Nevertheless, much that was useful came out of this phase; in particular, the details of MASCOT 3 design checks and the experiences with mapping MASCOT 3 to Ada were useful input to the next phase.

The fourth, and what became the final, phase of the project was in a much better position to succeed. The decision to use PCTE had been made. The design editor and DBI specifications were slightly less unstable than previously. Given that the end of the Eclipse Programme was 15 months away, the project had a clear deadline and had to accept the short time scale and limited resources. Also there was acceptance that the tool set being developed was not a 'product', but a prototype demonstrator for Eclipse.

9.3 OVERVIEW OF MASCOT

In the remainder of this chapter a certain level of understanding of MASCOT 3 is assumed. We therefore present a short overview of the MASCOT method.

9.3.1 History

The origins of MASCOT can be traced back to the period 1965 to 1970. The originators were involved in the development of embedded real-time systems during this period. During the development the possibility of creating an alternative method of software development was investigated.

MASCOT, as a method, was subsequently developed by Ken Jackson and Hugo Simpson at the Royal Signals and Radar Establishment (RSRE) over the period 1971 to 1975. The first official definition of MASCOT [82] was produced by a group of individuals formed from several companies and MOD establishments. The document defined what became known as MASCOT 1.

The development of MASCOT 2 began in 1980. Again it was developed by a group of individuals from several companies and MOD establishments. Software Sciences was one of the companies involved. The Official Handbook of MASCOT [61] published in 1980 and reissued in 1983, is the standard reference for MASCOT 2.

Since 1981 the technical development of MASCOT has been under the control of a joint committee (JIMCOM). It is under this committee that the development of MASCOT 3 has been carried out. The definition team was formed from various companies and MOD establishments and again Software Sciences were heavily involved. The definition of MASCOT 3 is contained in a new version of the handbook [62]. A less formal and more concise description is given in [110].

9.3.2 The Method

MASCOT has been widely used for the design and implementation of real-time concurrent systems. The method is largely language-independent and has been successfully employed with languages such as Coral, Pascal, and RTL2.

The MASCOT acronym stands for a **M**odular **A**pproach to **S**oftware **C**onstruction, **O**peration and **T**est. The approach encompasses:

- a design representation;

- a design derivation method;

- software construction in a manner that is consistent with the design;

112   CHAPTER 9. DEVELOPMENT OF THE MASCOT 3 TOOL SET

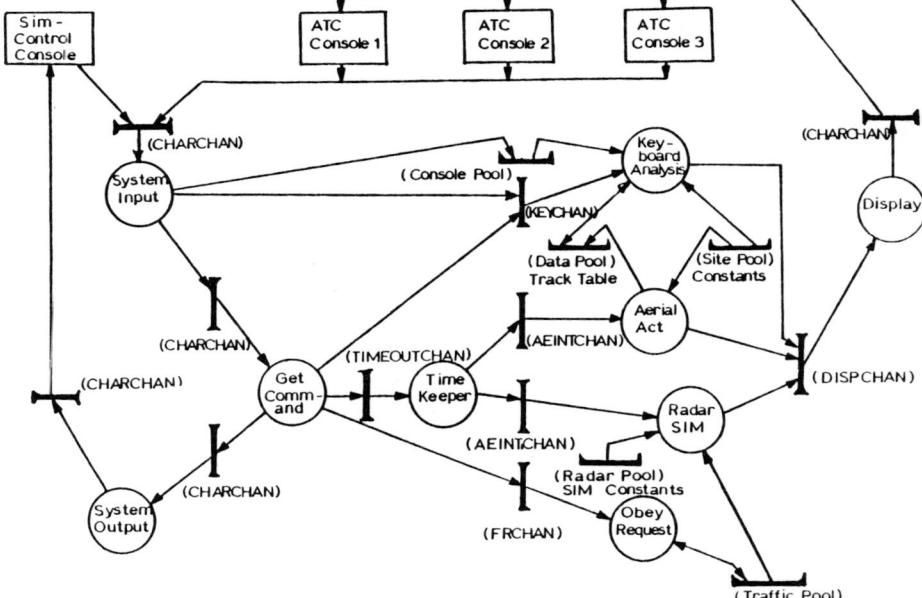

Figure 9.1: Simple MASCOT 2 System

- a means to execute software such that the design structure is manifest during execution;

- facilities for software testing in terms of the design structure.

The MASCOT design representation is characterised by the use of graphical dataflow networks to express the static structure and inter-communication of components within a system design. Figure 9.1 gives an example of the graphical representation for a simple MASCOT 2 system. The algorithmic details of a MASCOT design are expressed using an appropriate language, such as Coral, Pascal, RTL2, and more recently Ada.

The practical use of MASCOT 2 over many years had identified a number of deficiencies in the method. The most noticeable are:

- imprecise interface specification;

- direct dependencies between elements of the design;

- a 'flat' network for expressing the design (although some support environments have extended the MASCOT 2 notation to support hierarchical decomposition);

- inability to express designs for large multi-processor systems.

9.3. OVERVIEW OF MASCOT

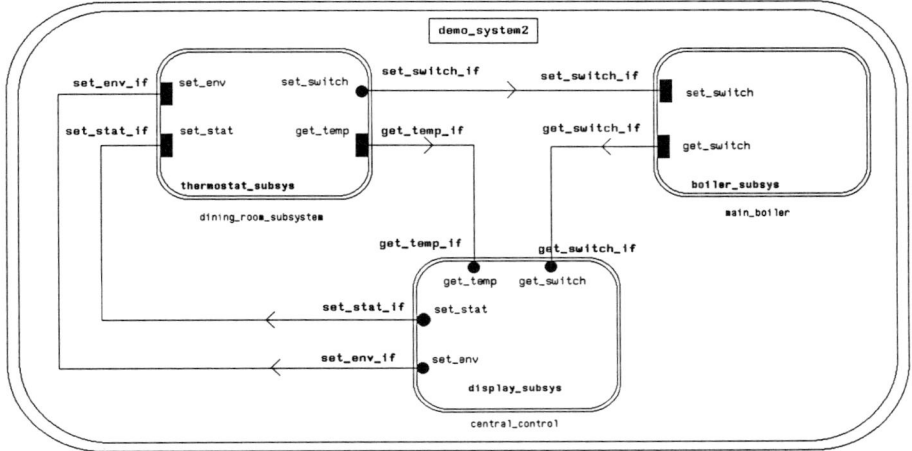

Figure 9.2: Simple MASCOT 3 System

The aim of MASCOT 3 has therefore been both to consolidate existing features of MASCOT 2 and to provide a common solution to the above deficiencies.

9.3.3 MASCOT 3 Representation

A MASCOT 3 design expresses, in an hierarchical manner, the dataflow between elements of a software system. At the lowest levels of the design the individual processing elements are identified. Figure 9.2 gives an example of the graphical representation for a simple MASCOT 3 system. The elements representing concurrent threads of execution are known as *activities*. A feature of MASCOT is that activities cannot communicate with each other directly. They must communicate through passive elements of the design known as *IDAs*. The two common forms of IDA are *channels*, which support a producer/consumer mechanism of transmitting data, and *pools*, which support the storage of sharable data. One other important class of processing element is a *server*. Servers provide abstract interfaces to hardware devices.

A *subsystem* enables a network of design elements, including other subsystems, to be defined. The top-level network, which has no external connections, is called a *system*. Thus a system may be decomposed through a hierarchy of subsystems into elementary components, i.e. into the activities, IDAs, and servers comprising the design. Figure 9.3 shows an example of a MASCOT subsystem

An important feature of MASCOT 3 is that the processing elements, or *components* of a design are derived, or instantiated, from *template* modules. The template modules, therefore, can be thought of as defining component types. So it is possible, and usually advantageous, to have multiple instances of a template within a MASCOT 3 design.

Template modules, like Ada packages, have a *specification part,* which defines the external interface of (instances of) the template, and an *implementation part,* which defines the implementation details corresponding to that specification. The external

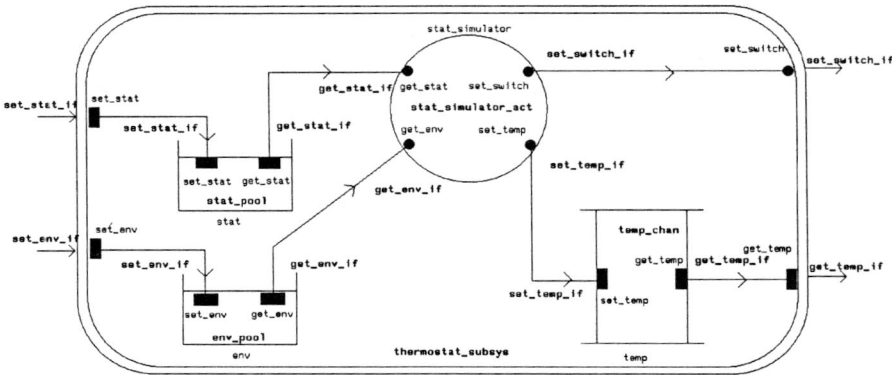

Figure 9.3: Simple MASCOT 3 Subsystem

interface of a template is expressed in terms of *ports,* which define the facilities required by the template, and *windows,* which define the facilities provided. Note that this is a distinct improvement over Ada. Ada packages have no specification of their required interface; the requirement is expressed merely as a collection of named packages.

Both ports and windows are defined in terms of access interfaces. For a composite template the implementation part is expressed as a network of components, i.e. instances of other templates, with dataflow *paths* connecting them. For a simple template the implementation part is expressed in terms of some suitable programming language, i.e. Ada for the Eclipse tools.

There is another class of module known as a *specification.* Specification modules, as their name implies, have no implementation part. The types of specification module are *definitions,* which enable a collection of global constants and types to be defined, and *access interfaces,* which define the procedural interface for a dataflow path. Keeping interfaces as separate modules is an important feature of MASCOT 3. It enables the connections between higher-level components to be specified without regard to the exact procedures involved. The interface modules can be completed as part of the lower-level detailed design process.

An important feature of MASCOT 3 is that of *Status Progression.* Each module has a status indicating the degree of progress made in the definition and checking of the module and of any other modules to which it refers, and hence its fitness for use by other modules. There are three primary statuses: *Registered* indicating that the module exists and has a name and class, *Introduced* indicating that the module has a legal specification part, and *Enrolled* indicating that the module has a legal implementation part. The Introduced and Enrolled statuses have Partial and Full categories indicating the status of the modules on which they depend. For example, the Fully Enrolled status indicates that a template module and all of the modules on which it depends (directly or indirectly) have legal specification and implementation

9.4. SUPPORT FOR MASCOT 3 115

parts. The MASCOT Handbook defines a precise set of pre-conditions for a module to attain each status.

One final feature of MASCOT 3, which deserves mention here, is that of the *MASCOT Database*. This is the central repository for all MASCOT modules and their various outputs. It enables modules to be reused easily both within a system and between different systems. A more detailed look at the reusability aspects of MASCOT 3, and their relationship to the reusability guidelines discussed in chapter 12, can be found in [28].

9.4 SUPPORT FOR MASCOT 3

The MASCOT method is quite extensive, ranging from initial documentation, through design expression, to testing on multiple-processor target machines. This section describes the extent to which the MASCOT method is supported by the Eclipse tool set.

9.4.1 Design Language

By 'design language' we mean the language which is used for expressing the algorithmic details of a MASCOT 3 design.

It was decided that the tools should support the use of Ada as the design language. This decision was, in a sense, pre-determined. The original Alvey proposal specified Ada. The use of Ada was an early consideration in the design of MASCOT 3. Considerable work had been done on developing mappings from MASCOT 3 designs to Ada packages, see [58]. A final factor was that the Ada cross development project was integrating the Telesoft Ada compiler into Eclipse. It seemed eminently sensible to make full use of an integrated compiler.

9.4.2 Scope of Method

The MASCOT acronym covers the aspects of operation and testing of MASCOT systems. We decided that the scope of the Eclipse tools should be confined to that of design manipulation and software construction. This was a well-defined area of the MASCOT approach and minimised the overlap with the Ada development system. The functionality of the tools would therefore concentrate on the editing and checking of designs, and on generation and compilation of Ada. Given the limited resources to develop the tools, we felt it better to concentrate on these phases rather than trying to cover all steps of MASCOT. Thus the functions of system building, preparation for, and execution on target processors would be the domain of Ada Cross Development tools.

Another fundamental and significant decision was that the tools would support only the mandatory subset of the MASCOT 3 design representation. There were a number of reasons for this. First, the mandatory subset includes a sufficiently rich set of module classes to express almost any MASCOT 3 design. The excluded composite module classes can usually be expressed in terms of other MASCOT or Ada constructs. Secondly the mandatory module classes include modules that are graphical, modules that are completely textual, and modules that have graphical and textual parts. Thus the feasibility of supporting all module classes would be demonstrated. Finally, at that time during the project the MASCOT 3 definition was not finalised; we were receiving various updates and draft issues of the Handbook. Much of the material in the Handbook was still undergoing change. The mandatory subset, however, remained relatively stable. Therefore, given the instability within other areas of Eclipse, the mandatory subset offered us a low risk option for the initial tool set.

9.4.3 Design Representation

Given the use of powerful Sun work stations within Eclipse, it was a natural decision that the system should support the capture and manipulation of MASCOT 3 designs graphically where possible. For the textual elements of a design a number of possibilities were considered. The Handbook defines a textual design representation language (we christened this as DRL, in line with the standard for Eclipse acronyms!). This form could have been used directly, by parsing and 'compiling' to an internal representation in the conventional way.

We decided, however, to present the design in a more structured fashion. Definition with-lists and access interfaces would be presented in a forms-like manner using the Eclipse Applications Interface. Ada text could be manipulated in a free-text area using an editor, such as vi. This approach avoided the need for parsing the textual design information; the user would do this, by filling in the separate fields.

Having decided on a combined graphical and structured text representation for modules, that would imply no support for the textual DRL defined in the Handbook. To rectify this situation a tool to output DRL was proposed. This would, at least, allow for the export of MASCOT 3 designs. To import designs a DRL input facility would be required. This was not considered to be essential for the initial tool set.

9.4.4 Design Checking

An interesting area was that of design checking. Since the Eclipse design editor was specified to provide a certain amount of local checking, and together with the future potential for such facilities as assertion checking and highlighting the diagram with errors, there was an argument for incorporating the checking functions into the design editor.

The MASCOT 3 Handbook has a well-defined set of checks that must be applied to modules for them to achieve a particular status. However, the checking required to do full status progression involves use of an Ada compiler. Also, as well as status progression there is the reverse process of status regression (or demotion). This involves impact analysis functions and report generation, etc. Thus to put all of the status functions into the editing tools would involve a considerable amount of extra functionality. It was therefore decided to have a separate tool concerned solely with the status progression facilities.

However, we did not want to forsake the possibility of using the design editor's checking capability. Therefore we accepted a certain degree of overlap between the design editor and the status tool, and decided to use the design editor to perform purely local design checks on the module. The status tool would do the necessary global and hierarchical design checks.

9.4.5 Ada Generation and Compilation

The previous section identified that to do full design checking it is necessary to use an Ada compiler — to ensure the validity of those module parts containing user-written Ada. This in turn requires Ada units to be generated and compiled to provide the necessary compilation environment. Given the prohibitive costs of Ada compilation, in terms of both elapsed and processor time, it seemed a pity to waste this compilation effort. Therefore the design decision was made that the Ada compilation of all module parts, i.e. including the graphical parts, would be done during status progression.

The choice of Ada mapping which made this 'incremental' compilation model possible is described in section 9.5.

9.4.6 Version and Configuration Control

Another area requiring consideration was that of versioning, and hence for configuration control. The MASCOT 3 Handbook does not address versions. We felt that for realistic use of the tools, some form of support for versions was essential. A reasonable set of requirements would seem to be: that there should be at least one MASCOT Database, that there should be versions of modules, and that there should be controlled sharing of versions between users.

The relationship between the Eclipse two-tier database, the MASCOT Database(s), module versions, and configurations thereof is examined further in section 9.6.2.

9.4.7 Run Time Features

The various activities comprising a MASCOT 3 design do not communicate with each other directly. They communicate through passive components, i.e. through IDA's, channels, pools and servers. The semantics of MASCOT require that the interfaces provided by passive components must preserve the integrity of any data within the component. The designer of IDA-like modules thus requires some means for achieving mutual exclusion between callers, i.e. from active components. There are two main ways that this might be achieved.

The first is to use a language-independent set of facilities. Both MASCOT 2 and MASCOT 3 define a standard set of interfaces called the *MASCOT Kernel*. These facilities are based on a *Control Queue,* and the primitives *Join, Wait, Leave,* and *Stim.* These primitives are sufficient to provide a simple and efficient means for achieving mutual exclusion. An Ada implementation of these standard primitives could be provided as part of the tool set.

However, given the use of Ada, there is the second possibility of using standard language features. Ada tasks provide independent and parallel threads of execution within a program. Communication between tasks is achieved using the *rendezvous* mechanism. Thus, in Ada, the implementation of an IDA-like module could use an additional monitor task to control access to the data encapsulated by the module. Each activity would be represented as an active Ada task which would access shared data by making a rendezvous with the passive Ada task controlling the IDA.

We made the decision that, for simplicity and on cost grounds, the MASCOT tool set would assume the use of Ada tasks within IDA's. This was deemed to be sufficient for a demonstration prototype. It was however accepted that for large MASCOT 3 systems a MASCOT kernel would be required. The corresponding large number of Ada tasks would probably be unacceptable to system performance.

9.5 MAPPING TO ADA

The process of generating a complete Ada program corresponding to a MASCOT 3 system requires some form of mapping from MASCOT modules to Ada compilation units. The report [128] identifies numerous possible mappings. We wanted a mapping which displayed the properties that:

- the MASCOT system structure was obvious in the Ada program/package structure;
- no source transformation of the user-written Ada was necessary;
- incremental compilation of the Ada on a module-by-module basis was possible;
- allowed for compilation-efficient reuse, i.e. where a module is shared between configurations so too should its compiled outputs.

The mapping selected for use by the tool set is based on the use of generic packages to represent template modules. The similarity between the style of these packages and those for reusable Ada components is examined in [28].

The rest of this section gives a short description of the mapping.

Definitions

Definition modules map to library package specifications. References to other (definition) modules are through the Ada context clause.

Access Interfaces

Access interface modules have no direct library unit corresponding to them. However, for the purposes of checking the access procedures, a library package containing the subprogram specifications is generated and compiled. Its compiler outputs are discarded.

Template Specifications

The specification part of template modules map to generic library package specifications. Windows and ports map to local packages as follows.

Each window interface provided by the template maps to a local package declaration within the library package. The local package declares a subprogram for each access procedure of the interface.

Each port interface required by the template maps to a local package declared in the private part of the library package. The local package declares a subprogram for each access procedure of the interface. The subprogram declarations rename generic formal subprograms of the library package. Thus dependencies on (the subprograms of) other template packages are expressed as generic formal parameters. The mapping

9.5. MAPPING TO ADA

```
generic
    -- port subprograms
    with procedure INIT1;
package CHAR_CHAN is
    -- window
    package PUT_W is
        -- subprograms for put_if
        procedure PUT (...);
    end PUT_W;
    -- window
    package GET_W is
        -- subprograms for get_if
        procedure GET (...);
    end GET_W;
private
    -- port
    package INIT_P is
        -- subprograms for init_if
        procedure INIT renames INIT1;
    end INIT_P;
end CHAR_CHAN;
```

Figure 9.4: Ada Mapping of Channel Specification

thus achieves de-coupling of Ada library packages in the same manner as MASCOT 3 template modules.

Figure 9.4 shows a simple template and its corresponding Ada file.

9.5.1 Simple Template Implementations

The implementation part of a simple template consists of user-written Ada. For activities this is the body of a ROOT procedure. For other modules the Ada contains package bodies corresponding to the local window package declarations. The mapping to Ada is simple; the user-written Ada forms the body of the template library package.

9.5.2 Subsystem Implementations

The implementation part of a subsystem maps to the library package body for the template. There are three main functions that the Ada has to achieve: instantiate templates to form components, establish dataflow paths between components, and provide the 'motive force' for activities.

Components map to local package declarations instantiated from their template generic library package. Dataflow paths are established by supplying the visible subprograms of components providing window interfaces as generic actual subprograms of components requiring port interfaces. Certain subterfuges are required to avoid cyclic dependencies.

In order to give activities an independent thread of control it is necessary to declare a local task for each activity component. The body of this task calls the ROOT procedure of the activity. Thus, on elaboration of the package body, each activity is started as an independent task.

9.5.3 System Implementations

The implementation part of a system template maps to a library subprogram body. This acts as the Ada main program for the MASCOT 3 system. The body of the subprogram is the same as for a subsystem implementation.

9.6 DESIGN OF THE MASCOT DATABASE

The initial stage of the design phase concentrated on defining an Eclipse database representation of the various elements in a MASCOT 3 design. It is worthwhile to look at some specific aspects of the representation, viz:

- modelling the MASCOT 3 Database and module naming,
- version and configuration concerns,
- diagram representation,
- module status and dependences,
- relationship to Ada outputs.

9.6.1 MASCOT Database and Module Naming

The MASCOT Handbook definition of MASCOT Database is:

> The collection of all MASCOT modules, their status, and their derived products known to a particular support environment.

A number of possible representations were considered. These are examined below.

Scheme 1

The first possibility considered was to allow the (objects representing) modules to be created in PCTE object store wherever users wished. Users would thus be able to achieve, for example, functional grouping of modules. There would be a single MASCOT Database, i.e. some subset of the object store.

A major problem with this scheme is the question of how modules are identified. MASCOT 3 modules have names; names are the means by which modules refer to each another. With modules strewn around the object store, there would need to be a fairly elaborate naming scheme so that modules could be uniquely identified. A natural scheme might be to use the PCTE path name to a module as its name. However, PCTE path names are relative, i.e. they merely define a navigation route

9.6. DESIGN OF THE MASCOT DATABASE

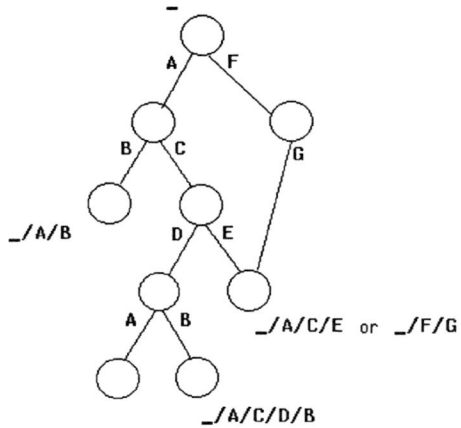

Figure 9.5: Pathnames to Modules

from one object to another. Thus there are potentially many different path names to an object, depending on the start object and the navigation route taken. Even starting from the common root of the PCTE object store, there are still potentially many path names to an object. (Note that in CAIS [129], it would be possible to use the 'primary' path to an object as its unique name). For example, consider Figure 9.5. One of the modules shown could be accessed with two different path names.

Whilst the use of names for modules based on path names fits in well with PCTE, the scheme poses a number of problems both for the user and for the tool set. Although not defined by the MASCOT Handbook, there is an implication that module names will be simple identifiers. Module names appear on MASCOT diagrams both as access interface labels and as template labels. Elaborate path names would clutter up the diagram. Also the Ada mapping strategy, discussed in section 9.5, requires that there be some mapping from module names to Ada package names, which themselves must be simple identifiers. Therefore some form of mapping table would be required to understand the MASCOT module to Ada package correspondence.

Scheme 2

A variation of this scheme, making the module mapping table explicit, is shown in Figure 9.6. Here, module objects are named through a key from a distinguished MASCOT Database object. This scheme still allows modules to be created anywhere in object store, but inter-module references are always by their simple name from the database object. Moreover, this scheme is much more in the spirit of the MASCOT Handbook and simplifies the mapping to Ada. It makes possible the trivial identity mapping between MASCOT module names and Ada package names.

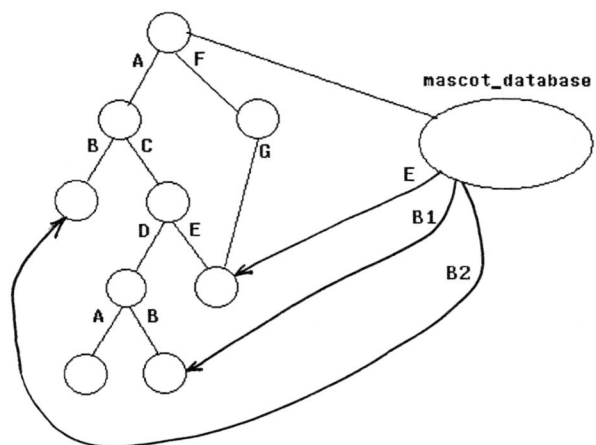

Figure 9.6: MASCOT Database with Simple Module Names

Scheme 3

A further variation of the second scheme above is to use the distinguished MASCOT Database object as the host entity for modules, i.e. the modules depend for their existence on the MASCOT Database. This arrangement, shown in Figure 9.7, would still give a simple naming scheme for modules. An advantage is that the MASCOT tools would be better able to provide support for creation and deletion of objects corresponding to modules. The MASCOT Database object is, in effect, like a module directory. The user would still be able to create local references to modules (although we would not see this as a necessary or desirable thing to do). We decided to adopt this design for the Eclipse tool set.

A refinement of this scheme would be to support a hierarchic structure for the MASCOT Database, i.e. to introduce the notion of sub-database objects. This option was kept as a possible upgrade path, but dismissed for the initial version to keep the naming scheme simple.

Having introduced the notion of a database object, it seemed a natural step to support potentially many MASCOT Databases. The tools would be invoked in the context of a particular database object. This design choice, although perhaps not strictly in the spirit of the definition of MASCOT Database given above, gives users maximum flexibility in setting up their development environment. An installation may be set up with a single MASCOT Database, giving maximum potential for reuse of modules between different development teams. It may be that there are security or geographical constraints requiring that developments are carried out within separate MASCOT Databases.

So, in summary, the approach adopted has been:

9.6. DESIGN OF THE MASCOT DATABASE

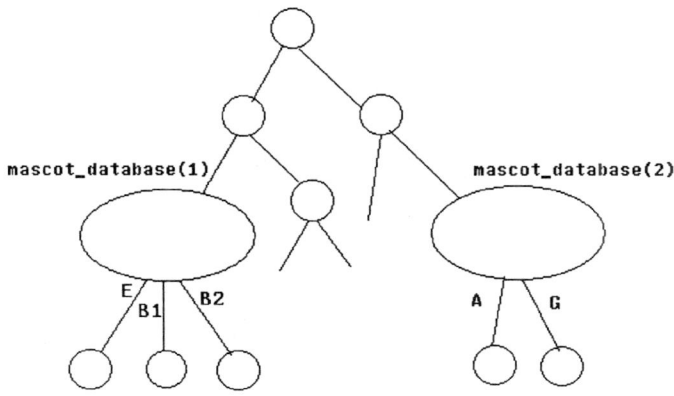

Figure 9.7: MASCOT Database as Host Entity

- to allow potentially many MASCOT Databases,
- to support only a single level of modules within the MASCOT Database,
- that modules depend for their existence on the MASCOT Database,
- that module names are simple identifiers unique within a MASCOT Database,
- that MASCOT tools provide functions for the creation and deletion of modules.

9.6.2 Module Representation

For the purposes of the discussion above, a module was regarded as a single abstract object. In concrete terms, i.e. in terms of actual PCTE objects, this is not the case. Let us now examine the design decisions behind the database representation of modules.

We had expressed the requirement that versions of modules should be supported. For specification modules, which have only a specification part, this presents no problems. A template module however, like an Ada package, has a specification part and an implementation part. So an activity template, for example, has a graphical specification part and a text-based implementation part.

What, however, are versions of a template with regard to its specification and implementation parts? If both parts were versioned together, i.e. each new version of the template resulted in a new version of the combined specification and implementation parts, then this may be inefficient. If only the implementation part required revision, unnecessary status checks (including Ada compilations) would result. If only the specification part required revision, an unnecessary copy of the implementation part would result. For maximum flexibility and efficiency (particularly with respect to Ada compilation), we made the design choice to version the specification and implementation

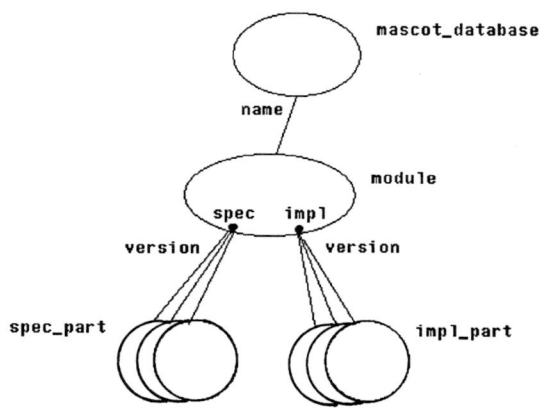

Figure 9.8: Possible Object Representation of Module

parts of a template independently. Thus the notion of a module, in terms of objects, is as a collection of specification part versions and implementation part versions. The latest version of a module can be regarded as the latest versions of its parts.

In PCTE object terms a convenient representation of a module might be as in Figure 9.8.

In this figure the module object has one set of links to its specification part versions, and another set of links to its implementation part versions. Both sets of links are keyed by some version identifier.

However, it was necessary to change this model to take advantage of the Eclipse kernel support for versions. The Eclipse two-tier database supports the concept of an *item* as a collection of versions keyed by an integer version number. The database interface provides support for version selection using a *primary* version link. The configuration control interface provides support for the sharing and development of versions in multiple configurations (see chapter 4 for details).

Using items, then, it was straightforward to model a specification module as a single item. To model a template module it was necessary to use a pair of items: one for the specification part versions and one for the implementation part versions. To enable navigation between specification and implementation parts, the two items would need to be linked by a one-to-one relationship. Since all modules have a specification part then the link from the MASCOT database would be to the specification part item. Figure 9.9 shows the object representation of a template module.

Some example path names for navigating to and between versions are:

```
name/+.part          -- database to latest spec version
name/.impl/+.part    -- database to latest impl version
../.impl/+.part      -- spec version to latest impl version
../.spec/+.part      -- impl version to latest spec version
```

9.6. DESIGN OF THE MASCOT DATABASE

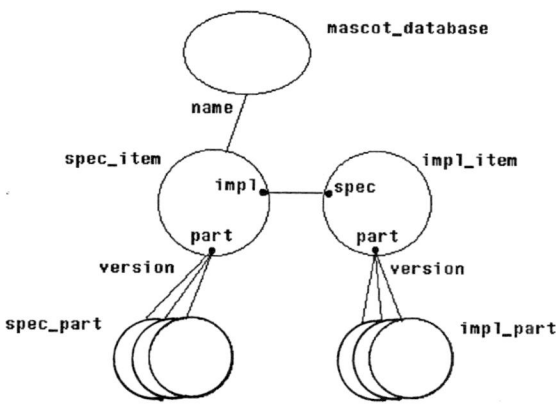

Figure 9.9: Representation of Template Module

9.6.3 Module Parts

The choice of representation for module parts was fairly straightforward.

definition a file containing Ada text of definition(s), typically a collection of named numbers, type definitions, and constant objects.

access interface a fine structure object representing an ordered collection of access procedures. As part of the process of mapping to Ada, the tools need to know about the individual access procedures. We made the design decision to constrain the user to edit access interfaces as structured objects. This avoided the need for the text editor to parse Ada subprogram declarations.

template specification a fine structure object representing the template boundary diagram.

simple template implementation a file containing Ada text of implementation. For an activity this will be a ROOT procedure. For an IDA-like module this will be a set of package bodies corresponding to the windows provided by the template.

composite template implementation a fine structure object representing the composite template network diagram.

For the diagrammatic parts above an initial design was of a MASCOT-specific second-tier schema. This required a procedural interface between the generic design editor and the MASCOT-specific data. A revised design for the design editor introduced a generic schema for diagrams, but with method-specific node types. The correspondence between names was established in GDL.

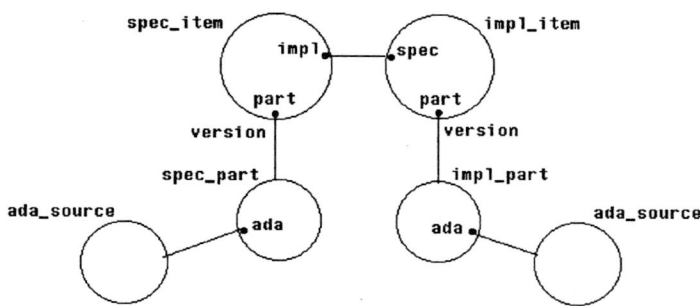

Figure 9.10: Generated Ada Files

9.6.4 Ada Outputs

A feature of the Ada mapping selected is that, by using generic packages, there is a one-to-one correspondence between MASCOT module parts and Ada compilation units. Specification parts map to package specifications, and implementation parts to package bodies. Thus it is straightforward to store the generated Ada file with a composition link from the module part, i.e. the module part is its host entity. This is depicted in Figure 9.10.

The Status Control tool, as part of the status progression operations, both generates the Ada corresponding to checked module parts, and compiles the generated files to further ensure their validity. An interesting design problem was how to handle the compiled outputs and the Ada program library structure.

A property of most Ada program library systems, in particular the Eclipse one, is that they do not support versions of compilation units. Rather, they usually support multiple libraries (or library versions in the case of Eclipse) in which compilation units may be shared.

The MASCOT Database exhibits a similar property. The status of a module and the validity of the generated Ada source file is not a property of some particular version of a module. It is a property of some particular collection of versions of module parts.

It was realised that the two structures could be united by having a single Ada program library item (i.e. a collection of versions of a program library) corresponding to a MASCOT Database. Within any configuration of the MASCOT Database, all modules in that configuration would be compiled into a single program library (version). Thus the program library would reflect the compiled state of the Ada source for the latest version of each of the module parts within the configuration. A simplified view of this structure is shown in Figure 9.11.

Having arrived at a workable design for uniting the MASCOT Database and its Ada program library, it was tempting to consider the impact of supporting a range of Eclipse integrated compilers. The extension to the data model was trivial. Instead of linking to a single program library, there would need to be one program library per compiler. In PCTE terms there would be a composition link keyed by some compiler identifier. The MASCOT 3 tool set would be invoked with the compiler identifier

9.6. DESIGN OF THE MASCOT DATABASE

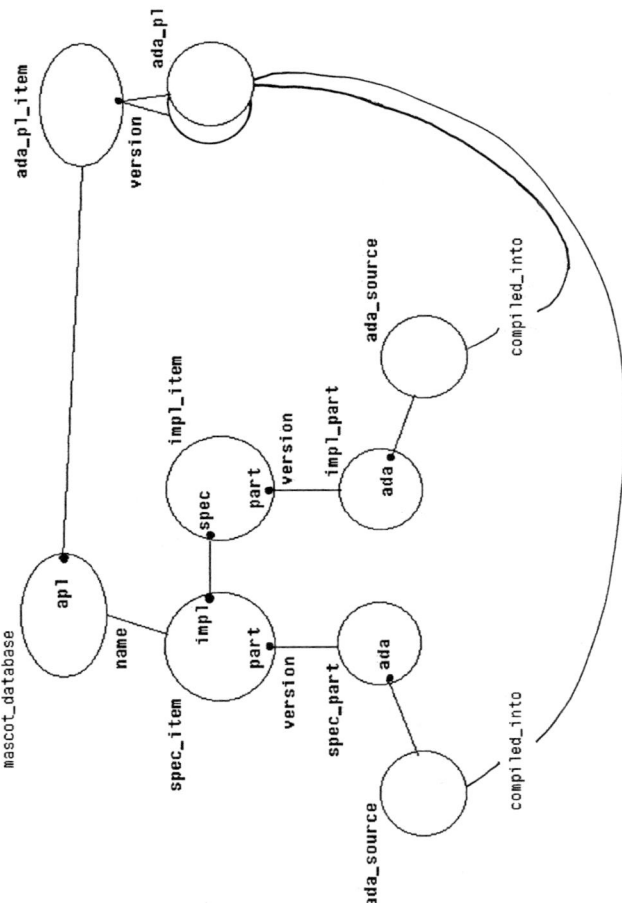

Figure 9.11: Ada Program Library Relation to MASCOT Database

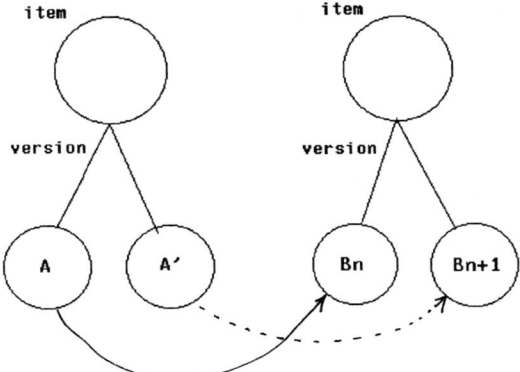

Figure 9.12: Version-to-Version Dependencies

as a parameter. This would enable the selection of a program library and compiler accordingly. (In fact the compiler identifier could be used to influence the mapping strategy, or even be used to support target languages other than Ada.)

9.6.5 Module Dependences and Participation

A great deal of effort was expended on this area. Modules are not free-standing components, there are numerous references between modules. For the purposes of design checking and impact analysis, these dependences need to be modelled in the database.

One of the problems with representing dependences between versions of modules is that of version propagation. Consider the situation shown in Figure 9.12, where a version of module A depends on some version of module B. As module B is revised, module A also needs to be revised so that the new dependence can be represented. This version propagation needs to be applied to all (direct and indirect) dependents of B. Such propagation could be prohibitive in terms of database space.

An idea from early work on the Foundation project was the notion of *participation*. The essence of this idea is that dependences are always from a version to an item, i.e. from a specific version of a dependent module to a collection of versions of the dependent module. The advantage of this scheme is that the dependent module can be revised without having to revise dependent modules. The scheme is depicted in Figure 9.13.

Adopting the idea of participation for MASCOT modules is straightforward. The specification part item, which all modules have, is the one that participates in designs.

A more interesting design choice is the extent to which information of the dependent item is used in the dependent version. For example, consider the case where a subsystem S depends on another subsystem T. The problem is what information, if any, is duplicated between the component C and its template T. The case where there is no duplication of information, we termed *reference participation*. The case where there is complete duplication of information, we termed *copy participation*. Participation by reference has the advantage that the component and its template are always consistent. Participation by copy has the advantage that the appearance of the com-

9.7. THE TOOLSET

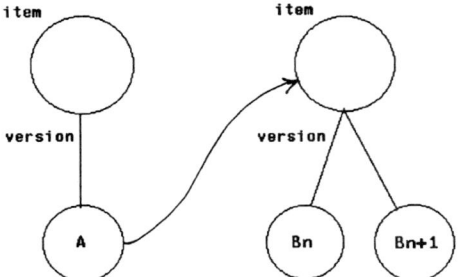

Figure 9.13: Version-to-Item Dependencies

ponent, i.e. its drawing information, could be different to that of the template. The disadvantage is that the two need to be checked for consistency.

Our initial design was a compromise approach, to try and get the best of both worlds. We opted for participation by reference of design information, but participation by copy of drawing information. The objective being to get permanent consistency between components and their templates, but still to have the flexibility of the component having a different layout to its template.

Unfortunately this scheme had a number of problems.

- From a design editing point of view, the subsystem diagram consists of an arbitrary number of fine structure objects — one for the subsystem and one for each of the templates referenced. It was not clear whether the Eclipse design editor would cope with more than one fine structure object.

- Anonymous components would need to be treated specially to fit into the scheme.

- If the number or type of junctions on the template were altered, the drawing information for all of the components based on that template would need to be brought into line with the new set of junctions. Such reconciliation would be far from straightforward.

- Whilst it seemed a reasonable goal to maintain consistency between components and their templates, it did seem a little bizarre to allow editing of templates by editing a component (cf. editing a type by editing an instance of it). The scheme would be more suited to dataflow diagrams where the decomposition is in terms of modules that are actual components, instead of templates for components.

After much deliberation the final design adopted was for participation by copy of both design and drawing information. The additional consistency checking required in design checking was accepted as an inevitable but simpler overhead.

9.7 THE TOOLSET

This section gives a description of the tool set architecture and the functionality of the individual tools.

9.7.1 Architecture

We had no real experience or understanding as to what the architecture of a tool set in the context of an IPSE should be. Neither was there any general Eclipse guidance in this area. In a sense this was one of the overall objectives of the Eclipse programme to research and establish an architectural model. Starting from first principles, three possibilities were considered: the tool set, the 'supertool', and a hybrid approach.

The tool set was perhaps the most conventional, in as much as there were any conventions to follow. There would be a master tool invoked from Eclipse. From that the various tools of the tool set could be invoked. Each of the separate tools would offer some logical grouping of functions. Overlapping of functionality between the tools would be avoided. Such an approach would enable further (Eclipse or foreign) tools to be easily added to the tool set. Thus the tools would be loosely integrated through the data they operated on.

The 'supertool' was the other extreme. There would be a single tool from within which all functions could be invoked, the window layout would change as appropriate from function to function. One supertool could spawn another for multi-window working. This approach had the advantage that a single tool could be 'reused' between functions, e.g. a module could be selected, edited, checked, have its status progressed, and the generated Ada viewed all within the same tool. Also a much tighter integration between the functions of the tool could be achieved. However, this approach was rejected on the grounds of the resultant process size of the tool being too large, since the code for all functions would need to be bound into the single tool. Another disadvantage with such a tightly integrated tool would be the difficulty in incorporating new functionality or adding foreign tools. This would require intimate modification of the tool. (It would perhaps have been a useful exercise to re-evaluate this approach in the light of our experience with Eclipse. The technique for calling sub-tools synchronously as separate processes was developed much later. This technique could have made the 'supertool' approach feasible.)

A possible compromise or 'hybrid' approach was considered. This entailed retaining the separate tools, but enabling all tools to be invoked from each other. Thus the master tool could be dispensed with. Whilst this approach had possible advantages, e.g. one less tool, it was rejected on the grounds of increased screen clutter, and because the invoked (sub-)tool would be dependent on the invoking tool for its existence. (Again, it now appears that such an approach could have been made to work. The tool menu would not actually have taken up much screen space, and the Eclipse server starter software would have enabled the invoked sub-tool to have an existence independent of the invoking tool.)

9.7.2 User Interface

One of the striking features of Eclipse tools is the consistency of their user interface. The MASCOT 3 tools themselves have a similar format for their presentation. This is achieved using common FDL for their layout.

The principles of interaction which we have adopted within the tools are as follows:

- only make allowable functions available to the user, i.e. menus, menu entries, and buttons are dynamically tailored and switched on and off to be appropriate

9.7. THE TOOLSET

to the current context or selection.

- apply immediate checking wherever possible, e.g. module names are checked as valid on input rather than as part of design checking.

- request confirmation for all potentially long actions or where significant loss of information might result.

- offer checking or analysis without committing updates, e.g. module status checks and impact analysis reports.

- reports produced and viewed asynchronously in separate window.

The MASCOT 3 tool set has an extensive network of help messages. This was possible, at relatively little cost, using the Eclipse help facilities. There are links to other general Eclipse and Ada help information. We also used the facility of associating help information with certain error messages. This enabled us to keep error messages succinct, but leave the user with the option of obtaining further explanatory text.

9.7.3 Graphical Editing

An area where we had strong views was on the style of interaction for graphical editing. These views were very much influenced by the first version of the CDL design editor (see chapter 12). The CDL editor had a number of features which we liked and wanted to copy in the MASCOT 3 graphical editor. (This is not surprising since the first version of CDL and MASCOT 3 are graphically very similar.) In particular we liked the 'active' grid and its use in placement of symbols, text, and paths. We liked the automatic placement of junctions down the vertical edges of template symbols. Another feature applicable to MASCOT 3 was the automatic filling-in of interface labels upon path creation. The CDL editor thus assisted the user in constructing neat diagrams, i.e. giving the impression of having been drawn by a competent draughtsman, and also reducing the possibilities for constructing incorrect designs.

However, these desires had to be foregone. We had to make the choice between using the Eclipse design editor, or writing our own MASCOT 3 graphical editor. The resources available to the project were such that the latter possibility was a non-starter. It was a feature, and indeed an underlying design aim, that the Eclipse design editor should not be prescriptive. Features such as automatic placement, implicit design updates, etc., were considered by the design editor team to be undesirable, the rationale being that the user should be able to sketch designs in a free-hand and unconstrained manner. Although we felt that much better functionality could have been achieved for MASCOT 3, we accepted the approach offered by the 'generic' editor.

9.7.4 Locking

An important aspect of the tool set was the design of the database locking scheme. It was a requirement that the tool set would be usable by large development teams. Moreover, to achieve maximum potential for reusability of modules, the teams would be developing within the same MASCOT database. Therefore a scheme was required which would not unnecessarily limit tool concurrency but would still ensure the integrity of the tool set managed data.

The facilities provided by PCTE are:

- activities which act as a scope within a process (can be unprotected, protected, or transaction activities),

- implicit locking, where, given the type of the local activity, each read or write operation automatically acquires an appropriate lock,

- explicit locking, where the tool locks all PCTE objects explicitly.

PCTE transaction activities initially appeared to offer the ideal solution. The ability to abort a transaction activity gave us the possibility of rollback. Multiple writers were automatically banned. The problem was that a transaction activity implicitly read-locks all objects read during the activity. So, if a tool reads an object within a transaction, any other tool attempting to write to that object would be locked out.

This was not acceptable and so we decided that tools would use unprotected activities, as a means of block-structuring the tool and ensuring the ultimate release of acquired resources. Within these unprotected activities, all objects to which write access was required would be explicitly write-locked by the tool. This would prohibit multiple writers, but allow uncontrolled read access by other tools. Transaction activities would only be used around single user operations, e.g. unregister module.

9.7.5 The Tools

Having made the decision to adopt a tool set approach, we then considered the division of functionality between tools. Some functions were straightforward. There would clearly be a graphical editing tool, and a textual editing tool for non-graphical parts of modules. The database search functions were naturally the domain of a separate tool, likewise the DRL generation facility. There would be a separate tool involved with the status progression, Ada generation and compilation.

The functions for version and configuration control could possibly have been combined with the status functions in a single tool; they have much in common as regards impact analysis and report generation. However, the two sets of functions are orthogonal, i.e. they can be applied to modules quite independently. Also one could envisage an initial MASCOT 3 tool set in which there was no support for versions. Therefore the version and configuration control functions were also packaged as a separate tool.

So, in summary, the tool set comprises:

- Master Window

- Graphical Editor

- Textual Editor

- Status Control

- Version/Configuration Control

- Database Search

9.7. THE TOOLSET

- DRL Generation

These are described in the following sections. Screen layouts of the user interface to the tools are given in Figures 9.14 and 9.15.

9.7.6 Master Window Tool

The Master Window tool provides the entry point to the MASCOT tool set. It is invoked from the Eclipse Master Window from the tool set menu. The invocation establishes an operational environment for the tool set, i.e. the current MASCOT database, the current configuration, and the default Ada compiler. All of the tools operate within this environment. A user could conceivably invoke multiple Master Window tools with different environments.

The Master Window provides two main functions: module selection and tool invocation. The selection of a module is achieved by entering the name of a module into a sign, or choosing from a pick-list containing the set of existing modules within the MASCOT database. In keeping with the philosophy of doing immediate checks wherever possible, the name is checked on input. If the name is valid and the module does not exist, the user may register the module in the MASCOT Database.

There are two menus for invoking tools. One provides for a display tool, appropriate to the current module, to be invoked. The menu is not available unless there is a current module. The other menu, which is always available, provides for the non-display tools to be invoked.

Tool invocation is also required by other tools in the tool set, e.g. the editing tools can invoke other editing tools, and reports are always presented by invoking an asynchronous viewing tool. The Master Window tool also acts as a tool invocation agent on their behalf. This is achieved by using the PCTE message passing facilities.

9.7.7 Display Tool

The Eclipse design editor requires that a fine structure object representing the diagram exists when the tool is invoked. Also, when the first version of a module part is created, it is possible to derive an initial skeleton for the module part. For example:

- the graphical part of a template module can always be given an outline with a correct symbol and with the correct template name label. In addition the template can sometimes be embellished with information from the corresponding specification or implementation part, or from a component created prior to its actual template (i.e. top-down design).

- an activity implementation part can consist of a skeleton Ada ROOT procedure body.

- an IDA-like implementation part can consist of a skeleton Ada package bodies with null subprogram bodies corresponding to each window provided by the template.

Since the editing tools can be invoked from the Master Window or from within each other, it was decided to common-up this functionality into a single tool referred

Eclipse Standard System Facilities
Help
Exit
Version
"ECLIPSE ver
Username
ecldemo
Software Sciences
CAP
Aberystwyth
Lancaster
Strathclyde
Time
11.57
Date
16 Feb 88
System Facilities
Eclipse Mascot 3
Master Window
Module Name
demo system2
Module Class
System
Module Status
Partly Enrolled
Compiler
Intel 80286
Mascot Tools
Display Options
Eclipse Mascot 3
Status Control Tool
Promote Operations
Demote Operations
Mascot 3 Configuration
Control Tool
Module Part
IMPL
Version
1
Config Status
unpublished
Issue
Publish
Acquire
Delete
Eclipse Mascot 3
DRL Viewing Tool
demo_system2
View DRL
Eclipse Mascot 3
Database Search Tool
Name Pattern
*
Module Group
Template
Introduced
Config Status
Any Status
Search Type
List Modules
List Level
Brief
Versions
Latest
Search
design editor
Eclipse Master Window
console
Eclipse

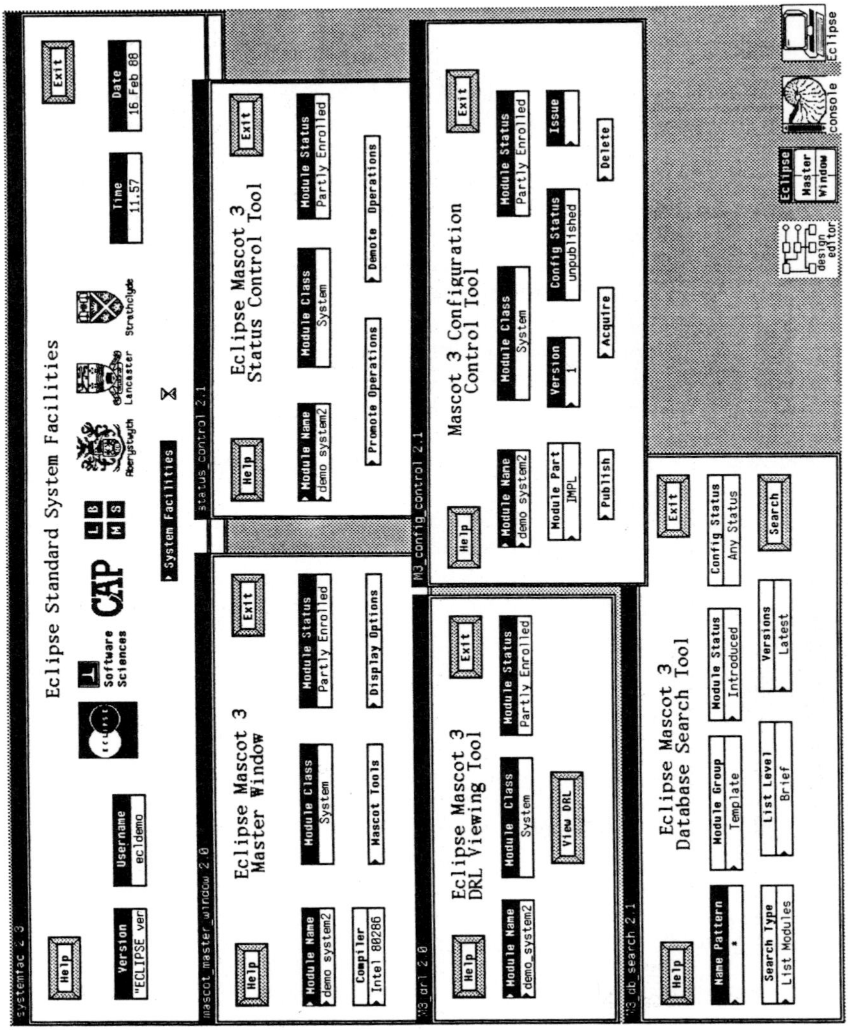

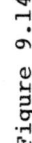

Figure 9.14

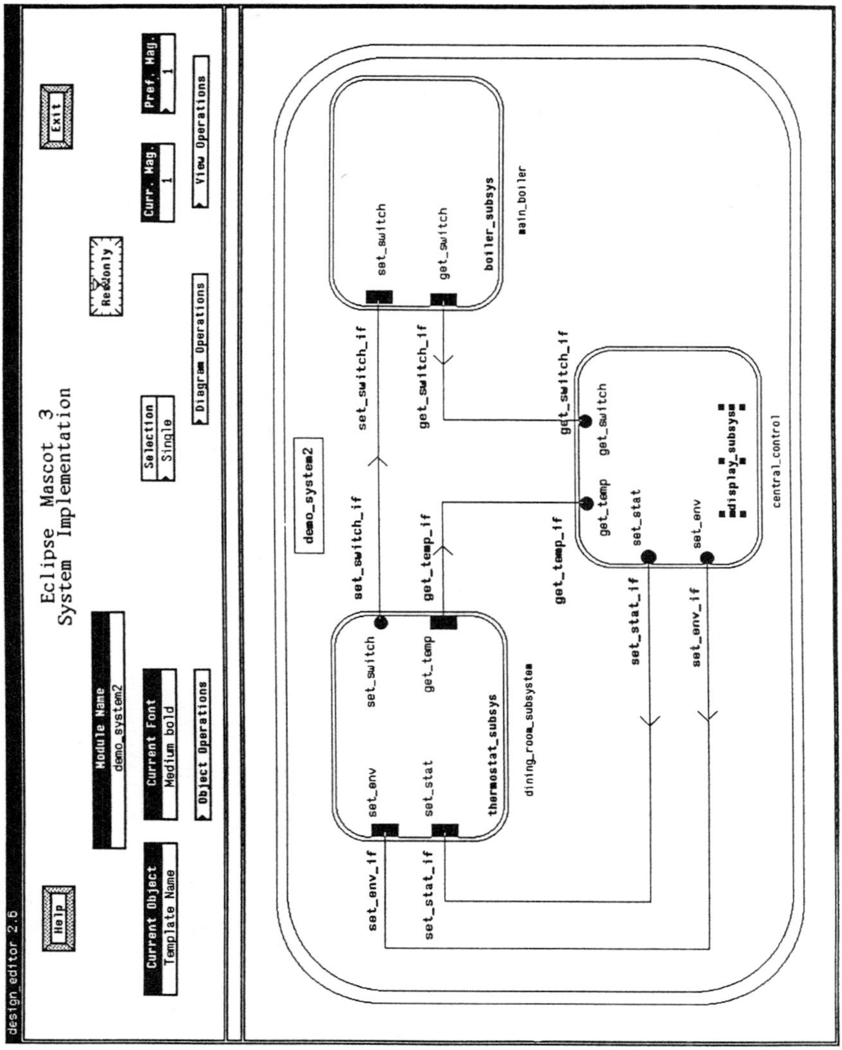
design_editor 2.6
Help
Current Object
Template Name
Module Name
demo_system2
Current Font
Medium bold
Object Operations
Eclipse Mascot 3
System Implementation
Selection
Single
Diagram Operations
Curr. Mag.
1
View Operations
Exit
Pref. Mag.
1
demo_system2
set_env_if
set_stat_if
set_env
set_stat
thermostat_subsys
set_switch
get_temp
dining_room_subsystem
set_switch_if
get_temp_if
set_switch_if
get_switch_if
get_temp_if
get_switch_if
set_stat_if
set_env_if
get_temp
set_stat
set_env
get_switch
display_subsys
central_control
set_switch
get_switch
boiler_subsys
main_boiler

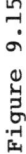

Figure 9.15

to as the Display Tool. This (sub-)tool is called synchronously and does not interact with the user, i.e. it is windowless. It creates the first version of the module part, if necessary, determines whether the editor is to be called in edit or view mode, and starts the editing tool appropriate to the module part.

9.7.8 Graphical Editor

This is actually a family of tools, all instantiations of the generic Eclipse design editor. These correspond to the various kinds of MASCOT 3 diagram. As well as the familiar system and subsystem implementation diagrams, we have chosen to treat each of the template specifications as a different diagram type. Although this results in nine different diagram types, it gives stronger typing of the GDL specifications and thus less scope for user error, e.g. an activity template specification can only be one of the valid activity symbols, and can only have ports, etc.

We were also mindful of the amount of screen space occupied by the design editor window. The default window size occupies nearly all of the screen. Whilst this may be suitable for system and subsystem diagrams, the template specification diagrams are usually quite small. A very useful feature of FDL is that it is possible to redesign the screen layout independently of the tool. Thus we, the MASCOT project, were able to define a half-screen variant of the design editor for the template specification diagrams.

A standard feature of the Eclipse design editor is the ability to invoke the editor in 'view' mode. We used this facility to ensure that the MASCOT module status rules are observed. Thus the specification part of an Introduced module, and the implementation of an Enrolled template, can only be displayed in view mode.

Another feature of the Eclipse design editor is the 'open' facility. This enables navigation from one instance of the design editor to another. We have used the facility to allow navigation:

- from the implementation part of a module to its specification part,
- from the specification part of a module to its implementation part,
- to the specification or implementation part of a selected module.

Such navigation includes the ability to invoke the appropriate textual editing tool.

The MASCOT-specific code involved in this operation enables initial template generation to be performed where the destination object does not exist. Thus, when doing top-down design, opening a subsystem component to its template specification causes a specification part for the template to be created that is consistent with the component.

As well as top-down design, we have utilised a design editor facility to promote bottom-up design. The 'paste' facility enables a diagram to updated with a set of nodes and links. In MASCOT 3 terms we have used this facility to allow creation of a component within a subsystem that is an instance of an existing template. The template specification details, including all junction and textual labels, are copied into the diagram as an anonymous component.

The Eclipse design editor has a 'check design' capability. This enables method-specific code to perform checks on the (design represented by the) current diagram.

design_editor 2.6
Help
Eclipse Mascot 3
Activity Specification
Exit
Module Name
room_temp_act
Readonly
Curr Object
None
Curr Symbol
None
Selection
Single
Curr Mag
1
Pref Mag
1
Diag Ops
View Ops
get_temp_if
get_temp
room_temp_act
screen_put
screen_put_if
M3_text_display 2.1
Help
Mascot 3 Text Tool
Exit
Module Name
room_temp_act
Module Class
Activity
Module Status
Fully Enrolled
View
Open
Definitions
Packages
with [demo_defaults
with [
with [
with [
with [
with [
Annotation [
procedure root is
next_time : time;
temp : temperature;
begin
-- update the screen at fixed intervals with the current
-- temperature
next_time := clock;
loop
-- determine next clock point
next_time := next_time + stat_interval;
-- get temperature setting now
get_temp.get (temp);
-- now suspend until end of interval
delay next_time - clock;
-- update the temperature on the screen
screen_put.put (long_integer (temp), 56, 10,
restore_cursor => true,
highlight => true);
end loop;
exception
when constraint_error =>
put_line ("Constraint Error in room_temp.root");
when numeric_error =>
put_line ("Numeric Error in room_temp.root");
when program_error =>
put_line ("Program Error in room_temp.root");
editor
console
Eclipse

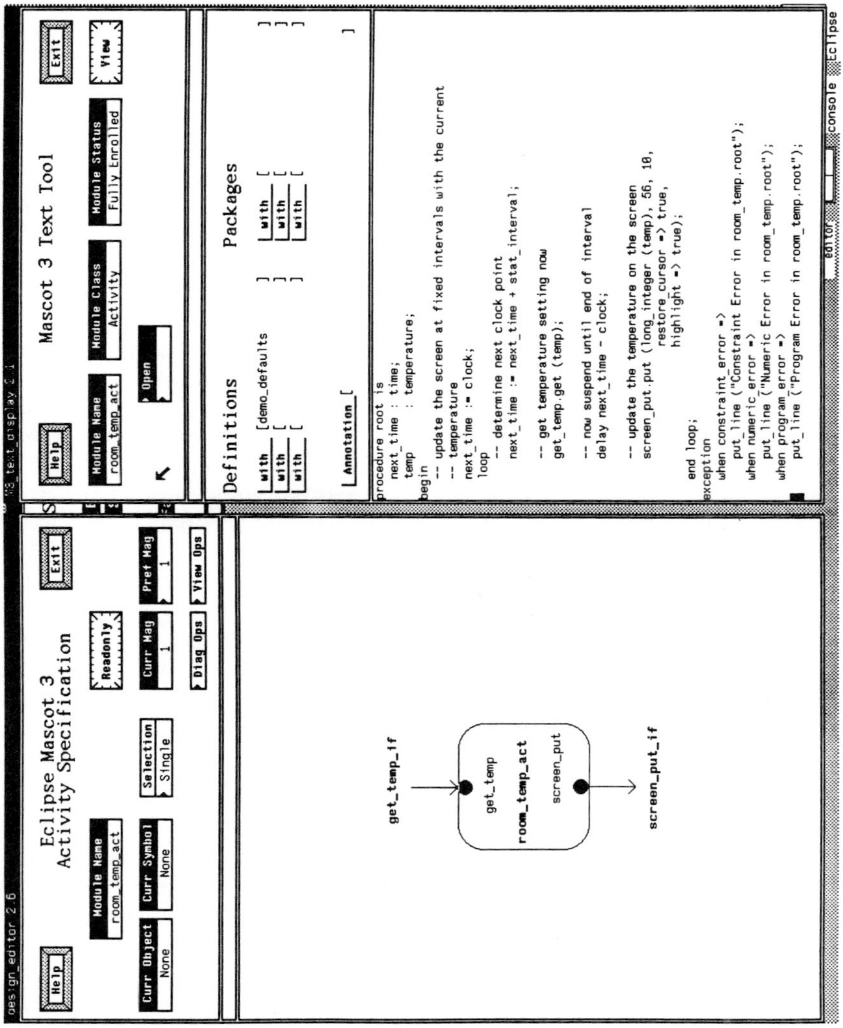

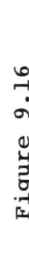

Figure 9.16

Although the MASCOT 3 tool set has a separate design checking tool, it was still felt to be useful to have a local checking capability in the editor. The user can treat such a facility as a confidence check. Also the first version of the design editor did not have an assertion checking capability, thus the 'check design' function could provide such checks, albeit in a delayed manner.

9.7.9 Textual Editor

Since Eclipse had no generic textual editing tools, the MASCOT 3 textual editor was purpose built. As described in section 9.4.3 it was a specific design decision to manipulate the textual part of modules as a structured object, without having to have a 'compile' phase.

The structure of the textual module parts is quite simple. All of the module parts have a 'with list' specifying dependencies between modules. The 'with list', like an Ada context clause, specifies a list of dependent modules. We chose to represent this structure as a pageable collection of single-line scalars using the Eclipse user interface. The update action on each scalar would be to check that the string conformed to the syntax of an Ada identifier, that it was not a reserved word, and that the string referenced an existing definition module. If the module did not exist the tool would offer the user option of registering it as a new definition module.

The more interesting structured part is that for access interface modules. They consist of a collection of access procedures, i.e. Ada subprogram specifications. Each procedure is split into its name, parameters, and return type (for a function). The strategy for representing this structure is to have a pageable set of triples. Each triple consists of a single line scalar for the procedure name, a multiple line scalar for the parameter list, and a single line scalar for the return type. An example editing frame for an access interface module is shown in Figure 9.16. Whilst this has avoided the need to 'compile' the text, the presentation as an Eclipse control frame leaves a lot to be desired.

A property of the Ada mapping chosen (section 9.5) was that no transformation of user-written Ada was necessary. Therefore, the Ada text for definitions and simple templates could be manipulated as free-text until the actual compilation stage in the status control tool.

Thus there are two variants of the textual editing tool. For an access interface module there is a structured 'with list' frame and a structured access procedure frame. For a definition module or a simple template there is a structured 'with list' frame and a free-text frame. In the absence of an Eclipse text editor we have built the MASCOT textual editor to allow vi to be used in the free-text frame.

Certain additional facilities have been incorporated into the tool to be compatible with the graphical editor. The tool supports invocation in edit or view mode. In view mode the user interface items of the structured frames are made read-only, and the vi editor is invoked with the read-only flag. An 'open' facility is provided allowing an editing tool to be invoked on a selected module.

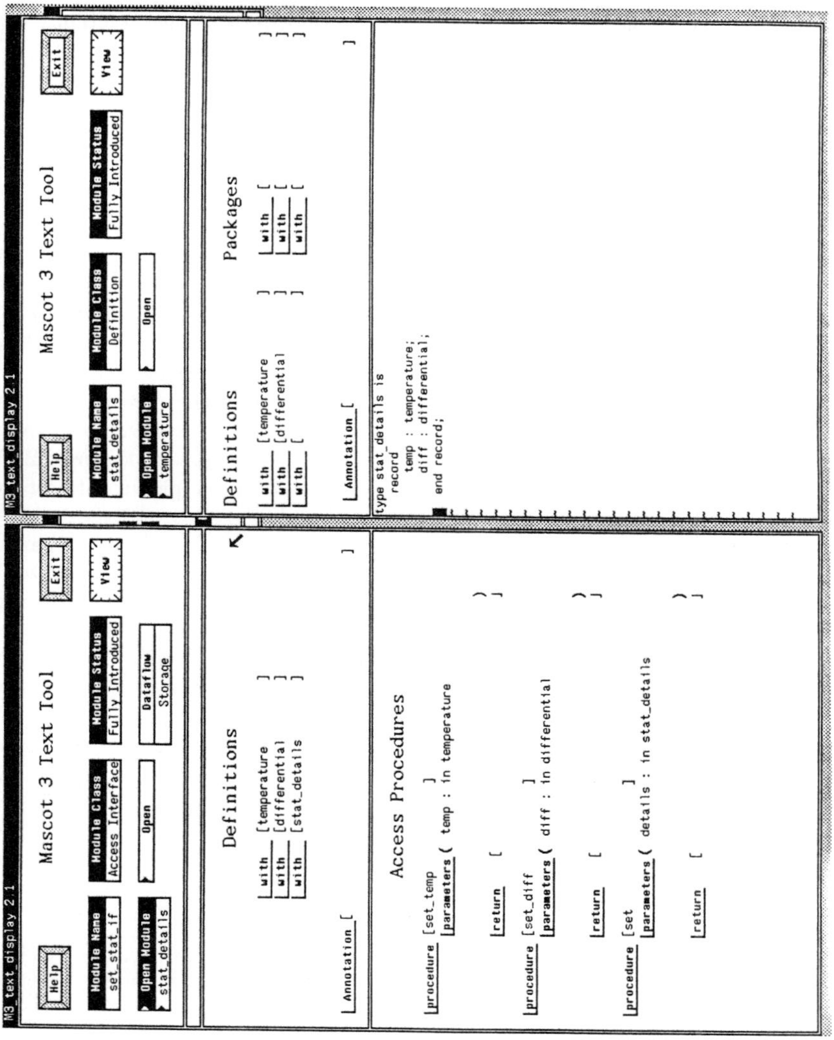
M3_text_display 2:1
Help
Mascot 3 Text Tool
Exit
Module Name
set_stat_if
Module Class
Access Interface
Module Status
Fully Introduced
View
Open Module
stat_details
Open
Dataflow
Storage
Definitions
with [temperature]
with [differential]
with [stat_details]
Annotation [ ]
Access Procedures
procedure [set_temp]
parameters (temp : in temperature)
return [ ]
procedure [set_diff]
parameters (diff : in differential)
return [ ]
procedure [set]
parameters (details : in stat_details)
return [ ]
M3_text_display 2:1
Help
Mascot 3 Text Tool
Exit
Module Name
stat_details
Module Class
Definition
Module Status
Fully Introduced
View
Open Module
temperature
Open
Definitions
with [temperature]
with [differential]
with [ ]
Packages
with [
with [
with [
Annotation [ ]
type stat_details is
record
temp : temperature;
diff : differential;
end record;

Figure 9.17

9.7.10 Status Control Tool

The status control tool is functionally the most complex. At the user interface level the tool appears quite simple. There are two menus providing status promotion functions and status demotion functions. The status promotion menu offers the functions:

- Register

- Introduce Checks

- Introduce

- Enrol Checks

- Enrol

As well as offering the standard functions for status promotion, there are also functions to perform checks on the module without actually promoting its status. Only those functions that are appropriate to the current module's status are made available.

Registration of a module establishes a new module within the current database with a given name and class. Checks are made that the module does not already exist. In data terms a new configuration item for the specification part of the module is created, and for a template module, a configuration item for its implementation part. Note that no versions of its module parts are created.

Introduction of a module is concerned with the checking of the specification part of the module. There are a number of necessary pre-conditions, defined in the Handbook, that need to be checked. In addition the tool also issues warnings of unusual design features, e.g. unexpected sources and sinks of data. The Ada package specification corresponding to the module specification part is generated. As a final check of the specification part, the Ada package specification is compiled. Following successful introduction the specification part of the module is 'frozen', i.e. made read-only.

Enrolment is similar to Introduction except that it is the implementation part of the template module that is checked, and an Ada package body that is generated and compiled. Following successful enrolment the implementation part of the module is 'frozen', i.e. made read-only.

The status demotion menu offers the functions:

- Unregister

- Revise Specification Impact

- Revise Specification

- Revise Implementation Impact

- Revise Implementation

As well as offering the standard functions for status demotion, there are also functions to perform impact analysis on the MASCOT Database without actually demoting the module status. Only those functions that are appropriate to the current module's status are made available.

9.7. THE TOOLSET

The Unregister module removes a module from the current database. The function requires that all module part versions in all configurations have been deleted.

The Revise Specification function can be applied to a module that has an Introduced status. It causes the specification part of the module to be 'unfrozen', i.e. allowing further updates. The module and all its dependents have their status demoted appropriately.

The Revise Implementation function is similar except that it is applied to a module that has an Enrolled status. It causes the implementation part of the module to be 'unfrozen', i.e. allowing further updates. The module and all its dependents have their status demoted appropriately.

9.7.11 Version/Configuration Control Tool

In its initial version this tool provides a rudimentary configuration control capability for MASCOT 3 modules. The tool provides 'atomic' operations on module parts, i.e. on the versions of single MASCOT configuration items. A module part can be Published, Acquired, Released, or Withdrawn. These operations use the corresponding Eclipse functions (see chapter 5).

The operations are sufficient to control configurations of a MASCOT Database. However, for realistic use, the functions would need to be enriched to operate transitively on collections of module parts, e.g. publish the complete set of module parts comprising a subsystem.

For acquisition and release there are impact analysis functions to enable the resulting impact on the configuration to be determined. The reports are produced in the same manner as the status control tool.

The other function which this tool provides is that for deleting versions of modules. Either the latest version can be deleted, with or without impact analysis, or unused old versions can be purged (their deletion can have no impact).

9.7.12 Database Search Tool

One of the limitations of the Eclipse development was the absence of a general database query facility. (This would have been available in an SDS-2 implementation but was lost by the move to PCTE.) We considered it essential for the user to have some means of listing or querying the MASCOT Database. The other reason for producing this tool was that it would provide a vehicle for demonstrating the Eclipse database pattern matching facilities.

The tool enables a report to be produced listing the modules in the current MASCOT Database which satisfy certain user-selected criteria. The criteria which may be specified are:

name a name pattern to be matched — default is '*', i.e. all names;

class the class of the module, including abstract classes such as specification, template, etc. — default is any class;

status the status of the module — default is any status;

configuration status whether unpublished, published, or acquired — default is any status.

In addition to these criteria there are various listing levels controlling the amount of information in the report. There are brief and full listing levels: brief gives only the module name and its class; full gives name, class, status, version information, creation date, etc. For a full listing either all versions can be selected or only the latest version.

In implementation terms the tool is reasonably straightforward. The set of keys from the MASCOT Database object are traversed filtering out the required modules according to the criteria above. Unfortunately not all of the criteria are based on simple database attributes. This means setting up a database iterator with those criteria that can be specified as patterns, and the remaining criteria are filtered out by the tool. Having established modules of interest the various attributes are examined to produce a report.

The tool also has the capability to produce reports based on module dependency searches. These are intended to augment the impact analysis functions of the status and configuration control tools. The tool can, given a selected module, produce a report of dependent modules, i.e. modules depending on the current module, or of dependent modules, i.e. modules depended upon by the current module. The implementation of these functions is not so straightforward. It requires the tool to traverse the hierarchy of module dependency relationships. There are no Eclipse database functions to perform this iteration.

9.7.13 DRL Tool

This simple tool provides for output of text corresponding to the design information for a fully checked module. The text conforms to the syntax for the textual Design Representation Language as defined in the MASCOT Handbook. The generated text is displayed as a report in the frame of a separate tool. This flat text representation is not stored in the MASCOT Database.

We recognise that a useful enhancement to this tool would be to support an input function. This would then provide for export and import of MASCOT 3 modules.

Currently the text representation does not specify positional information for the graphical design elements. A useful extension to the textual design language would be to define a standard for including such information. For example, graphical information could be incorporated as formal comments in the text.

9.8 CONCLUSION

The MASCOT project did eventually, after previous unsuccessful attempts, implement a tool set in support of MASCOT 3 and Ada. The culmination of the work was a successful demonstration of the tools at the Alvey Conference in July 1987. The demonstrations were received with considerable technical and commercial interest. In fact interest was such that, following completion of the Alvey Eclipse Programme, Software Sciences have continued to develop and market the tool set as a product.

With hindsight, the false starts on the project were inevitable. These were not entirely wasted effort; the prototype reports and a number of working papers were

9.8. CONCLUSION

of subsequent use. The lesson is clearly that tool builders need stable specifications of underlying software components before design and development can realistically commence.

The MASCOT graphical editing capability is probably the most visually impressive feature of the tool set. The editor has an impressive set of editing functions. This is one of the advantages of a generic tool — enrichment of the generic functionality is bestowed on all instantiations of the tool. An important feature of the graphical editor is that the design information is manipulated directly, hence the term *MASCOT design editor*. A disadvantage of the generic approach is that the editor is not particularly sensitive to MASCOT 3. An area of future work would be to enable parameterisation of the editor with more method-specific functionality.

The integration of the graphical and text editing tools has been achieved reasonably well. A disappointing area of functionality has been that of editing structured text. Our decision to use the Eclipse User Interface in a forms-like manner was not particularly successful. For the future, we would identify the requirement for a generic text, particularly structured text, editing capability.

One of the most powerful features of the Eclipse environment, from a tool builder's point of view, is the two-tier database. The ease with which the MASCOT Database structure has been modelled is a consequence of the first-tier PCTE OMS facilities. The ability to represent fine-grain data (e.g. diagrams, access procedures, etc.) within files achieves both integrity of data and efficiency of access. From a user point of view the visibility of data enables additional tools to be written more easily.

A striking feature of the MASCOT 3 tools, and indeed of all Eclipse tools, is the consistency of their user interface. The interface is consistent both in terms of appearance and interaction style. The ability to modify the interface without modification to the tool has been used to great advantage by the MASCOT project. We would similarly expect an end-user to adjust the interface to suit their own preferences.

The implementation of the tool set represented a significant software development effort. The tool set comprises over 50 components amounting to some 40,000 lines of C code.

The tool set is more than a prototype. We see no reason why it could not be used effectively by projects of all sizes. The Ada generation and incremental compilation capabilities are tasks that would be laborious and error-prone by hand. The ability to manipulate the MASCOT diagrams directly is a distinct improvement over manipulating the textual form of diagrams.

The tool set is open in that it does not dictate any particular development strategy. Rather, the data structures and functions enable a variety of development scenarios to be set up.

By any measure the MASCOT Project exceeded the original objectives outlined in the Alvey proposal. A comprehensive tool set in support of MASCOT 3 was produced, including tools additional to those identified in the proposal. On reflection we perhaps lost sight of the original objectives, and aimed at a level of functionality which would exploit and demonstrate more of the underlying Eclipse software. The fact that we were successful is an indication of the capabilities within Eclipse.

Chapter 10

The LSDM Tool Set

John Estdale

10.1 BACKGROUND

LBMS (Learmonth & Burchett Management Systems Plc) were invited to collaborate in the Eclipse project to produce method support tools for the early phases of the software life cycle. LBMS maintains and supports LSDM, the LBMS Structured Development Method for systems analysis and design, which is widely used in the UK and is growing in popularity worldwide. The UK government method SSADM (Structured Systems Analysis and Design Method) [77] is closely related to LSDM, having been developed originally by LBMS and the CCTA.

LSDM is used mainly in commercial data processing, particularly for transaction processing, so LSDM users are more likely to be familiar with large IBM mainframes running CICS and COBOL than with Sun work stations, PCTE and C.

10.2 WHAT IS LSDM?

LSDM is a top-down step-by-step approach which defines three separate views of any information system: in terms of information flow, the underlying data structure and the sequencing of events. Analysts are encouraged to develop these system views independently and then relate them together, identifying additional requirements and inconsistencies for further analysis. The products are combined and refined further to derive the eventual system design. The various stages are shown in Figure 10.1.

In the pencil and paper version of LSDM, each system view consists of one or more *diagrams* and a number of accompanying *forms* on which further details about design objects can be recorded.

Data Flow Diagrams (DFDs) provide a snapshot of an information system, showing all the possible flows of data within the system and across the system boundary. Thus they show the sources of data, the processes which operate on it, the data stores which hold it between processing operations and the recipients of the results. Hierarchical

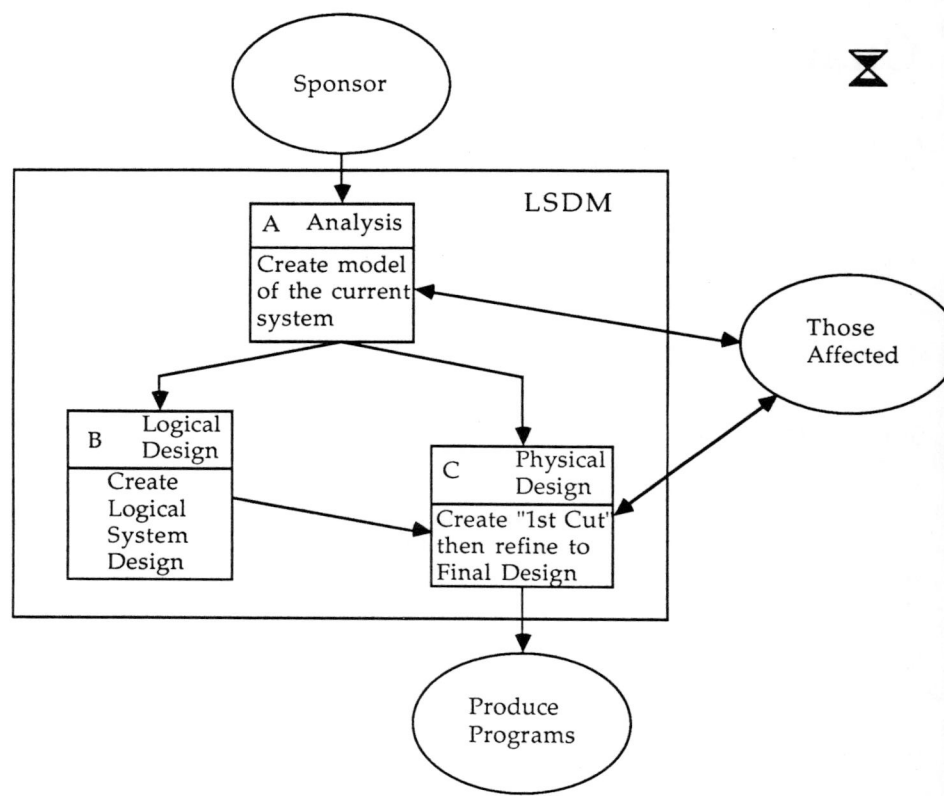

Figure 10.1: Stages of LSDM

10.2. WHAT IS LSDM?

decomposition is accommodated by allowing each process to be broken down in a further Data Flow Diagram.

Data Flow Diagrams are used to depict existing systems and new proposals. They can be used for computerised systems, clerical systems and those which are a combination of the two.

A Logical Data Structure diagram (LDS) shows the underlying structure of the data in an information system using the *entity-relationship* model. An *entity* or more accurately an entity type, is a type of real-world object about which information is to be held, e.g. customer, order etc. A *relationship* shows how one such entity is related to another, i.e. that an occurrences of some other entity (the *detail* Normally the existence of a detail is dependent on the continued existence of its master: the detail is then said to be *owned* by that master. Some occurrences of the detail may not relate to an occurrence of its master, i.e. the master is *optional*. Thus one customer may own many orders, but need not be assigned to a salesman. This also allows a detail to be created before its master, if that is needed.

Some entities may be details of more than one master. A relationship to one master may preclude relationships to others: *exclusive* relationships. Conversely one master may have relationships to many details and again the relationships to one detail may exclude others.

Entry points into the data structure can also be shown. This may involve the addition of an *operational master* to provide another, keyed access path to a detail. The traditional example is 'date', normally a pure key, with no associate data.

The Logical Data Structure is inherent in the entities chosen, regardless of the system(s) processing them, so tends to be reasonably stable over time. The question of how formalisable the external world really is, is left for students of metaphysics to debate [56].

A Logical Data Structure diagram is produced during analysis and is ultimately used to generate the schemas for the target Data Base Management System.

Finally the Entity Life History diagram (ELH) shows all the various sequences of events that may have an effect on any occurrence of the entity type concerned, from its first appearance in the system to its eventual removal, e.g. a line of stock is introduced, orders are fulfilled, stocks replenished and so on, until eventually the item is discontinued. Each such event would generally be recorded on a computer by some kind of update transaction.

Events and *clusters* i.e. groupings of events may be sequential, optional, repeatable, alternative and so on. There is provision for events or clusters which could occur at any time, interrupting the normal event sequence permanently or temporarily. A permanent interruption is the equivalent of an exception in Ada. Temporary interruptions may start a sequence of their own, i.e. a 'parallel life'. More complex sequencing rules can be specified via state indicators which list those states that could have preceded any given event.

Entity Life Histories are mainly used in the design stages, but can also be used during analysis to capture sequence information.

A variety of other techniques are practised downstream of these, including Relational Data Analysis, Composite Logical Data Design, On-Line Dialog and First-Cut Physical Data Design. These are not discussed here as they are not supported by the Eclipse LSDM Tool Set.

10.3 EARLY STAGES

When Eclipse started, LSDM was still a pencil and paper method, so it was not clear what software support might involve. Being dependent on the development of the Eclipse environment, the first two years were spent collaborating with the projects responsible for the components needed, i.e. bottom-up design. This was not ideal as the amount of work was not enough to maintain continuity of thought or personnel.

Meanwhile LBMS decided that LSDM CASE (Computer Assisted Software Engineering) tools were urgently needed, and therefore built, two products for the IBM/PC called AUTO-MATE and DATA-MATE, covering systems analysis and data analysis respectively.

With Version 2 of Eclipse, the research to find some means of linking LSDM and MASCOT was dropped. LBMS has since undertaken an initial study into using SSADM with MASCOT for RSRE and the CCTA. However, the opportunity to achieve data integration between the tool sets was lost, leaving the LSDM tool set isolated. Nevertheless, as sales of the early releases of AUTO-MATE proved, stand-alone support for the method is still well worth having and support for automatic system generation can be added at some future date.

10.4 FACILITIES

Early in 1987 work began on the Eclipse LSDM Tool Set. LSDM had been revised and extended several times. AUTO-MATE and DATA-MATE had grown into a large, all-embracing product called AUTO-MATE PLUS. It was decided to develop a range of tools to support the major elements of the systems analysis stage of LSDM, on the grounds that the resulting tool set would be a good demonstration of Eclipse, that it would be useful in its own right and that it would form a good base for further development. The aim was to make maximum use of the Eclipse environment, both the kernel and the tool builder's kit, whilst conforming to the Eclipse house style and not worrying unduly about LSDM features that were hard to support. The result is that an experienced Eclipse user should find it easy to operate the LSDM tool set, but an AUTO-MATE user would have to learn the Eclipse *modus operandi* first.

The tool set enables users to develop diagrams of the three views and to record associated information. Automated support provides the means to draw the diagrams quickly and easily. They can then be viewed, edited or tidied, output and stored for future reference and revision. Other system details are captured via computerised forms, which can be retrieved, viewed, amended, printed and so on. Some examples are shown in Figures 10.2 and 10.3. These notional documents may be inter-related and then 'navigated' to give more sophisticated access to the information held.

Thus the purpose of the Eclipse LSDM Tool Set is to reduce the analyst's workload by managing the data collected and providing easy access for recording, correcting, refining, and printing it.

design_editor 2.1
DFD Design Editor
Help
Exit
Name
EXAMPLE.DFDs
Curr Object
None
Curr Symbol
None
Selection
Single
Zoom
1
X
2
Add Main
Diag Ops
View Ops
Example Data Flow Diagram
KEY:
External
Two Way Flow
Process
One Way Flows
Data Store
<Name>
<Ref>
<Location>
<Process Name>
<DS Ref>
<Data Store Name>
LSDM_master_window 2.0
LSDM Master Window
Create Design Model
Delete Design Model
Design Model Name
LSDM
Design Model Class
Architecture
Mode
Edit
System View
Example
System Detail
EXAMPLE
LDS DE
DFD DE
Ent Desc
Rel Desc
ELH DE
Data Store Desc
Process Desc
Data Flow Desc
Information: Entity created successfully
Eclipse
Master
Window

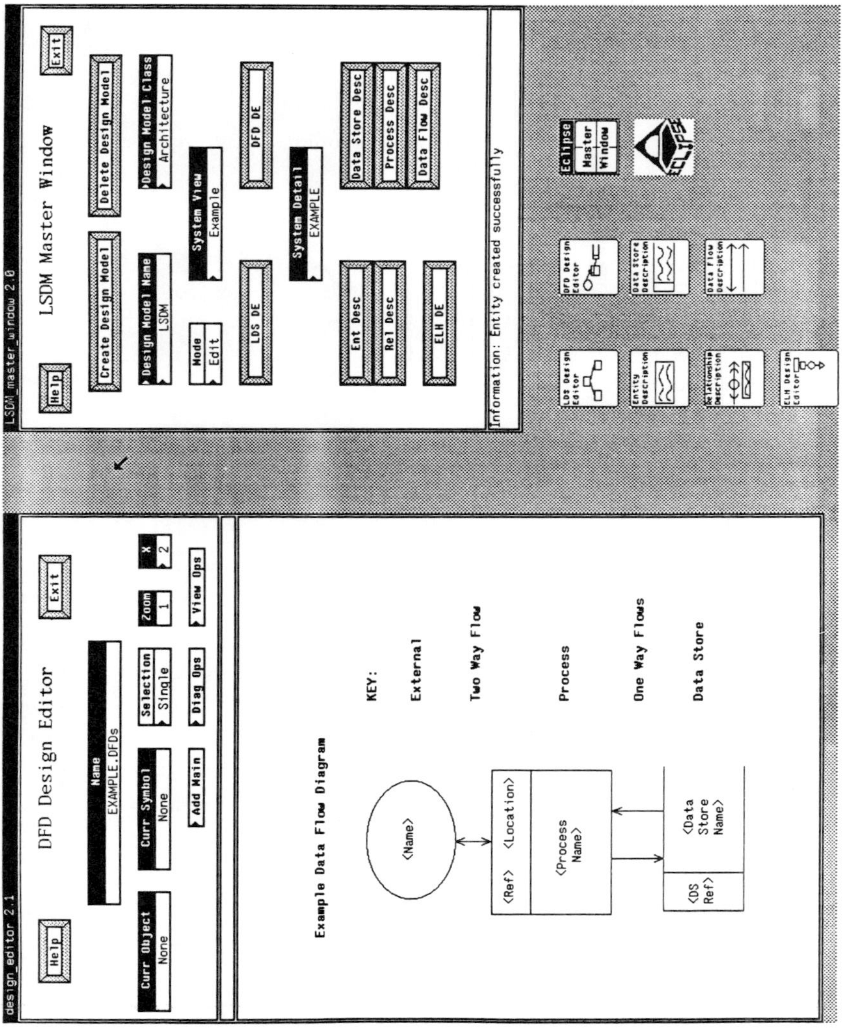

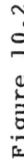

Figure 10.2

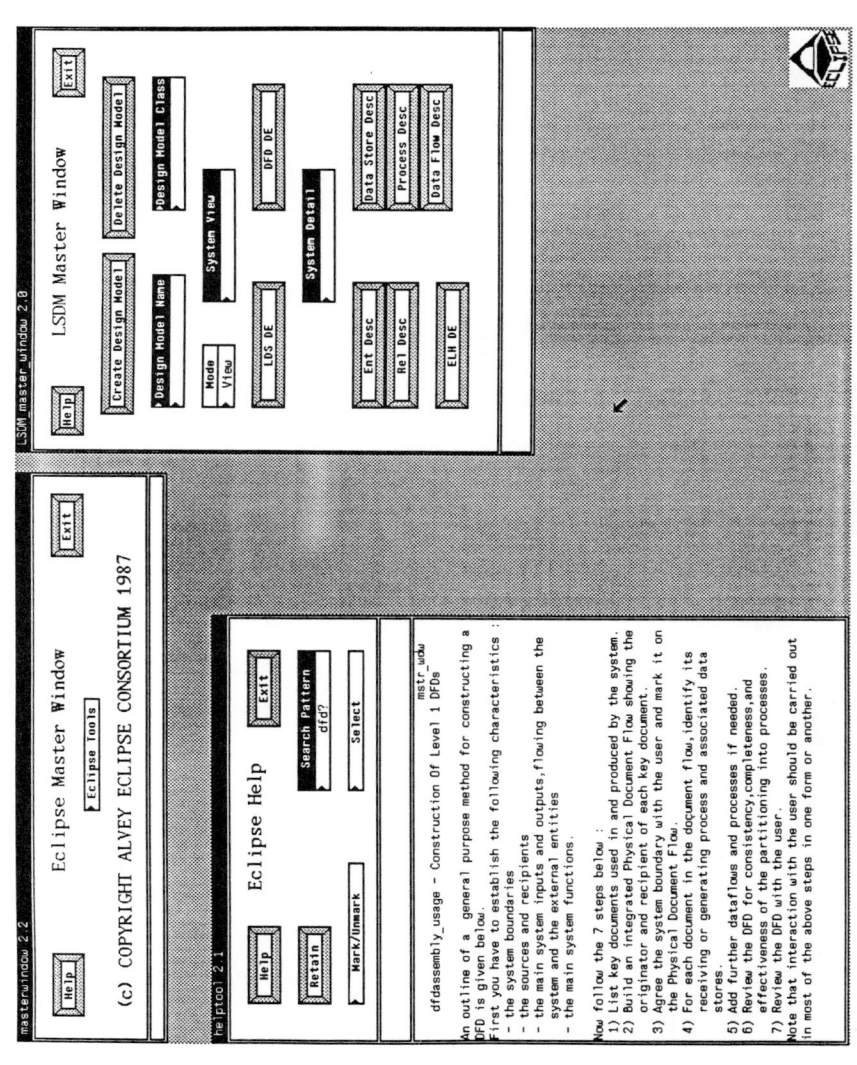

Figure 10.3

design_editor 2.1
Help
ELH Design Editor
Name
EXAMPLE.ELHs
Curr Object
None
Curr Symbol
None
Add Main
Life History of an LDS
LDS Diagram
Create LDS Diagram
Open
Edit Opera
Replace
Close
Delete
Design Editor
Name
EXAMPLE.LDSs
Selection
Single
Zoom
1
X
1
Diag Ops
View Ops
Exit
A simplified LDS for LDSs
LDS Diagram
Access Path Entry Point
Op. Master
Entity
Relation
Op. Master Relation
Master
Detail
Excl. Group
entity_desc 2.1
Help
Mode
Edit
Entity Description
Exit
Entity Name
LDS_DIAGRAM
Volume
20
of
Size in Bytes
4000
Insertions
2
Amendments
20
Deletions
1
per
Volatility Period
Week
Description
The LDS diagram shows entities and their relationships. As the design develops, Operational Masters and Access Path Entry Points are added. Relationships may be normal master-detail, or optional, or part of an exclusive group, i.e. a group of mutually exclusive rel:

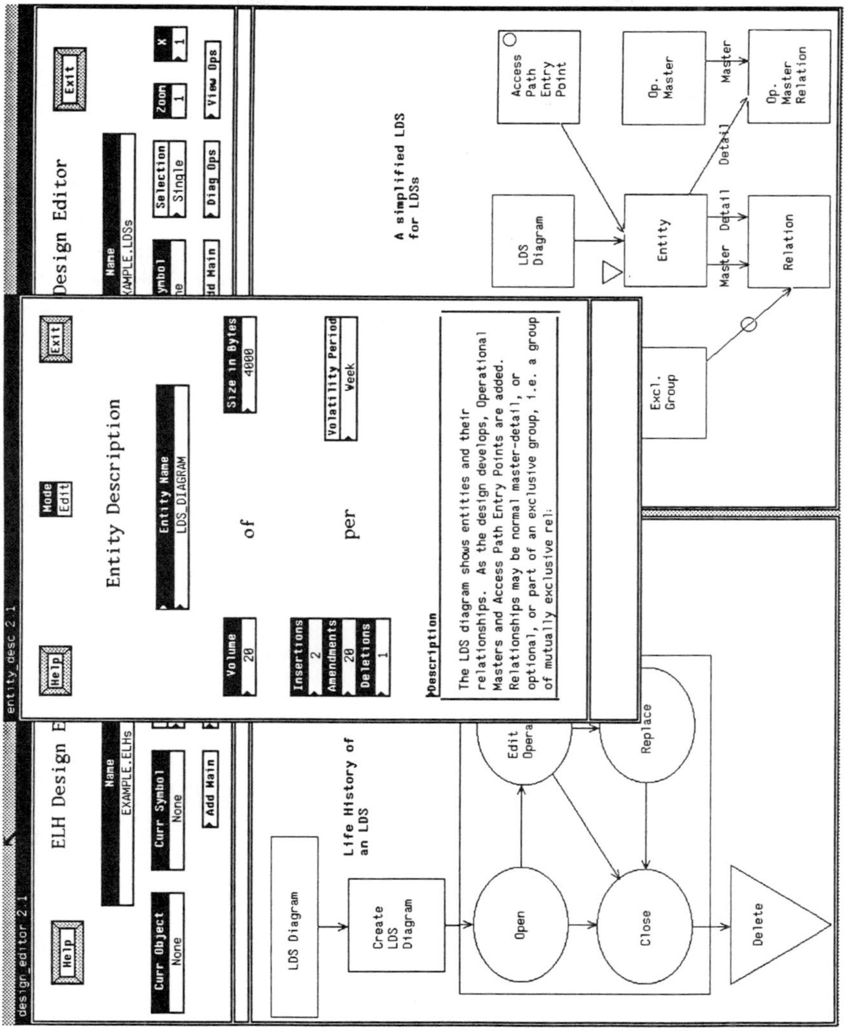

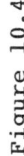

Figure 10.4

10.5 APPROACH

The intention was to construct the proposed tool set emulating future independent tool builders and thus uncover the practical difficulties of utilising each components. The functionality of the Eclipse components had been influenced by the requirements of the tool sets. Now they had to be used as they stood or rather, as they could realistically be expected to become within the timescale. The LSDM tool set therefore consists of a tool administering a master window control panel, and a collection of specialist design and forms editors (see Figure 10.4), using the Eclipse facilities. Each view or form is handled by a separate tool, enabling the user to see any combination of information(s) he wishes.

The team had a head start in having some Eclipse knowledge already, but this was less advantageous than one might expect, as changes in personnel, the move from version one to version two (see section 2.2) and the sheer size of Eclipse meant that every member was faced with a substantial amount to learn. Fortunately the functional specifications were good and the software, when distributed, was generally reliable.

However, most components were still being developed. When the early releases arrived, the corresponding user guides, tool builder's guides and installation details were not yet available, so the learning period for each component was long: weeks could pass with no visible sign of progress. Team members resisted asking the developers for advice, partly because they were all at other sites, so started off as total strangers, but also because it was hard to formulate answerable questions, rather than just saying "I am getting nowhere. Help!"

A lot of effort went into an electronic mail system, to access the Eclipse mail facilities at Lancaster University over a dial-up line. Unfortunately it could take days to achieve a successful transfer, so the system fell into disuse. Messages were phoned and files sent on cartridge tape. It was found that an overnight parcel service was more reliable and that the enormous capacity of a cartridge tape encourages people to send additional files in case they might be useful!

10.6 LESSONS FOR TOOL BUILDERS

Working for a while in any environment changes one's outlook. Facilities that are easy to provide become the norm even if they were previously infeasible. The designer has to concentrate on those that are difficult but attainable, even if they could not even be contemplated before. The following sections are a personal selection of lessons learnt, from that unavoidably biased standpoint.

Eclipse is an evolving system, so new releases may invalidate some of the points made. Nevertheless, they represent real experience of Eclipse, which will hopefully be of benefit to other potential tool builders. They should also be of some interest to those planning to build tools for environments other than Eclipse. Every designer has to map an original conceptual requirement down to code executing in some environment. Mismatches are most easily recognised when porting, because there is then a concrete definition to follow. However, ideally applications should not merely be ported into an environment, but should be redesigned to fit. Moreover, some of these issues are encountered whenever a service is available, not just in a fully- fledged IPSE.

The division into topics is somewhat arbitrary, but the aim is to give a two-dimensional view of Tool Building, by Eclipse interface or component and by software life cycle phase.

10.7 THE TOOL BUILDER'S ENVIRONMENT

10.7.1 Portable Common Tool Environment (PCTE)

PCTE is, of course, not part of Eclipse, but is the environment in which Eclipse runs. The tool builder needs to study it carefully. Designing tools for PCTE's network object store requires one to decide what use to make of object types, attributes and links. To do so, the designer must overcome the traditional 'mind-set' imposed by the hierarchical file stores of most other operating systems.

Using PCTE is a curious experience. Pathnames are exactly that: objects do not have names of their own. Once one has traversed a link, there is no guaranteed way back. This is reminiscent of the 'Adventure' game, in which one can easily get lost 'in a maze of twisty little links, all alike'. Links can easily be mis-directed, so the object type becomes a useful hint as to what an object represents. A traditional hierarchical directory listing is not organised to identify alternative paths to the same object.

Initially the developing PCTE was expected to be very unreliable, with regular corruption of the object store. Surprisingly this did not occur during the LSDM development (although it happened afterwards), perhaps due to the use of well-proven software as the base for developing PCTE. Nevertheless, with no supported archiving method at the time, schemas were rarely amended, to avoid the risk of making objects inaccessible.

10.7.2 Two Tier Database

The Eclipse data model and database facilities were adequate for LSDM's needs. The data model for LSDM is defined as an LSDM Logical Data Structure. The relationships described in section 10.2 do not directly map on to the links of the Eclipse data model. A basic LSDM relationship is one-to-many with ownership. This maps onto an Eclipse composition link. However, in LSDM an entity occurrence is dependent on the continued existence of all its related masters (unless a relationship is optional). In Eclipse, an occurrence will continue to exist until the last composition link to it is removed. Additional code is therefore necessary.

Although the two tiers are integrated to the extent of providing a common interface, the two are distinguishable by the presence of the Local Root (This is an unfortunate restriction, since removing it would effectively turn the second-to-first tier links into links providing an unlimited hierarchy of related and over-lapping groups. Users who may wish to change their choice of tier, should define suitable standards.

The equivalence of the first and second tier provides a range of design options. The choice depends on precisely those aspects which differ: performance, concurrent access, configuration control and obscure functional differences. It is not uncommon for a user to have a considerable number of design objects of the same type: a thousand entity LSDs are not unknown. These have to be treated as second tier entities, which can be indexed, instead of first tier objects, which have to be searched linearly. It is now felt that the LSDM tool set probably treats too many of its design objects as second tier entities, i.e. trades the level of user configuration control, for the expected performance of second tier facilities.

PCTE and hence the Eclipse Database, do not support specific representation of *undefined* for each attribute type. Thus the LSDM tool set defined default initial values throughout, even silently creating a form on the first attempt to access it. This was a mistake for a data capture tool: there is definite significance in the fact that a field has not been filled in yet.

Unlike some other environments, neither PCTE nor UNIX make it easy to build processes which are proof against misuse by users. A tool which fails to 'log off' from the Eclipse database interface correctly, can leave a network of corrupt fine structure databases, but these are not flagged in any way. The correct approach is to delete all the open FSDs and the database work area and reboot. This is tiresome during development, so most people just delete the work area and run it again! Any unexpected results thereafter get blamed on the crash and worse still, its effects spread. It then becomes impossible to enforce a disciplined attitude to testing. It took several months to gain such confidence in Eclipse's reliability that the developers would investigate every unexplained problem.

10.7.3 Configuration Control

Much time was spent debating where version control could be useful. The key question is what should constitute each type of separately versionable item, i.e. the granularity problem described in 4.3.3.

No satisfactory solution has yet been devised. The main problem stems from the fact that design objects are commonly cross-referenced or associated in various ways defined in LSDM. A solution which treated the objects as versionable and ignored the changing relationships would not be useful. Obviously such relationships could be encoded as very fine-grain data, but this is complicated by the problems, discussed earlier, of maintaining them during changes to their owners.

At present, the user must be recommended to archive his design database at significant points in the development.

10.7.4 Message System

The message system provided everything needed. It is recommended that each tool have its own window on the screen, in case it needs to tell the user about any problems. Any tools which do not, have to rely on others for their communication, which is rather more complicated.

10.7.5 Applications Interface

The Applications Interface was successful in shielding the LSDM tool set from all lower-level user interface considerations. It provides a strong house style, not just for the appearance of Eclipse tools, but also for a number of direct end-user facilities. A common style is useful to the designer, not just the end-user, because following it

10.7. THE TOOL BUILDER'S ENVIRONMENT

reduces the design options. The control panel metaphor is a nice way to control tools and can be used to support basic forms.

Nevertheless the Applications Interface provides a number of options and there is still room for legitimate debate within the Eclipse house style. For example, the LSDM forms tools have an Edit/View mode sign, whereas the design editor, which was being produced at the same time, has a 'Read-only' light (Figure 10.3). The former tells the user what mode the tool is operating in, whereas the latter warns him of a restriction. Arguably the tools should instead have an 'editing allowed' light to tell the user of the availability of extended facilities.

The original tool set design followed the desktop metaphor, having one window to represent each sheet of paper. However, forms seem rather passive, with no buttons, lights or other active control panel features. Once on display, the commonest operation is 'overwrite', which is not explicit.

This was superseded by the idea of the *forms editor*, which provides a genuine control panel for managing and navigating between all the forms of a particular sort and a *form-area* for the current form itself. Such a Forms Editor can move rapidly between forms and can be replicated if necessary. This approach greatly reduces the number of windows (and corresponding tools) to be managed.

This split between control panel and form-area is not properly brought out in the visual appearance of the Forms Editor illustrated in Figure 10.3. Whereas it is easy to adjust the appearance of an individual field in a window, it takes more effort to change the frame structure within a window. Changing the type of an object, e.g., from menu selection to button, can also be awkward, when the code contains assumptions about that object's attributes. Suitable standards could probably be devised to help, e.g. avoid using relative names for user interface objects.

The forms editing tools follow the 'WYSIWYG' principle, interpreted here as 'What You See Is What You've Got (on the data-base)', so each field is validated immediately on completion. If it fails, the error is reported and that field remains selected. If the field selection is abandoned, the previous (valid) value is restored. If an acceptable value is input, the database is immediately updated.

Various fields in the LSDM Master Window control panel are initially blank because there is no sensible default. However, blank is not an acceptable value, so any attempt to insert it fails validation.

It may be misleading if values already processed are left on display. However they may be useful defaults for future operations. Furthermore, the control panel metaphor suggests that a tool should display its full context or state, see for example the Design Model fields on the LSDM Master Window shown in Figure 10.2. It is then frustrating if these fields cannot be edited to change the context. If there are several connected fields involved, should the tool react to each change, or delay until some sort of context change is invoked? The former may mean expensive operations are done needlessly. The latter requires an Eclipse 'light' or perhaps a 'change context' button to appear, to indicate that the context displayed is now out of date. The LSDM Master Window tool deals with this by merely validating fields when they are changed and leaving all significant work until one of the function buttons is 'pressed'.

Another possibility is to show both the current context and that proposed. Some real-world control panels have both because it takes time for an intended context to be attained. However, the analogous control panel in our case, is one for which a desired operation may be so involved that it cannot be started instantaneously and therefore requires to be set up in advance, rather like the presets on a theatre lighting control board.

Of course, displaying both contexts uses more screen space, so the conclusion is that each tool's user interface should preferably be designed to have only a single, current context.

Most LSDM forms include a description field for formatted text. In AUTO-MATE PLUS these regularly run to several screens-full. How many control panels could support this?

Reports are also needed, for summarised or derived information which cannot be directly updated. These have an even greater variability of length. Note that there is no implication that forms must be filled in interactively, or that reports exist only on paper. We found it helpful to think of all of these styles of user interface as a sort of spreadsheet, each field having an input function and a display function.

In comparison with normal terminals, the 19" Sun screen initially seems enormous. However, its usable display area is about one-tenth of that of a desk! This is much too small to dedicate sufficient space for the longest possible contents of every field. Convenient and easy-to-use facilities are still required for viewing and editing a large item in a small area of the screen. The problem is particularly acute with multi-column forms containing multi-line elements, where most of the form may be white space.

10.7.6 Help System

Eclipse provides a powerful end-user help tool, so it is sensible to use it for all on line help. Good help material is always expensive to produce. The Eclipse help tools support networks of help texts, which although very useful, can be difficult to structure for easy navigation by any user who asks for help. Thee are so many aspects to every topic: definitions, when to use, how to use in the current method step, how to use the tool(s), what to do about error(s) etc.

10.7.7 Shapes Editor

All the main LSDM symbols were easily prepared with the shapes editor. It is particularly convenient to be able to use 'stretchy' ellipses. There were problems with the exclusion arc, a small arc oriented on a relationship link to indicate an exclusive group. The physical goods flow arrow, a broad arrow link, to show a flow of goods which is information not otherwise available, could not be provided at all. The initial version of the shapes editor did not support particular links needed for SSADM (the 'crow's foot' and the parallel bar), so we had to delay our plans for an SSADM variant of the tool set.

10.7.8 Graphical Description Language (GDL)

LSDM's diagrams can be modelled as graphs (not necessarily planar) and so fit neatly into the graph model of GDL. The strong typing, with no type conversion mechanism, does however present problems in use, as it effectively prevents a user of the design editor changing one type of symbol to another. For those used to simple picture editors

10.7. THE TOOL BUILDER'S ENVIRONMENT

this might seem like a major disadvantage. The advantage is that the design editor can offer users just those options relevant in the current context. For example one or more objects have to be selected before an operation can be applied to them. Again, the 'add subordinate' operation has to be selected before the possible subordinates are offered. In this way, even text labels are typed, increasing the opportunities for checking and further manipulation. In this situation, it is not clear whether a useful type conversion mechanism could be devised.

GDL is sufficiently rich that alternative solutions are possible. Do two different method symbols really represent different types or are they just alternative representations of one type, which GDL also supports? In some cases there is a third option, which is to treat the difference between two symbols as a picture label, which can be added or removed to alternate between them, e.g. LDS entities and Operational Masters (see Figure 10.2).

Each link is directed, in the sense that it must be drawn from a source node to a destination node. Arrowed links are particularly elusive: is an arrow in one direction really a different type of link from an arrow in the other, and from a two-way arrow? The answer is 'yes' on a Logical Data Structure, where an arrow indicates which entity owns the other, i.e. the structural relationship between the nodes it connects. It is less clear on a Data Flow Diagram where a link shows an information flow, which is structural information, while the arrow-head(s) merely indicate its direction, not that one node is a 'pusher' and the other a 'puller', or whatever.

Types were defined for LSDM to fit GDL's hierarchical type model. Levels in LSDM are generally unlimited, so could not be depicted using level-specific symbols. The problem is dealt with in a variety of ways: nested diagrams for DFDs, relationship links for LDSs and nested cluster boxes for ELHs. The deepest level of nesting of subordinates is probably on a Logical Data Structure: the optional label on an exclusion arc, on a relationship, between two entities.

10.7.9 Design Editor

The Eclipse design editor coped with the complexities of the three LSDM diagram types which the tool set supports and the results look good, which is a prime requirement! It provides operations to add, move and delete nodes, links, labels, annotations etc. and to manage the user's view, as well as facilities to print the results.

Computerisation reduces the effort needed to maintain a diagram and makes complex symbols easy to draw. The industrialised design editor also looks after LSDM's repetition variants: some symbols may be replicated on a diagram to reduce the untidiness of having links which cross. While a design object has more than one occurrence of the symbol representing it, that symbol is slightly altered to remind the viewer.

One can also point at a symbol on a diagram and open it up to the form(s) or diagram describing the underlying design object. This is an important aspect of tool integration from the end-user's point of view, but is visually rather unsatisfactory, as the forms are so large that they hide much of the screen and an individual form is not visibly tied back to the symbol opened. Perhaps the symbol should be 'popped open' like a menu or an icon.

For the longer term, dynamic window resizing must be considered. The naive approach of cropping, or adding a border, is not suitable with the control panel metaphor, where one would have to place all the fields in a 'minimal' corner. One solution might be to reduce all the contents equally, but this is much harder to support, particularly in the Sun's multi-font environment, where few sizes are provided in each font. Rather better, would be to allow the user to manage which frames of a window are displayed, so that rarely required fields are not automatically visible.

Positioning is never significant in LSDM: any isomorphic graph has the same meaning. This makes it easier to analyse the diagrams, even when produced using an untyped picture editor.

The limited repertoire of operation menus ensures that only supported operations can be requested. Semantically incorrect, i.e. inappropriate, operations are not made available to the user, removing the most obvious source of error. More subtle errors can be detected by writing assertions about designs, i.e. statements which if not true cause a diagnostic. These proved to be rather less of an advantage than expected, partly due to the way that LSDM diagrams are constructed. Thus the tool set has to take a very *laissez-faire* attitude when the analyst is sketching an existing physical system, but could enforce much tighter rules when he is specifying a logical system design. Assertions also have to be used for any label validation required. Stand-alone checking tools have to be written to check consistency and completeness between diagrams and forms, as assertions are currently not able to provide this.

A generic design editor can be required to perform method-specific code at virtually any point. For example, the traditional problems of handling names containing a mixture of upper and lower case and spaces. Are they to be rejected, treated as significant, ignored, or visibly converted? Similar problems apply to the purely pictorial elements too.

Hierarchical Data Flow Diagrams present an interesting challenge to the would-be designer of a generic design editor. There is a need to show the context of a process being decomposed and to allow the data flows to it to be reconnected to the processes to which it is decomposed. Thus either the context must be read-only with link editing allowed only at the process end, or ideally, changes should permeate outwards to the higher-level diagram. Perhaps we should think of it as one diagram, with a 'logical zoom' operation, as well as the more normal physical one.

10.8 LIFE CYCLE SUPPORT

10.8.1 Design

Eclipse provides a highly sophisticated environment. To make good use of it, an imaginative flexible designer is required. It is quite easy to ignore Eclipse facilities and write great quantities of UNIX-compatible C. However this ignores the integration aim of an IPSE. The Eclipse Kernel should really be used complete, but the designer has more flexibility with the Tool Builder's Kit and can choose which components to use and which to discard.

Computerisation affects all applications, including analysis and design methods. Requirements have to be carefully defined. Some clerical tasks become unnecessary. Working documents, including those whose main purpose is recording progress or checking completeness, get radically altered. Forms for cataloguing become reports on what is stored. Features which cannot easily be computerised are replaced.

10.8. LIFE CYCLE SUPPORT

Eclipse tool sets normally start with a control panel type tool which sets up the operating environment for any other tools and therefore has to be invoked first. This encourages top-down coding and testing.

Designing a set of separate tools allows parallel use by the end-user and parallel development.

Note that the Applications Interface permits operations to be requested in any sequence, so the user interface (and even program side-effects) must be designed with this in mind.

10.8.2 Coding

There are a number of unique languages to learn: DDL to describe the Database schema, FDL for the User Interface, GDL for diagrams and even help frames have a syntax. Each is fairly simple, but their effects are not, so plan to have an expert for each in your programming team.

Some C will also be needed, to initialise and terminate each tool and to manipulate the C interface to other Eclipse components, normally the Database, Applications Interface, Message Handling and Help. So much of each tool is provided by these components that there is not much C to write and independent testing of it is rarely worthwhile. A background in using UNIX system for program development is valuable, but knowledge of UNIX system calls is not required: the LSDM tool set only calls PCTE directly to create processes.

Eclipse tools always interface to the end-user via the Applications Interface. Normally the FDL is got working first, so that the rest of the tool can be correctly invoked as it is added. The tool is then connected to the database, adding messages as necessary. Help can be added later. Thus incremental development is suggested.

10.8.3 Debugging

The normal debugging facilities of Sun UNIX are available. In addition, Eclipse components take exception-handling very seriously and most log a whole flood of messages. Amongst these it can be impossible top pick out the real errors. The specification of complex requirements in argument strings or worse still, in separate files, means that a failure tends to take place deep inside a component, obscuring its precise cause. It is not easy to relate a diagnostic to a particular call or set of arguments passed across the interface. One can find oneself longing for less reliable software, which would crash and produce a traceback! This is not particularly a criticism of Eclipse, but a common problem when a service is supplied via a procedural interface which ignores the change of context.

FDL makes it easy to add extra facilities to a tool for debugging, which can be removed later. Alternatively they can be hidden until the right incantations are given. A PCTE command processor field is particularly useful as it allows investigation of the tool's environment.

The interface to the Database and Applications Interface use tokens to provide multiple pointers into the data. Mistakes here can produce puzzling effects.

10.8.4 Integration

Under Eclipse, many components assume a considerable environment, requiring a number of small objects, hence an Environment Specification, Schema Definition Set and installation instructions are essential, even for System Integration. Lacking these, we had to ship the entire project to Macclesfield for a fortnight to achieve successful installation.

All tools should be written to cope with faulty installation. Even if rarely needed after general release, it will be essential during integration. This implies checking the return code from every interface routine.

Many components are supplied in two parts, A C Interface to be linked into the end-user tool and a separate process to provide the actual service. Obviously the two have to be consistent.

Generic software such as the design editor, has the disadvantage that it is unusable until it has been instantiated, so a simple test version is needed to test installation. Each instantiation also has to be tested and documented. Nevertheless, it is very easy to create new design editor for new types of diagram, so much so that it is worth trying to make as much data as possible diagrammatic!

10.8.5 Validation

The descriptive languages can be tested in the same way as 4th Generation code, verifying that each phrase has the desired effect. It was felt that the complexity of the design editor and the possibility of unintentional side- effects warranted checking which operations were available when and testing each one very LSDM-defined object.

10.8.6 Prototyping

It is unlikely that anyone could design a good Eclipse tool set without having reasonable experience of Eclipse. When the first tools started working, they did not 'feel' as expected. Admittedly a paper simulation of the user interface would have helped. Nevertheless, a team's first Eclipse tool set will probably be a prototype, whether planned that way or not. At the very least, time should be allowed for revising the user interface and help material, so that the most obvious usage problems and stylistic anomalies can be alleviated.

10.9 SOME CONCLUSIONS

The Eclipse LSDM Tool Set has no genuine users at the time of writing, but is a useful demonstrator and performs very acceptably. The user interface is good, especially for diagram editing, in spite of some current deficiencies. Eclipse itself is solid and easy to use, with good help facilities. Users do not need a knowledge of PCTE.

Eclipse provides a comprehensive, integrated, Fourth Generation Environment for the tool builder. It is very sophisticated and therefore takes time to master, but in the long run should be very productive. Clearly it has its shortcomings, but these have only been revealed by its successes. It is improving all the time and has many capabilities that the LSDM tool set did not even use. However, the savings on a single

10.9. SOME CONCLUSIONS

project may not be significant. This is not a unique criticism of Eclipse: it probably applies to any sophisticated environment.

As an R & D project, participation in Eclipse has been successful. It has clarified our ideas on what a method support environment should include and has produced some demonstrable software.

Chapter 11

The System Structure Language

Ian Sommerville and Ronnie Thomson

11.1 INTRODUCTION

It is now fairly generally accepted that software environments which are intended to support the development of large software systems should be based on some form of project database system where all of the information associated with the software development is recorded. In general, the associated data base is very complex and is made up of a large number of entities and tens or hundreds of relationships. Each entity or relationship may have associated attributes. Usually, the software engineer working on part of a project is aware of only a relatively small number of entities, attributes and relations and it is very difficult for him or her to form an overall understanding of the system structure recorded in the data base.

The aim of the work described in this chapter is to develop a notation which will allow the structure of systems which are held in the Eclipse database to be described. This description should be understandable to the software engineers involved in software development and maintenance. The notation, described here, is called SySL (System Structure Language).

In the terminology of [25], SySL is a notation for programming in the large. It is intended to describe the structure of any system (not just software systems) which is recorded as attributed entities and relationships in the Eclipse database.

The system structure language is intended to describe the static structure of large software systems and may be looked upon as a development of module interconnection languages such as those described by DeRemer and Kron and by Tichy [124]. Module interconnection languages are used for specifying the static structure of systems in terms of how one system module makes use of other modules. They are principally intended as a high-level description of the software system. The features which distinguish SySL from simple module interconnection languages and notations for configuration description such as the Cedar system modeller [68] are as follows:

- SySL is tightly integrated with an underlying database. It describes configurations of database items rather than files. In essence, a SySL description is a description of database structures in a form which is readily understandable without detailed knowledge of the underlying DBMS.

- SySL allows the description of both specific systems and classes of system which may be represented in the database. Thus the user may view system configurations at varying levels of detail.

- SySL has an associated tool set which supports the construction of SySL descriptions, system building and database checking. The language was designed with automated tool support in mind and its practical usability is dependent on its tool set.

One example of a class of tool which we intend to build as part of the SySL project is a system building tool like the UNIX Make system [34] or the Cedar System modeller [68]. These tools use explicit notations for describing the build system structure. It seems to us that by extending static structural descriptions in SySL with build information abstracted from the project database, it will be possible to automate the process of system building.

In the remainder of this chapter, we illustrate SySL by example and describe the toolkit which has been developed to support it. Space does not allow a full description of SySL here — further information is available from the authors [115].

11.2 THE LANGUAGE

The Eclipse system allows very complex relationships between database entities to be set up with many of these relationships actually created by software tools. Although the user of the system may have access to the database schema and to the query language, it is, in general, extremely difficult for him or her to get any kind of overall picture of the part of the database of interest and the relationships which are (or which ought to be) maintained there. In many cases, it is also very difficult to check that relationships between items which should exist actually do exist and that items have a particular set of expected attributes. Thus, the aim of our work was to develop a notation which allowed the static structure of systems to be made apparent and to develop an associated toolkit to assist with activities such as system building, database validation and system viewing.

The fundamental assumption underlying our work is that a universe of entities exists in a project database and users are interested in particular configurations of these entities, the classes to which these entities belong, the structure of members of these classes and constraints on individual entities and entity configurations.

SySL includes constructs to define the following:

- classes of database items which are defined by enumeration of explicit items or by class unions;

- the structure which is associated with all members of a particular class;

- the specific configuration of individual members of a class;

11.2. THE LANGUAGE

- the interface published by individual members of a class;
- constraints on classes in general or on individual class members.

A SySL description consists of a number of class definitions where individual classes are defined, structure definitions where structure is associated with particular classes, assertions which place constraints on the attributes associated with class members and a large number of component descriptions where the static structure of the components making up a system is described.

A component description is a description of the static structure of a particular software component which is part of the system whose structure is being defined. Depending on the underlying implementation, a component may be a procedure, an Ada package, an 'include' file or whatever — SySL does not prescribe how a component is represented. As far as SySL is concerned, any item in the database may be considered as a system component.

However, we do support the notion of a primitive components and compound components. We define a primitive component to be a component where the database item represents a single logical system element such as a procedure or a function. A compound component is a component where the database item is a packaging of a number of logical components. Examples of this type of component include Ada packages which make several procedures/functions available through their interfaces and C 'include' files where several functions are contained in the same file.

We believe that users of an IPSE take on different roles at different times which means that they are interested in understanding the structure of systems at different levels of detail from the very abstract (what is the general standard structure for a specifications document? say) to the concrete (what is the particular organisation of the SySL specification document?). Thus a key feature of SySL is the ability to express system structure at different levels of detail. For example, the description below might be part of the SySL specification of a personal work station.

```
structure WORKSTATION is
PROCESSOR,
MEMORY,
BACKPLANE,
DISPLAY,
-- square brackets mean optional item
[DISK_SYSTEM],
-- [ ]* means 0 or more items of this type allowed
[ETHERNET]*,
POINTING_DEVICE,
KEYBOARD,
-- tape is optional
[TAPE],
OPERATING_SYSTEM;
end structure
```

This specification of the structure of a work station indicates that it is made up of a number of components some of which are optional (indicated by square brackets). In this abstract description, the names used in the description are class names (distinguished by the fact they are written entirely in upper-case letters). Thus, work stations in general are made up of processors, memories, backplanes, displays, etc. The writer of the description has not chosen to associate particular item names with these class names, that is, to specify which particular processor is used, what sizes of memory are available, etc. This specific information is provided as part of a concrete description of a specific work station.

Classes are defined explicitly by enumeration and may have an associated structure as defined above. For example, the class WORKSTATION and the class PROCESSOR may be defined as follows:

```
class WORKSTATION is (MOON_WORKSTATION,
VENUS_WORKSTATION,
MARS_WORKSTATION)

class PROCESSOR is (m68010, m68020, ns32032)
```

The class WORKSTATION is defined in terms of sub-classes MOON_WORKSTATION, VENUS_WORKSTATION and MARS_WORKSTATION (any unescaped sequence of upper-case letters, underscores and digits is taken as a class name) and the class work station is defined as the union of the classes MOON_WORKSTATION, VENUS_WORKSTATION and MARS_WORKSTATION. The class PROCESSOR, on the other hand, is described explicitly as being made up of the items identified by the names m68010, m68020 and ns32032.

A structure may be associated with any class via a structure declaration. This means that the structure of all items in that class must correspond with that defined. For example, the declaration below associates a structural description with the class MEMORY:

```
structure MEMORY is
MEMORY_MANAGEMENT_UNIT,
-- + means that there must be one or more items
[MEMORY_BOARD]+;
end structure
```

This definition states that items of class MEMORY are composite items made up of an item of class MEMORY_MANAGEMENT_UNIT and a number of items of class MEMORY_BOARD. Notice that following a bracketed item with a '+' means 1 or more instances of that item, following it with a * means zero or more instances. The upper bound on the number of instances may be specified by following the '+' or '*' with an integer as shown in the MOON_WORKSTATION example below.

The definition of a work station structure allows for the possibility that some elements of the structure may be empty. Thus, not all work stations need be equipped with a tape drive, some may be connected in a network and may be diskless, etc. However, not all possible options are allowed so we allow the user to make assertions

11.2. THE LANGUAGE

defining disallowed structures. For example, the following assertions would normally be associated with the structure WORKSTATION.

```
-- Diskless work stations must have an ethernet interface
assert WORKSTATION: not (Not_present (ETHERNET)
  and Not_present (DISK_SYSTEM))

-- Work stations with a tape must also have a disk
assert WORKSTATION: not(Not_present (DISK_SYSTEM)
          and Present(TAPE))
```

Assertions are always associated with particular classes and the assertion mechanism is a general one. As well as specifying constraints on system compositions, it may also be used to associate particular attributes with classes. For example, the following assertions state that items of class DISPLAY must have an attribute called RESOLUTION which may have the value '1192/768' or the value '1000/800'

```
assert DISPLAY:  Has_attribute (RESOLUTION)
assert DISPLAY:  Has_value (RESOLUTION, '1192/768')
   or Has_value (RESOLUTION, '1000/800')
```

The work station description above is very general indeed and might apply to any of the personal work stations which are now available. We can define a more detailed work station description as shown below.

```
structure MOON_WORKSTATION is
PROCESSOR => (m68010, m68020)
MEMORY => MOON_MEMORY
BACKPLANE => multibus,
DISPLAY => (monochrome_display, colour_display),
DISK_SYSTEM => (d71Mb, d130Mb, d430Mb, null),
POINTING_DEVICE => OPTICAL_MOUSE,
OPERATING_SYSTEM => (unix4.2bsd, unixsV)
end structure
```

Again, this is a generic description but at a less abstract level than the description of work stations in general. Parts of the structure of class WORKSTATION have been instantiated either to specific database items or to sub-classes. Class names which are associated with a previously declared type name introduce a sub-class. Thus, MOON_MEMORY is a sub-class of the class MEMORY, OPTICAL_MOUSE is a sub-class of the class POINTING_DEVICE, etc. This class network is reflected in the Eclipse database where each item must have an associated type (class name) and specialisations and generalisations of types are supported. It is assumed that those parts of the structure of work station which have not been instantiated are unchanged and are inherited directly from the description of the structure of WORKSTATION.

The description may be further refined to refer to specific individual work stations. For example:

```
system ians_moon: MOON_WORKSTATION is
PROCESSOR => m68010,
MEMORY => s2mbytes,
DISPLAY => monochrome_display,
DISK_SYSTEM => d71mb,
ETHERNET => e12345,
OPTICAL_MOUSE => m1234,
KEYBOARD => k1234,
OPERATING_SYSTEM => unix4.2bsd;
end system
```

This defines a specific work station configuration where all of the names must refer to specific items in the Eclipse database rather than item classes. In practice, of course, the items in the database for hardware systems are descriptions of the hardware.

We have deliberately introduced this section on SySL with a hardware example to illustrate the flexibility of the notation. However, we anticipate that the language will be most used for describing the structure of software and documentation systems. As part of the evaluation of SySL, we have written a complete description of the structure of the UNIX kernel and anticipated that this might serve as a source of useful examples for this paper. In fact, because there is no associated database, the UNIX system is represented as a large collection of files and its structure is flat and uninteresting. It has not proved particularly useful for assessing features of the language.

Instead, we use examples taken from an electronic mail system which is currently being developed in Ada. This system provides the usual mail facilities of sending and receiving mail, uses menus for user interaction, provides comprehensive on-line help facilities and makes use of a number of abstract data types. Initially, it is possible to define the expected structure of (generalised) systems written in Ada:

```
structure ADA_SYSTEM is
-- packages of shared constants, types, variables, etc.
[SHARED_COLLECTION]*,
[ABSTRACT_DATA_TYPE]*,
[SUB_SYSTEM]*,
MAIN_PROCEDURE;
end structure
```

This specifies that a system of class ada_system should be made up of a number of items defining shared collections of types, constants, etc, packages defining abstract data types, packages defining sub-systems and a single item of type 'main_procedure'. The classes declared here are a union of sub-classes as follows:

```
class ADA_PACKAGE is   (SHARED_COLLECTION,
ABSTRACT_DATA_TYPE,
SUB_SYSTEM)
```

11.2. THE LANGUAGE

A possible assertion which might be associated with the class ADA_PACKAGE is:

```
assert ADA_PACKAGE: Has_attribute (Ada_package_spec) or
Has_attribute (Complete_Ada_package)
```

This assertion states that to be used as part of a system, the Ada package must either be a specification or a complete (specification + body) package. Package bodies alone may not be included.

The highest-level description of the electronic mail system is:

```
system Electronic_mail_system: ADA_SYSTEM is
external (print_spooler, sort_command);
provides (Em_system);

SHARED_COLLECTION => Em_types
 Em_constants
-- No abstract data types visible at this level in
-- this system
-- Define the sub-systems
SUB_SYSTEM =>   Menu_manager
Send_mail
Receive_mail
Help
Mailbox_manager
MAIN_PROCEDURE => Em_system
end system
```

This description starts with a SySL external declaration which specifies that this system requires access to items which are not controlled by the Eclipse database. Here, it makes use of a print spooler and a sort command which are presumed to be provided by the operating system. Declaring these entities as external indicates that they are an integral part of the system but are not Eclipse database items.

The 'provides' declaration is used in a SySL description to specify which names used in the package are made visible to system users. Here, we specify that the name Em_system is published as the interface to Electronic_mail_system and may be used in other SySL definitions. The use of a name in a 'provides' declaration implies that that component is part of the component item and that its use in a structure description does not represent a reference to another Eclipse item. Thus, the item identified by the name Electronic_mail_system contains the main_procedure called Em_system. The description continues with a list of the Eclipse items which make up the electronic mail system. Thus, the sub-systems Menu_manager, Send_mail, etc are separate and distinct items for which SySL definitions should exist.

Notice that the Electronic_mail_system has been identified as a system whereas the Mailbox_manager below has been identified as a component. The difference between these is that components may be parts of systems but systems may not be part of components. Whilst this distinction is not strictly necessary, we believe that it reflects a natural human structuring mechanism.

The components of the electronic mail system are also described using SySL. For example, the Mailbox_manager sub-system may be described:

```
component Mailbox_manager: SUB_SYSTEM is
provides ( Get_from _mailbox_of,
             Discard_expired_mail_from,
    Put_item_in_mailbox,
    Move_mail_to_mail_list );

SHARED_COLLECTION => Em_types
  Em_constants
ABSTRACT_DATA_TYPE => Mailbox
        Mail_list
PROCEDURE =>  Get_from_mailbox_of
Discard_expired_mail_from
Put_item_in_mailbox
Move_mail_to_mail_list
end component
```

Here, the component description specifies which procedures may be called by users of that component and list Eclipse items which are used by the Mailbox_manager sub-system. Mailbox_manager provides four procedures called 'Get_from_mailbox_of', 'Discard_expired_mail_from', 'Put_item_in_mailbox', and 'Move_mail_to_mail_list'. It makes use of the Eclipse items named Em_types, Em_constants, Mailbox, and Mail_list.

The Receive_mail component is described in SySL as follows:

```
component Receive_mail: SUB_SYSTEM is
provides (Present_mail, File_mail, Redirect_mail);
requires ( Mailbox_manager);

SHARED_COLLECTION => EM_types
    EM_constants
SUB_SYSTEM => Send_mail
PROCEDURE=>
Mailbox_manager.Discard_expired_mail_from
Mailbox_manager.Get_from_mailbox_of
Present_mail
File_mail
Redirect_mail
end component
```

In this description, the requires declaration specifies the name of an item that is required and implies that the component being described makes use of facilities provided by that item. It is rather like an Ada with clause. Here we specify that the

11.2. THE LANGUAGE

item Mailbox_manager is required and, within the definition, we specify which procedures from Mailbox_manager are actually used, namely Discard_expired_mail_from and Get_from_mailbox_of. These names should be published in the provides declaration of Mailbox_manager. The provides clause specifies that the Receive_mail sub-system provides the procedures Present_mail, File_mail and Redirect_mail.

In our final example, we show the SySL description of the Mailbox abstract data type.

```
component Mailbox: ABSTRACT_DATA_TYPE is
provides (Append_item, Remove_item, Clear,
Is_empty, Get_owner);

PROCEDURE => Append_item
Remove_item
Clear;
FUNCTION => Is_empty
Get_owner
end component
```

This component is entirely self-contained and does not use any other Eclipse item. All of the modules making up Mailbox are specified in the provides list and are thus assumed to be part of the Mailbox item itself.

11.2.1 SySL and Configuration Descriptions

As can be seen from some of the above examples, SySL allows the user to specify alternative compositions for particular items. Thus a MOON_WORKSTATION may include the item d71mb of type DISK_SYSTEM, the item d130mb of the same type, the item d430mb, or no DISK_SYSTEM at all. However, it must be emphasised that SySL only allows for alternative items to be specified so that similar system structures can be defined. SySL does not provide facilities to specify that a particular version of a system or a component is made up from particular versions of its parts.

In fact, the facilities provided by the Eclipse system make such implicit version specification unnecessary. As discussed above in the section on Eclipse, it is normal for all items in a Eclipse data base to be versioned with each distinct version termed an object. In all cases then, an item name really means one of the objects associated with that item but the binding of the name to a particular object is not made when the system is defined but is made at run-time when the object is actually referenced. Thus, if some name X, say, is used in a SySL system, the user's current context is evaluated and the database object named X in that context is selected. If some other version of the component X is required, the context must be changed (using system commands) to ensure that it refers to the version of X which is required.

The tools which process a SySL description always do so in an environment defined by the user's current context. The current context contains the names of items which are referenced in the SySL description plus the association of these item names with particular objects. The evaluation context may be saved with a SySL description so that future processing will always access the expected objects but the normal default for initial SySL descriptions is to bind the name to the latest version of the referenced item. Thus, one context may refer to the system being developed, another may refer to the previous version of the system, another may refer to the system delivered to some customer T. Thus, a complete specification is made up of a SySL description and the context which binds this to the Eclipse database.

11.3 THE SySL TOOLKIT

SySL is a notation for describing systems represented in a project database and is thus useful in its own right. It provides a source of information to project developers by collecting together information about the structure of the various components and their relationships into a form which is both readable and easily accessible to all concerned. Traditionally this type of information is buried throughout the project in source code and informal documentation and as a consequence it is difficult to gain an overall understanding of project structure.

However, it is obviously more useful if the language is supported by automated tools. To enhance the usability of the language a means must be provided for system descriptions to be kept in a consistent state. The process of change should be quickly reflected in the system description. Therefore, a powerful language-oriented editing system has been provided. This enhances readability by providing a structured approach to viewing descriptions. Additionally, it removes the burden of updating descriptions by letting the system carry out, automatically, changes which are initiated by the user.

In order to provide such facilities we must have some way of representing a system description in a logical way which is internal to the SySL system. This is provided via the language processor which, as well as checking the consistency of the description, translates a SySL description to an internal directed graph representation. Integration of the SySL tools is achieved through each tool using this internal representation.

SySL, allows the user to describe the static structure of software systems and families of systems. From this the user can then use tools to control the versions which are used in system configurations, construct descriptions of a system using the editing facilities and from this build the desired system. A brief description of the various features of the system follow. Figure 11.1 shows the architecture of the environment.

- The SySL Language: this is the basis of the environment. An overview of the language has been given in section 11.2.

- Language Processor and Database Generator. The environment uses a database generated by the language processor. The database is a logical representation of the equivalent SySL description and has the form of a directed graph. Nodes in this graph represent entities in the system description and links between nodes represent relationships between entities. The language processor is used to generate the database and check the system description for consistency and completeness.

- Language Browser and Structured Editor. SySL is an important source of documentation on the system. The language browser provides a structured approach

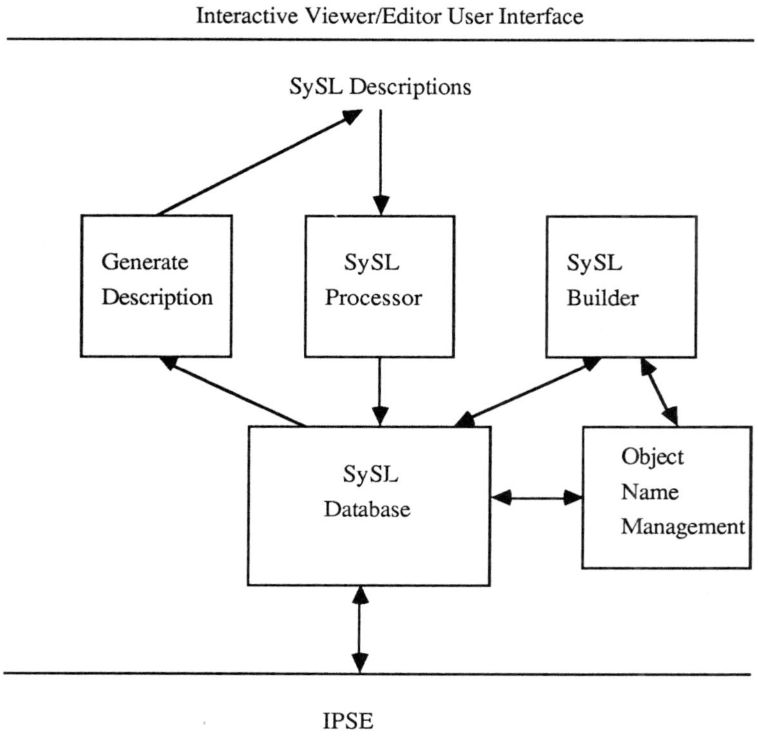

11.3. THE SYSL TOOLKIT

```
┌─────────────────────────────────────────────────────────┐
│           Interactive Viewer/Editor User Interface      │
└─────────────────────────────────────────────────────────┘
                       SySL Descriptions

    ┌───────────┐      ┌───────────┐      ┌───────────┐
    │ Generate  │      │   SySL    │      │   SySL    │
    │Description│      │ Processor │      │  Builder  │
    └───────────┘      └───────────┘      └───────────┘

                  ┌──────────────┐       ┌──────────┐
                  │              │       │  Object  │
                  │     SySL     │◄─────►│   Name   │
                  │   Database   │       │Management│
                  │              │       │          │
                  └──────────────┘       └──────────┘

┌─────────────────────────────────────────────────────────┐
│                          IPSE                           │
└─────────────────────────────────────────────────────────┘
```

Figure 11.1: The SySL Environment Architecture

to viewing the database structures. The editor system provides the user with a means of updating the database in such a way as to preserve the integrity.

- Object Name Management. SySL provides no explicit naming conventions for identifying version of components. We assume that the underlying IPSE provides such facilities. This tool provides the user with a means to map the SySL object names onto the IPSE database names and to view the IPSE object representation.

- System Building Facility. This tools allows the user to generate the information required to build a component and dependent components. The system is based on a rule base which contains the knowledge about the types of component and information required to build the components. This provides a flexible and extensible way of generating build information.

The important feature of the above system is that the SySL language and the supporting toolkit are integrated to provide a more uniform approach to understanding system structure. The environment is organised as an interactive system based on a database system which records the system structure. The above SySL tools manipulate this structure in performing specific tasks. The database is initialised by processing a SySL description. Modifications to the description cause the database to be modified immediately thus ensuring the consistency of the description.

The user access to the system is via a common user interface. This interface provides a means to view the textual representation of the SySL description and to interrogate the underlying SySL database. This user-interface also provides the user with access to the SySL environment tools such as the version name management system, build system and language browser. The types of commands which are available allow the user to analyse the description in a highly interactive way, modify the description, view the database representation and select particular components for the build system.

All interaction with the system and the underlying database attempts to guarantee the integrity and consistency of the underlying database system. Therefore, the system will not allow the user to change the description in inconsistent ways that may violate the interfaces to components. This ensures the completeness and the consistency of the description.

11.3.1 An Interactive System

The SySL environment is an interactive system. Immediate feedback on actions initiated by the user is provided. The environment editor provides the user with a powerful way of constructing and editing SySL descriptions. The system builder allows the programmer to immediately build the new system.

The other benefits of an interactive system are as follows:

- Creating and modifying SySL descriptions. The user can choose to modify a particular component or system. The SySL system will immediately display the information and related information and the changes that are made can be seen immediately. The change is propagated immediately into the database and becomes available to other SySL tools.

- Context relative display of SySL descriptions. The SySL system considers descriptions as highly structured objects and therefore tries to display the information in a sensible form by placing related information together. A display algorithm calculates where to place different parts of the SySL description so that related information is grouped.

- Interactive checking of SySL descriptions. The system provides the user with the ability to interactively check SySL descriptions. However the user can only make changes in such as way as to preserve the integrity of SySL descriptions. Immediate feedback on such changes is provided for the user.

- Change propagation. The integration of a language viewer and a structured editor allows the user to see immediately the effects of a change on the system. The editor has been developed in such a way as to take away much of the burden of keeping SySL descriptions in a consistent and complete form. Changes made to one part of the description are propagated through the rest of the description by the editor.

11.3. THE SYSL TOOLKIT

- Tool integration. If the SySL environment is to be used effectively, the various tools in the environment must be accessible in as unobtrusive way as possible. The user must be able to move between tools quickly and effectively. All tools have been integrated within a common interface and the user can easily access the facilities provided in each.

11.3.2 The SySL Language Browser and Structured Editor

A system structure description written in SySL provides an essential record of the project structure. It records component interconnections, dependencies between components and the relationships. As such it provides a focus for designers and implementors who wish to discuss their work and view it in context with the overall project structure and who wish to integrate their software with the system.

It is essential, therefore, that the user is able to view and understand the system structure in a more structured way than simply reading a textual description or using existing text editors. The provision of a powerful language-oriented viewing system helps the reader of a SySL description to prepare, read and understand the system structure.

The integration between the editor and the language makes it possible to include language facilities which will enhance readability and ease the task of maintaining the integrity of a SySL description. An editing facility is provided as part of the browsing system and helps keep the description consistent during user initiated operations.

Viewing SySL descriptions as Structured Objects

The basic assumption underlying the browsing system is that descriptions written in SySL are not simply text to be processed in a sequential manner but are themselves structured objects. The SySL language processor discussed above is used to translate the SySL description into an internal directed graph representation. Using this graph representation we provide a structured way of presenting the structure and to understanding this structure.

Existing text processing tools such as vi, ex, em, etc, which are provided on the UNIX system, and other similar text editing tools look upon text as a linear sequence of characters; no attempt is made to understand the text. Such tools do not provide a useful basis for program understanding. Language based systems provide a more intelligent means to language understanding [26, 53, 104, 15], etc. They are based around structured editor techniques and build a tree structure representing the user's program. They are useful for detecting errors, such as syntax errors and certain semantic errors, early during the programming phase.

The Smalltalk system browser [43] provides the user with a means of navigating through the class hierarchy. The system provides a top-down approach to viewing the classes, the ability to traverse the class tree does not exist. The SySL browsing system provides a flexible way of moving around the internal graph representation.

Using the directed graph representation generated by the SySL language processor we can use the relationship information recorded in the form of directed links between entities in the graph to provided a powerful description browser. In this section we discuss the features of a language browser, built for the language, which provides the user with a way of navigating around a SySL description. The system allows the user to traverse these relationships between entities in the graph. As well as operations based on the relationships between items the browser has simple text viewing operations which allow the user to move around a SySL description in an unstructured way.

The types of viewing operations which are available are as follows:

- Viewing entity definitions. This allows the user to view the definition of a SySL entity.

- Viewing entity references. It is important to be able to have some idea of the possible affects of a change on the structure of a system. This command allows the user to view those entities in which changes may affect.

- Viewing different component configurations. SySL allows the representation of families of related systems. Therefore, each component in the description may exist in a number of different configurations. This operation allows the user to view each configuration of an entity.

- Analysing component dependencies. Each component in the system has an interface which defines the dependencies between itself and other components. This allows the user to move around each of the dependent components.

- Viewing generic structures. SySL descriptions describe the structure of a system in a top-down manner thus showing the hierarchical decomposition of the system. This operation allows the user to move from a very abstract level of detail to a more specific level of detail and vice-versa.

- Moving through class tree. Similarly classes in a description form a network like structure. The ability to move through such a class network is provided.

- Viewing database representation. This facility is available once the user has bound the SySL description onto the project database name space. Once this has been done the user may view the database representation for such an object.

Structured Editing of SySL descriptions

SySL is used primarily to document structures recorded in the project database. It serves to highlight the dependencies and relationships that exist between components in the database. Therefore, SySL descriptions must be maintained and kept in a consistent state in order for them to be useful and they must document information which is present in the project database. To help with the process of maintaining a system description we have developed an editor which allows the user to edit and change a SySL description and maintain the consistency of the description.

Consider the case where we wish to add a new component description which is a member of the class MOON_WORKSTATION, for example pc_work station. The system would immediately realise that the component pc_work station had not been previously defined and would add details to the class MOON_WORKSTATION. It would then construct from the structure associated with MOON_WORKSTATION a template component description in which the user then instantiates with details about pc_work station.

11.3. THE SYSL TOOLKIT

```
class MOON_WORKSTATION is
(ians_work station, pc_work station)

structure MOON_WORKSTATION : WORKSTATION is
PROCESSOR => (m68010, m68020),
MEMORY => MOON_MEMORY,
BACKPLANE => multibus,
DISPLAY => (monochrome_display, colour_display),
DISK_SYSTEM => (d71Mb, d130Mb, d430Mb, null)
POINTING_DEVICE => OPTICAL_MOUSE,
OPERATING_SYSTEM => (unix4.2bsd, unixsV)
end structure

-- The new component template for pc_work station is as follows

system pc_work station : MOON_WORKSTATION is
PROCESSOR => (m68010, m68020),
MEMORY => MOON_MEMORY,
BACKPLANE => multibus,
DISPLAY => (monochrome_display, colour_display),
DISK_SYSTEM => (d71Mb, d130Mb, d430Mb, null),
POINTING_DEVICE => OPTICAL_MOUSE,
OPERATING_SYSTEM => (unix4.2bsd, unixsV)
end component

-- etc.
```

Figure 11.2: Results of edit on SySL Example

Figure 11.2 displays the result of the above edit on the example given in section 2.

All changes that are made to the SySL description by the user are made directly to the SySL database. The objectives of the SySL editor are as follows:

- Keep the description consistent and complete. Many changes that the user will initiate may involve searching through the description and checking that other parts do not need to be changed as well. For example if we change the interface to a component we wish to check and possibly change any references to such an interface. The editor should assume responsibility for such changes.

- Re-construct the description. Once a change has been made to the SySL database we must update the visual representation of this immediately. Therefore the editor should invoke the description re-construction system to generate the new version of the text incorporating any changes made.

- Check the semantics of changes. Certain changes that the user may invoke may not be consistent with with the description (such as, defining a component of a non-existent class). The editor should make the user aware of the consequences of such changes.

- Assume control of edit after initiated by the user. Immediately after the user has declared the type of edit required and specified the new information, the editor should assume responsibility for updating the components affected and any dependent components. Some changes may involve many smaller changes.

- Use the inheritance features in the language. Some changes can be simplified by using the inheritance features of the language. For example if the user wishes to add a new component which is member of a particular class then the system can deduce the generic structure of the component and sub-components which are already declared. Properties applicable for the parent class can be inherited by the new component.

11.3.3 The SySL Build System

The SySL system building facility allows users to generate the information that is required to build a described system or group of systems. The prototype system generates a UNIX makefile [34] which the user can then run to build the executable system. The UNIX make command, although primitive, does include features which makes it possible to optimise the amount of building required. Make uses timestamping as a method of calculating what has to be recompiled. Generating the makefile, therefore, does remove the need to optimise the building system. It also provides a certain degree of portability and therefore allows us to build target systems, that is, systems that are developed on one machine and run on another system.

There are three important subsystems within the SySL toolkit on which system building is based on.

- A SySL database: this stores the logical representation of the system structure and component dependencies.

- An object name management system: this provides the mapping between the logical representation contained in the database onto the physical representation contained in the project database. The object name management system handles the mapping onto component versions.

- A system build facility: this takes the logical representation and the information contained in the name management system and, using a rule base of translation rules, generates a UNIX makefile. This makefile describes how to build the system which is described in SySL.

Briefly the build system operates as follows. A SySL description of a system represents a logical description of the structure of the system. Each logical item in the SySL description is mapped onto a physical entity in the project database. This mapping must also identify the particular version that is to be used. The SySL language processor generates a logical structure of the system from the textual SySL description. The object name management system allows the user to map entities in

11.3. THE SYSL TOOLKIT

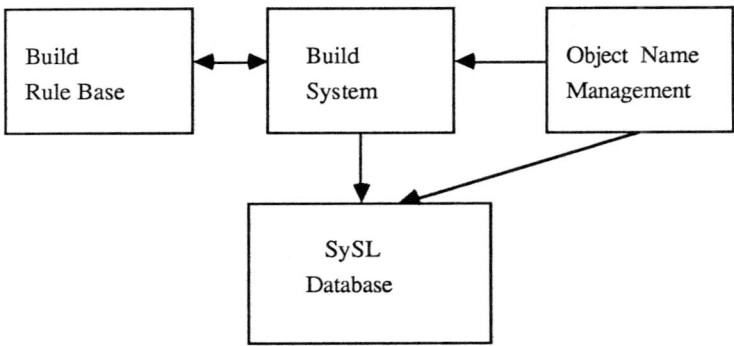

Figure 11.3: Architecture of SySL Builder

this logical structure onto physical entity versions. The build system then takes both the SySL database and the name management information and generates a UNIX makefile from this.

The SySL System Builder

Once all component references between the SySL description and the project database have been resolved the user can then invoke the system building facility provided within the SySL environment. The building facility generates the information required to build the system. The present prototype system (see Figure 11.3) generates UNIX makefiles [34], however the system can be adapted easily to generate other system building commands.

We have already described the purposes of the SySL Database and the object name management system earlier in this chapter. The rule base component in the above diagram contains all the knowledge that the SySL builder needs to know about building the various types of components. Information that is contained here includes the translations which take place, applicable operations, options to be used, etc. The Build system component uses the knowledge contained in rule base together with the component naming information in the object name management system and the dependency information in the SySL database to generate a UNIX makefile. The process of actually compiling each of the components and linking them in the correct order is handled by Make itself.

In providing an automated system building facility there are several important requirements.

- The system should be capable of building any system which can described using SySL. In large software projects SySL will be used to show the interrelationships between software components, documentation, design diagrams, etc., so this is an important requirement.

- Once the information on how to build components of various types has been recorded in the build rule base the user should be freed from having to maintain this information. This contrasts with other systems such as Make [34] and Jasmine [81] in which the user is required to maintain knowledge such as compiler used, options used, etc.

- SySL descriptions are used to describe a class network in which there are inheritance features. In the event that the user wishes to build systems for which building information is absent the system should use the inheritance features of the language to infer the information required to build the system.

An important feature with respect to the building of components is the object type which is an integral part of the object name management system. All objects within the object name management system are of a specific type, for example a standard file, text, source code, executable code, etc. Types can also be project specific. Object types are organised in a hierarchical fashion, from the very general type to a specific type. For example we could have a type called TEXT which has specialisations SOURCE and ENGLISH and the type SOURCE specialisations FORTRAN and C_SOURCE.

Associated with object types are the operations which may be applied to objects of specific types, for example the C language compiler, 'cc', may be applied to objects of type C_SOURCE. Object types provide a degree of type checking in the environment and provide a means of checking the validity of operations applied to certain objects.

Using the above idea of object types and command type checking, we can expand on this and add information about the building process, for example the transformation that takes place when building an object of a certain type. It seems natural to record the above information in the form of a rule base in which facts about various types of components is recorded and rules about how to build them, e.g, the transformations which take place, the options needed and information on how to infer new knowledge from existing information. This rule base forms the basis of the SySL system builder.

11.4 CONCLUSIONS

The language which we have developed appears to be a useful one to describe the structure of complex systems. It has been evaluated by describing hardware, software and documentation systems and is sufficiently general purpose to describe any type of system which may be represented in an Eclipse database.

As in similar systems the usefulness of such a description relies on the user maintaining it. This is dependent on the support provided via software tools. The toolkit which we have build provides the user with powerful facilities for updating the system descriptions and from this to automatically build the system. Therefore the process of generating new releases and new configurations of the system are significantly eased. In terms of providing a means to understand system structure the viewer system is a useful tool.

At the time of writing, an initial version of the SySL system is complete. To demonstrate the ideas we have developed a version of the system building facility which generates UNIX makefiles.

Chapter 12
CDL and its Tools

Frank Bott, Bob Gautier and Mark Ratcliffe

12.1 BACKGROUND

The genesis of the work described in this chapter lies in the idea of exploiting reusable software components to provide a mechanism for fast prototyping. As the Eclipse programme progressed, the software industry's growing interest in reuse caused the emphasis of the work to shift away from fast prototyping towards reuse in a more general context. The arguments in favour of promoting software reuse and the difficulties of achieving it are well known and do not need rehearsing here; see for example [64, 117, 102, 10].

It was known at the start of the project that a number of existing systems claimed to support software reuse and fast prototyping. It was natural, therefore, to start by investigating such systems. The results of this work are reported in [99]. In essence, it appeared that such systems had little to offer in the area of application work, however useful they might be for prototyping or reusing 'computer science' constructs such as abstract data types. There were three exceptions to this. So-called fourth generation languages (4GLs) have shown themselves to be very effective as rapid prototyping tools within the narrow application area they address, even though they may leave much to be desired from the point of view of language design. They provide a mechanism, in effect, for assembling systems by parameterising a fairly small set of complex reusable components — although the normal user of a 4GL would not perceive it in this way. The second exception was a system called RAPID/USE [133]. This includes a method of representing user interaction as a state diagram labelled with actions, from which program skeletons can be generated. While RAPID/USE has many weaknesses and does not directly address many of the problems in which we were interested, it provided the germ of an idea which was developed later in the project. Finally, one or two ideas from OBJ [42] were important in designing the first version of CDL.

12.2 GUIDELINES FOR REUSABILITY

It is clear that aspects of the way a piece of software is written can affect the extent to which the software is reusable. While some of these aspects are obvious, others are much less so. A significant amount of effort was devoted to identifying the factors which affect the reusability of software, with a view to producing guidelines for writing reusable components. It became apparent that Ada offered enormous advantages over other industrially important programming languages from this point of view. It was therefore decided to concentrate on producing guidelines for Ada. The results are embodied in [8]. An overview is given in [39].

We started writing the Ada guidelines without first defining our idea of what a reusable component should look like; as the work progressed, it became clear that component interfaces were very important to us, and that what we were actually doing was capturing ways of defining interfaces in a very implementation independent way, and ways of defining components in terms of those interfaces.

This led to trouble with the Ada language in several areas. Firstly, an Ada package specifies not only its interface but also some parts of its implementation (for example in the package private part); secondly, the generic mechanism for parameterising a component does not allow a group of types, functions and procedures (in fact, a package) to treated as a single parameter.

Problems such as these caused us much soul-searching, because we felt that Ada was best language available for writing reusable components, and, as we were running into difficulties, either Ada had to be inadequate or our approach was wrong. Examination of current work in component design and programming languages eventually convinced us that most of the trouble lay with Ada.

The guidelines we produced encouraged programmers to write Ada that would often be very verbose and which, we had to concede, would not in fact be very reusable, as a result of its verbosity and the sheer tedium of interfacing to it.

We tried to encourage construction of components implementing abstract data types, and our guidelines were aimed at strengthening the barrier between the abstraction defined by the component interface, and its implementation. We looked at the possibilities open to a component implementor and tried to come up with an interface style that would allow as many of them as possible. For example, since we felt that any abstract data type might be implemented using heap storage, we suggested that all interfaces should include a deallocation operation, which for many components would be a no-op. Sometimes, the obvious way of allowing all possible implementations was clearly counterproductive, and instead we appealed to a need for purity of abstraction to motivate our guidelines. An example of this appears in our guidelines for operation parameter mode choice, where we insist that parameter modes must be chosen in accordance with the effect that an operation has on the *abstract* value of a parameter, not the effect that some implementation may have on the *representation* of that value. This guideline increases implementation hiding, at some expense to the implementor, who as a result will often have to resort to dirty tricks in order to comply with parameter modes defined in an interface.

12.3 THE COMPONENT DESCRIPTION LANGUAGE (CDL)

As a result of the work done on the Ada guidelines, it was realised that, despite its strengths, Ada suffered from a number of deficiencies as a language for describing and

12.3. THE COMPONENT DESCRIPTION LANGUAGE (CDL)

using reusable components. For example, the fact that a generic package cannot take another package as a generic parameter leads to verbose and repetitious code. It was felt that the generation of such code could very profitably be automated and that some of the 'programming by pictures' ideas from RAPID/USE could be adapted to support this.

12.3.1 CDL Version 1

CDL stands for Component Description Language; in essence it is a language for describing interfaces and treats interfaces as first class objects. Since it regards components as being constructed recursively from other components, it also serves as a component design language. The first version of CDL was heavily influenced by MASCOT 3 (see chapter 9) and by OBJ [42] and was syntactically untidy. However, it fulfilled its purpose as a vehicle for demonstrating the feasibility of the ideas and for exploring how they might be developed. This version of CDL is described fully in [38] and more briefly in [40].

Our objective in designing CDL was to build a new language, which would provide a syntactically cleaner way of following the guidelines, and in which conformance with the guidelines would be either more convenient than in pure Ada, or better still, simply impossible to avoid.

The main source of inspiration for CDL was MASCOT 3, which was then undergoing its final review. A significant advance over its predecessor, this new version offered almost exactly the features that we were looking for, by means of a design language in which interfaces could be defined independently of components, and components could be defined in terms of the interfaces they used and provided. The MASCOT 2 entities called *activities, channels and pools* are retained in MASCOT 3, but these can now possess *windows*, which indicate the *provision* of a specific interface, and *ports*, which indicate a *requirement* for a given interface. Since activities are active, they may have only ports, whilst channels and pools, being passive, may have only windows.

MASCOT 3 also introduced hierarchical construction of components from others, and a new diagram construct to represent it, the subsystem. In MASCOT 3, any part of a diagram can be encapsulated in a subsystem, which can then be embedded in a larger diagram, where it will communicate with the rest of the network only by means of ports and windows. Since a subsystem can encapsulate both active and passive entities (as well as other subsystems), a subsystem may possess both ports and windows.

Although MASCOT 3 met our needs well, we did not want to commit ourselves to many of the details of the MASCOT semantics and we needed to be free to define and extend the design language in ways natural to the Ada programmer. Although inspired by MASCOT, in the end we used very little of it. We designed our own language syntax (with disastrous results, at least initially!), and discarded most of the diagram representation, retaining only the subsystems. This was because we felt that it should not be necessary for any component to publish its structure completely, so that all components should be adequately represented to their users as subsystems; activities would be subsystems possessing only ports, whilst channels and pools would be subsystems possessing only windows. We also shifted the emphasis on the function of ports away from their role in allowing flexible configuration of a system, and towards a role as mechanisms for parameterisation of components. It then became more natural to describe all components as subsystems with both ports and windows.

Our final technical departure from MASCOT 3 needs some background from our other main source of inspiration, the OBJ language [42]. OBJ comes from a world rather different to that of MASCOT 3; it is an algebraic logic programming language, with semantics based on rewrite rules. Nevertheless, it shares many ideas with MASCOT. Interface definitions, called theories in OBJ, are used to state requirements on components which may be provided as parameters to other components (known as objects in OBJ, hence the name of the language). The components themselves, however, do not name the interfaces they provide; instead, each component states its interface explicitly, and the interfaces of components are related to the theories by means of constructs known as views, which state mappings from component interfaces to theories, and may also be used to state mappings from one theory to another. It was the concept of a view that we wanted to capture in CDL, because it was a step in the direction of "gluing" together components whose interfaces do not match exactly. We saw views as special types of component which captured knowledge about how to adapt one interface to another, and which could be inserted between otherwise incompatible components to make them work together. This gave us our last adjustment to MASCOT 3. In a MASCOT 3 diagram, interconnected components must use the same interface, so a connection is labelled with the interface used on that connection (perhaps more naturally, the "protocol" of the connection). For CDL, we associated the interfaces with the ports and windows of components, not with connections, and introduced the concept of a view, a transformation from one interface to another, which could be placed on a connection to adapt the interface provided by the window end to the interface required by the port end.

In designing the first version of CDL from this mixture of ideas we made little attempt to disguise its pedigree; the result was clearly the offspring of MASCOT and OBJ, abandoned at an early age and raised by Ada. The new language was christened with the unremarkable name of CDL, for Component Description Language, but is always 'cuddle' to its friends. A set of prototype tools was implemented: a component librarian, a syntax checker and a diagram editor, all of which were demonstrated at the Alvey Conference in Brighton in July 1986. They are described in more detail below.

As for the language itself, with the benefit of hindsight and a couple of years more experience, its flaws seem countless, but as an experiment intended to help us develop our ideas it was a great success.

12.3.2 CDL Version 2

Our experience with CDL version 1 uncovered many restrictions, whilst at the same time indicating that the language was too complicated; there were too many basic concepts used to build the language.

A new language was designed, which, although it had the same basic aim of encouraging production of reusable components by reuse of interfaces, was conceptually much simpler, and syntactically cleaner. This language also addressed some of the areas of Ada that had not been covered by the first version, such as exceptions.

The simplification has allowed us to be more confident of producing a complete

12.3. THE COMPONENT DESCRIPTION LANGUAGE (CDL)

and reliable implementation.

CDL version 2 is fully described in [41].

The most obvious failing in version 1 of CDL was its syntax, which was much less verbose than Ada, but which was still clumsy, and used reserved words that were inappropriate to its users, factors which could make tutorials and presentations on the language little short of embarrassing.

Also, in writing the checking and Ada conversion tools we discovered many awkward issues in the semantics of the language, few of which were resolved during its lifetime. We ended up with an incomplete implementation of those parts of the language we felt we understood!

Finally, and most usefully, we discovered deeper flaws in the approach supported by CDL. We found that in allowing components to provide more than one interface we effectively had an interface composition mechanism, which could produce anonymous interfaces. To avoid this, it was necessary to define a new interface (theory) for each component, and then define each component as having only one window, providing that interface. Also, the explicit parameterisation mechanism in CDL meant that the designer of a component had to decide in advance which components were to be imported via parameters, and which would be bound permanently into the component. To avoid this restriction would have led to very verbose CDL, in the way that earlier attempts to write reusable components had led to verbose Ada.

With these problems in mind, we set out to redesign CDL, treating the first language entirely as a throw-away prototype, and putting rather more care into this second version. The first CDL was designed and implemented in about three months; by the time it was demonstrated in Brighton, the main features of the second version were taking shape, but it took more than a year for the new language to stabilise, a process which itself included some major revisions.

The new language offers a set of operators for building interfaces from smaller ones, and does away with the distinction between a component and an interface, allowing the designer to reference a CDL object either as a component (to use it in another) or as an interface (when a component will provide that interface). This makes it possible to say things like "This component is a new implementation of that component" without being forced to define separately the interface to the first component. Removal of this problem also makes the language much smaller.

Version 2 of CDL avoids the difficulties of explicit parameterisation by allowing all references from one component to another to be re-bound at will, by means of a general purpose rewriting operator. As a result, CDL no longer has a construct to parameterise a component by another, because all references to other components are treated as potential parameters, but are defaulted if no substitution is made.

The concept of a view, as a special language entity, has also been dropped, and the job of a view can now be performed by any suitable component.

The result of all these changes is a smaller, more elegant language which is much more powerful than the first attempt, but of which we can be much more confident of achieving a complete and reliable implementation.

Unfortunately, the flexibility in this new language has exceeded our ingenuity in writing Ada generics, so the Ada mapping produces non-generic components interconnected by 'with' clauses. In effect, our preprocessor performs generic instantiation prior to compilation, leading to large, possibly inefficient Ada programs. This indicates that CDL is close to (or possibly already beyond) the limit of worthwhile extensions to Ada.

12.4 THE CDL TOOL SET

A diagrammatic representation of CDL was developed showing components as nodes on a directed graph and interconnections between components as arcs of the graph. A diagram editor (CDE) was developed to manipulate this representation on a Sun work station; it provided facilities to insert or delete connections, to move components, to introduce new components from the library, to zoom into a component to see how it was constructed from smaller components or to zoom out to raise the level of abstraction.

A translator was also developed which would generate Ada package specifications for a complete system starting from the diagrammatic representation of the system as a component made up of smaller components.

These tools were demonstrated on the Eclipse stand at the Alvey Conferences in 1986 and 1987. Full descriptions of the tools are given in [38] and [101].

The facilities of CDE, although perhaps novel in operation are not new and are common to most diagram editors. CDE is different from other editors in that it was designed to support reuse. Full interaction with the component library is supported by the editor to facilitate and encourage reuse of library components. Prior to creating new components, the user can browse the library to determine what components are already available.

The main objects manipulated on the diagram are diagrammatic representations of Ada package specifications. Components can be composite, enabling the user to carry out a hierarchical decomposition of the system into smaller, more manageable units. In this way, components can be 'opened up' using the zoom facility in order to inspect their internal composition.

As with CDL, the most important concept within CDE is the separation of interfaces from the component in which they occur. Most components required (imported) certain interfaces in order to implement (export) others. In CDE, the requirements of a component were represented as ports while the operations offered were represented as windows.

The interfaces associated with ports and windows were the key to reuse within CDL and this was reflected by further automatic facilities provided by the editor. These facilities included the automatic inference of interfaces, when connections were made between ports and windows, as well as a system whereby compatibility between components could be maintained. If, for example, two incompatible interfaces were connected, the editor was capable of recognising the problem and would automatically create a component to resolve the incompatibility.

Other tools provided with the initial tool set included a component librarian and a CDL to Ada translator. The component librarian provided a textual equivalent of the diagram editor enabling the user to browse the library, retrieving or creating new CDL components and their associated interfaces. The translator could then be invoked to generate Ada package specifications for a complete system using the textual or diagrammatic representations that had been created.

Only a limited degree of integration with the rest of Eclipse was possible with the

12.4. THE CDL TOOL SET

tools supporting the first version of CDL. The Eclipse message system and standard control panel were used but there was no integration with the database because many of the tools were written before the design of this was finalised. For the tool set to support the second version of CDL, integration with Eclipse, in particular with the database, was seen as essential.

The tools to support the second version of CDL are similar in nature to the earlier tools, although their functionality is greater and they support a more powerful language. They are described in [100]. Their implementation, however, is very different, since they are implemented using the Eclipse PTI (Public Tools Interface). The whole philosophy of Eclipse demands that the tools for the second version of CDL should be properly integrated and there are, indeed, many advantages in doing this.

The implementation of the current CDL tool set has therefore followed the same approach as that taken by for the MASCOT tool set (see Chapter 9). All of the tools have been built on Eclipse with the generic design editor providing the main editing facilities.

The main design decisions for the second implementation, revolved around the component library which was implemented as a single database to be used by all CDL tools. As the design of the new CDL tool set progressed, the suitability of the Eclipse two tier system became very apparent. The component library was specified using the Eclipse DDL and then mapped onto PCTE. In this way it is possible to integrate all the tools, not just the design editor, into the system. Currently as well as CDE, the tools include a textual browser for the library and a CDL to Ada translator.

For reasons of efficiency, the fine structure of the diagram objects were not specified in PCTE; instead, these objects were further refined by defining IDLE schemas. Together with the top level DDL, these schemas were then used to instantiate the generic diagram editor to form the new implementation of CDE.

One disadvantage of using large generic tools such as the diagram editor is that the functionality is often restricted to very basic operations. The Eclipse design editor, however, allows functionality to be added through the inclusion of method specific code. Consequently, the new CDL tool set has been able to retain the facilities for encouraging reuse which were defined for the original editor.

Using Eclipse to its full advantage, the CDL system has been developed into a fully integrated tool set that is compatible with the rest of Eclipse. In the same way that a user invokes the MASCOT and LSDM tool sets, access to the CDL tools is through a Masterwindow available from the main Eclipse window.

Prior to invoking the tools, the user is requested to specify a library which is to be used. In this way, CDE is able to support a number of separate component libraries, the use of which is left to the discretion of the user. Having selected a library, the user can browse through it either textually or diagrammatically using CDE. Once within the tool, all the usual diagram editing facilities for creating or manipulating components are made available to the user. In addition there are also facilities for the textual specifications of components, generation of CDL text and translation to Ada. All of these latter tools are available from within the editor. Using the current CDL tool set, complete software systems can be developed quickly and in a way that encourages reuse.

The development of the CDL tool set has abundantly demonstrated the value of Eclipse as a tool building environment. The Aberystwyth team were the first real off-site users of Eclipse and the exercise proved invaluable to all parties.

12.5 CONCLUSIONS

CDL and its tool set have attracted considerable attention (as, indeed, have the Ada Reuse Guidelines). They offer a mechanism for designing large Ada systems at the component level, which encourages the reuse of existing components but is also applicable in an environment in which most (or even all) components have to be designed from scratch. The automatic generation of code is time saving and avoids abortive compilations. Both the level of sophistication and the technology used make the tools suitable for application in present day industrial environments; no similar tools are currently available. Commercial exploitation is therefore under active consideration.

On a more theoretical level, CDL demonstrates both the feasibility and the value of treating interfaces as first class objects.

Our view of CDL has evolved significantly since it was first conceived. We no longer view the textual form of CDL as being in some sense the primary form, with the diagrammatic representation as simply an aid to design. Rather, we regard the database structure as primary and the textual and diagrammatic forms as representations which may be used to help in editing the database. From this point of view, there is no reason why the user should not be permitted to extend or modify these representations. Indeed, we feel that if the use of reusable components is to be extended into a wide variety of application fields, it is essential that the user have this ability; otherwise, piecemeal extensions to CDL will continue to be necessary indefinitely. We are continuing to work on a system called JARGON to support this. It will also provide proper support for higher-order components, i.e. components, such as 4GL processors or syntax analyser generators, which generate other components.

Chapter 13

A Software Components Catalogue

[1] Ian Sommerville and Murray Wood

13.1 INTRODUCTION

The reuse of software components which have been developed in previous projects is one of those motherhood principles which is generally espoused but little practised, except in very specific areas of software development. There are powerful economic arguments for reusing an existing component rather than reinventing that component anew and [7] has suggested that we will only see very significant improvements in software productivity when software reuse is widely practised. Not only does the reuse of an existing component reduce the development cost of a software system, it should also reduce the testing costs as, presumably, that component has already been tested in some other system.

Given, therefore, that reuse is widely accepted as a 'good thing' and that it has a clear economic benefit, why then is it not more widely practised, particularly in the development of large and complex software systems? The reasons why software reuse is the exception rather than the rule are partly technical, partly human and partly a consequence of the way in which software is procured. In summary, the human problems are a result of the fact that software development is seen as a highly skilled activity and reuse implies some kind of deskilling; the economic problems are a result of the difficulties of deciding who owns an intangible object like a software component when that component is developed by X for Y.

Leaving aside these non-technical problems of software reuse, the technical problems of reusing software may be summarised as follows:

- It is more expensive and difficult to develop a generalised component for potential reuse than it is to develop a specific component for a specific system. Indeed, as relatively little software reuse is practiced, we don't really know what characteristics of a software component lead to or militate against future reuse of that component.

---

[1]The text of this chapter first appeared as [137]

- There are no effective catalogues of existing software components apart from ad hoc lists provided with specific systems such as UNIX. Where such lists exist, only very simple keyword-based retrieval systems are provided to assist the user in finding the required component.

- The nature of software components and system requirements is such that in many cases a software component is almost but not ideally suited for a particular task. Whether or not that component can be reused depends largely on the difficulty of modifying that component.

The work described here has concentrated on the problem of building a software component information base and an associated system to retrieve component descriptions from that information base.

The principal objective of our work was to develop a system which would retrieve information about software components for potential component reusers. The overheads of using such a system must be low and it must be usable by software engineers without specialist information retrieval training.

Our initial approach to software component retrieval centered around a hierarchic (enumerative) classification scheme. This initial experimentation highlighted a number of difficulties in describing software components in terms of individual keywords. Fundamentally individual keywords do not provide an accurate description of the software components 'purpose'. We also found it difficult to control the amount of information returned by this approach. At one extreme excessive information is returned due to the use of a general keyword classification; at the other little or no information is returned due to a mismatch in the user's and classifier's keywords. A further weakness of the hierarchic classification approach is that they do not cope well with changing data and are dependent on the availability of natural, well-defined classes. It is not clear whether or not well-defined classes exist for software components.

The work described in this paper takes a different approach to the development of a component cataloguing system. The classification and retrieval system is based on ideas derived from natural language processing where an attempt is made to understand the semantics of a component description or retrieval request. This gets round many of the problems of classifier and retriever using different keywords to describe a component yet allows the same term to be used to represent differ concepts. The system is implemented in Prolog on a Sun work station.

In designing a component catalogue or, indeed, any reuse support system, there are a number of factors which must be taken into account.

- Should the system be specific to a particular application domain?

- Should the system be specific to a particular design method or programming language?

- Should the system be stand-alone or part of an IPSE?

- Should the system be supported or unsupported. A supported system is one where some individual has a specific responsibility to maintain the component information base. He or she controls which components are entered into the system. In an unsupported system, users enter components into the catalogue.

The target user for our system was a software house which did not specialise in any particular application domain, method or language. It was intended that the system should be supported and that it should be integrated with an Eclipse. This meant that we had to devise a very general representation for cataloguing components as they could be drawn from a variety of application domains, could be developed using different methods and to different standards and could be implemented in almost any programming language. However, it also meant we could concentrate on retrieval tools with less effort devoted to the problems of cataloguing. Integration with an IPSE (Eclipse) meant that the component documentation was available in the IPSE database and that this information need not be maintained in the catalogue.

13.2 CLASSES OF SOFTWARE COMPONENT

The first thing that we have to do in setting up a software components catalogue is to decide what we mean by a reusable component. We have identified six types of reusable component. Notice that we use familiar terms but their meaning is somewhat more constrained than when such terms are used for programming language constructs. These classes are:

1. **Functions** A function is a stand-alone component which is an abstraction over an expression. It is evaluated from within an expression and its value is not dependent on its evaluation environment but only on the value of its parameter or parameters. Notice that functions in most programming languages may or may not fall under this definition depending whether or not they make use of external values in their evaluation.

2. **Procedures and value-returning procedures** A procedure is a component which is an abstraction over a set of statements although value returning procedures which may be used in expressions are also provided in some programming languages. Apart from the obvious difference that a function is used in an expression and a procedure as a statement, a critical distinction from the reuser's point of view is that a procedure is dependent on its environment and execution of the procedure causes some change to the environment. Value-returning procedures are something of a hybrid in that they are used, like functions in expressions and return a value yet are dependent on the environment in which they are used.

3. **Declaration packages** A declaration package is a component which is an abstraction over a set of declarations. This type of component is relatively little used as most programming languages do not provide a facility to encapsulate and name a set of declarations. Ada is an exception in this respect and this type of component is almost essential if procedures are to be reused — the environment required by the procedure to be reused is set up and named in the declaration package.

4. **Objects** An object is an abstraction over a variable where the object is made up of both the variable value and the allowed operations on that variable. Effectively, the object conceals the variable and the object interface is a set of procedures

or functions which are used to update or interrogate the variable value. Direct access to the value of the variable is forbidden.

5. **Abstract data types** An abstract data type is an abstraction over a type where the abstract type is made up of the type representation and a set of access and update procedures to objects of that type. Objects are normally created by declaring names to be of some abstract data type.

6. **Sub-systems** A sub-system is an abstraction over a program and it may be made up of components in classes 1 to 5 above and other sub-systems. Sub-systems are normally represented as processes but in strictly sequential systems, may be implemented as procedures.

We are not concerned with the reuse of entire application systems or operating systems within some other system. Whilst this is clearly a very cost-effective form of reuse (for example, it must almost always be cheaper to reuse rather than rewrite a database management system), we consider this to be more a problem of standardisation rather than reuse.

13.3 COMPONENT INFORMATION BASE

Automated support for software reuse is critically dependent on the availability of a component information base where all information pertaining to components and their reuse is maintained. This includes cataloguing attributes, component documentation and code and information about which systems have reused components. There must be tool support for retrieving information about particular components, adding new components to the information base and browsing through the available components to see if a suitable part is available.

We are particularly concerned with retrieving component information and, typically, a request for component information is made in two stages.

1. Access the component catalogue to see if components are available which may be reused. The user, typically, wants a small number of 'catalogue hits' at this stage.

2. Examine the documentation for each potentially reusable component to see if it is reusable without modification, reusable with modification or unsuitable.

The initial catalogue access should be straightforward and should not require the use of a complex query language (one of the major drawbacks to the use of bibliographic retrieval systems). The time taken to determine if any possible component is available should be short. It should not be necessary for the user to have developed a detailed component specification but he or she should be able to find possible components with only an approximate idea of the components function.

This latter facility is important if reuse is to be exploited. There is little point in a reuse system requiring a developer to write a detailed formal specification and then finding that no components match that specification. Rather, if a component which meets an approximate specification is available, it may be possible to adjust the detailed specification so that that component can be reused.

13.3. COMPONENT INFORMATION BASE

The work described here is concerned with this initial catalogue access so we have not been involved in trying to establish what documentation is needed in a reuse system, how reuse metrics can be derived and so on. Neither have we paid much attention to the problem of providing the catalogue librarian with tool support although it is now clear that this is a major problem which must be resolved in a fully developed system.

13.3.1 The cataloguing system

The primary requirement of the components catalogue is the ability to match users requests for software components onto descriptions of software components which satisfy these requests. Since software components have the property that they are flexible (their code or designs may be adjusted) the system must also have the capacity to match requests onto components which only partially satisfy the requirements and which, with alteration may be of use.

A second requirement is that the system should be usable with the minimum of training by any software engineer. If a large amount of effort is spent in training then the benefits from reuse are reduced; if this effort is comparable to the effort of writing the software from scratch then reuse will not be practised. We feel that this requirement rules out formal specification as a method of software component description and request specification. (There are two further problems in using formal specification as a method of software requirement description. Firstly, we cannot show in all cases that two syntactically different but semantically similar specifications describe the same component and, secondly, it is difficult to envisage formal rules to enable incomplete matching of components, that is, what is a close match between two formal specifications?).

The final requirement of the components catalogue is that the system should be extensible. Since the software development process covers a very wide range of application areas it is impractical to construct a demonstrable system that utilises software components from all areas. The methods used for component representation should be such that they can be applied without change to software components from similar domains and readily extended to handle new application domains.

Initially, we have concentrated on building a catalogue of components for classes 1 to 5 above, and of establishing a retrieval mechanism for such components. Although the economic benefits of reusing larger-scale components such as those from class 6 are obvious, there are great problems in classifying and retrieving such components. These components tend to be described in specific terminology. For example, say a user requests a 'tokeniser', ideally the components catalogue would know that this is more or less what the lexical analysis phase of a compiler does and that such a component would fulfil the user's requirement. To handle such components the catalogue must incorporate some semantic knowledge about how a component is used and about the component's logical function.

13.3.2 Component Knowledge Representation

Our aim in developing the catalogue was to produce a system which was easier to use and offered better information retrieval than keyword-based systems. This suggested that we required to find some effective means of representing knowledge about the software components. Natural language understanding / question-answering systems provide a mechanism for representation of natural language concepts, known as conceptual dependency. The fundamental idea behind conceptual dependency may be applied in a simplified way to the representation of software component descriptions and software component requests.

Lehnert [72] states

> Conceptual dependency is a representational system that encodes the meaning of sentences by decomposition into a small set of primitive actions.

The core of such an approach is a number of fundamental concepts which are sufficient to capture the semantics of any domain of interest. Schank [107] lists three types of concept — nominals, actions, and modifiers.

Nominals are considered to be things that can be thought of by themselves without the need of relating them to some other concept e.g. duck, book, New York, file, bit, etc. An action is that which a nominal can be said to be doing. There are certain basic actions which are the core of most verbs in a language. A modifier is a descriptor of the nominal or action to which it relates and serves to specify an attribute of that nominal or action e.g adverbs and adjectives. Each of these conceptual categories can relate in specified ways to each other. These relations are called dependencies.

A similar approach has been adopted by Waltz [132, 131]. He has implemented a natural language front end to a database using stereotypical structures known as concept case frames. Each concept case frame consists of the act (typically related to the verb) and a list of noun phrases which can meaningfully occur with the act. Each act covers a number of related verbs. These frames are used as tools to build a query to the database by filling in the slots of the template with information extracted from the current request, earlier requests, world knowledge and default values.

A practical realisation of this approach involves an analysis of the problem domain resulting in the distinct conceptual actions that can occur, the distinct conceptual objects that are acted on and the modifiers which describe these actions and objects. These are then related in the form of conceptual case frames for each action which have slots which specify objects that are meaningfully manipulated by the action in the domain of interest. In Waltz's system a natural language parser maps the verbs in textual input onto the conceptual actions and nouns onto the object slots.

An example is the conceptual action PTRANS which represents the transfer of physical location of an object. PTRANS has object slots requiring an actor, an object, an origin and a destination. The sentence "Jill took the disk from the drive" would map onto a concept case frame representing the PTRANS action as follows:

13.3. COMPONENT INFORMATION BASE

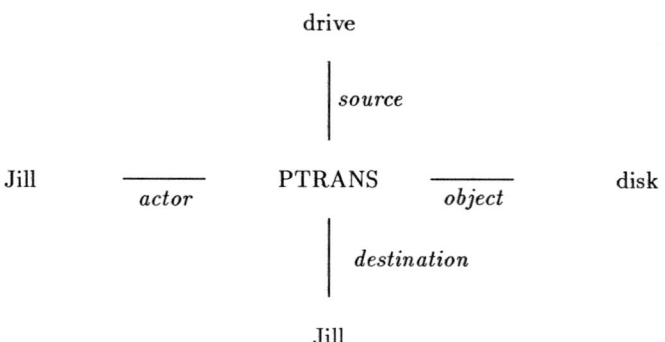

This would form the system's internal representation of the sentence capturing the semantics of the act to put. If the sentence had been "Jill removed the disk from the drive", the meaning would be the same. However, a sentence such as "John removed the file" would not be considered as a physical transfer as the term 'removed' has a different meaning in this context, namely deletion.

13.3.3 Component Descriptor Frames

Within the restricted natural language domain of software component descriptions there are only a limited number of basic concepts. Following Schank we can separate three fundamental types of concept — action, nominal and modifier. Actions correspond to the basic, fundamental functions that software components perform. Nominals correspond to the objects that perform the function (the software component itself), objects that the function manipulate, objects produced as a result of the function and objects that provide a context for the action. Modifiers describe actions and nominals. Corresponding to dependency relations or conceptual case frames we have our own *component descriptor frames*.

There is a component descriptor frame for each basic function that software performs, based around the action, with slots for the objects manipulated by the component. Since, in general, software components perform a function and furthermore it is this function which characterises the software component, a representation scheme which captures the function provides a sound foundation for the description of software components, the description of software component requirements and the matching of the two.

This is confirmed by the work of Prieto-Diaz [98] in his classification scheme for software. When considering descriptors for software components after a study of software descriptions he concludes "Program listings are characterised by describing the function performed by the program ...". He then goes on to use the function and the objects that are manipulated by the function as a basis for a software classification scheme.

A components catalogue based on these ideas requires an analysis of the software component domain resulting in a set of basic functions for software. There is a direct relationship between verbs in software descriptions and the basic functions of software components. There should be one basic function for each 'classification' of conceptually similar verbs, that is, verbs that describe semantically similar software functions. An example of conceptually similar verbs might be search, look and find. Also required is a classification of the objects manipulated by software component into classes or 'nominals' that represent conceptually similar objects. An example of a nominal might be file_part, that is objects that are parts of a file, typical members of this nominal classification are line, word, pattern, etc.

Having decided on the basic functions of the software component domain it is necessary to develop a set of component descriptor frames. For each recognised basic function of software there is such a frame which relates the objects to the function. In our classification of UNIX system components, we identified 25 basic functions such as control, communicate, search, etc. Other work, carried out in a different application domain (aerospace engineering systems), identified 10 actions of which approximately 40system domain.

Each frame has a variable number of slots, the number is dependent on the meaning of the function. For any software component function all or only some of the slots need be filled. In our current domain the number of object slots ranges from two to four. For example, the control function has two slots, the component itself and the object that is controlled. Diagrammatically the control function frame is:

$$\text{COMPONENT} \xrightarrow{actor} \text{action\_control} \xrightarrow{object\ that\ is\ controlled} \text{OBJECT}$$

An example of a UNIX command which is catalogued as a control function is the 'kill' command:

$$\text{kill} \xrightarrow{actor} \text{action\_control} \xrightarrow{object\ that\ is\ controlled} \text{process}$$

The print function has three slots, the component itself, the object that is printed and the object that is the destination for the print:

13.3. COMPONENT INFORMATION BASE

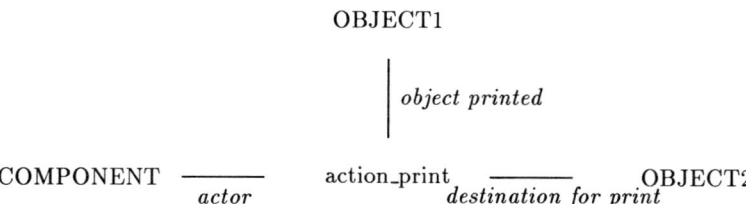

An example of a UNIX command which is classified as a print function is the 'more' utility which lists files on the user's terminal:

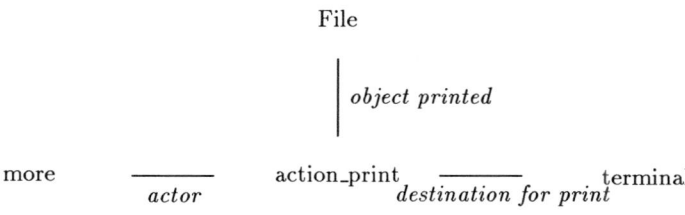

The communication function has four slots, the component itself, the object that is communicated, an object that is the source of what is communicated and an object that is the destination for what is communicated:

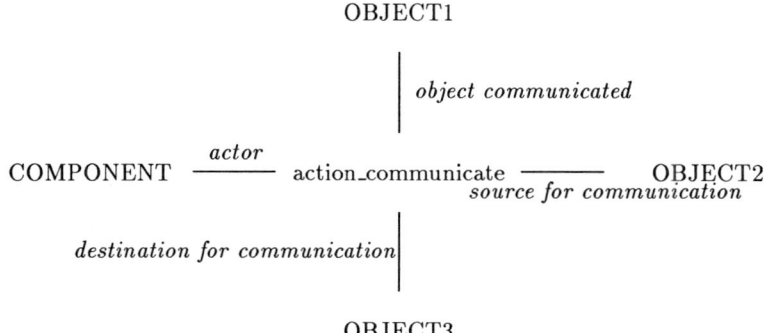

For example, the UNIX mail command is classified as a communication function:

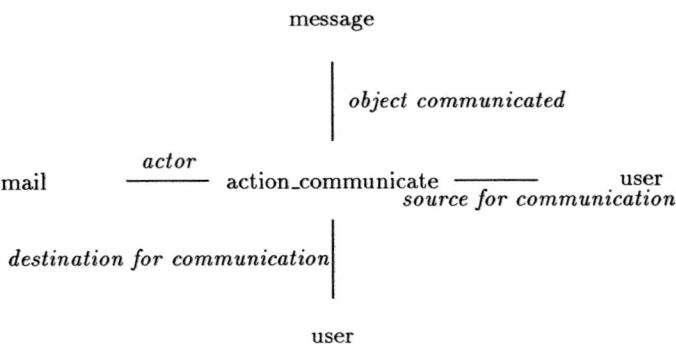

The conceptual action of 'searching' has three slots — one for the actor carrying out the search, the software component itself, one for the object that is being searched and one for any object that is being searched for. A completed component descriptor frame that captures the function of the UNIX software component 'grep', which can be described by the phrase 'searches a file for a specified pattern', is:

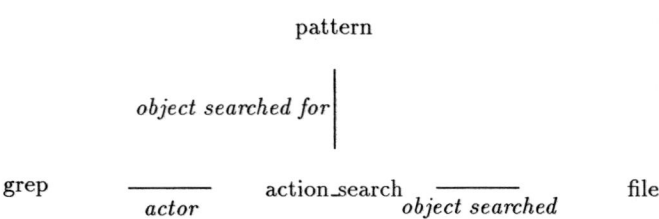

Thus the actor is the software component called 'grep', the object being searched is a 'file' and the object being searched for is a 'pattern'. The representation also includes an optional link for descriptors of objects and actions. For example a hypothetical component called 'fast_grep' that uses a binary chop to search an ordered file would be represented as:

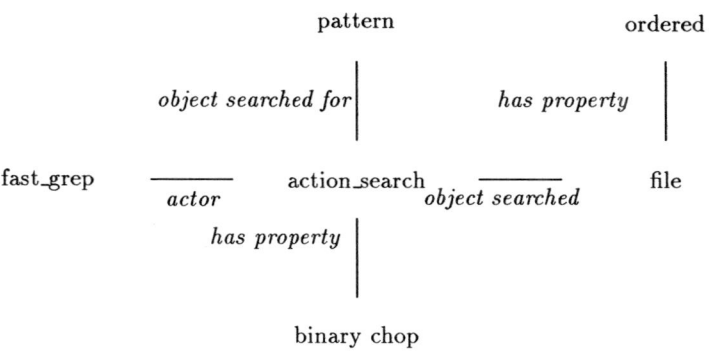

13.3.4 The Catalogue User Interface

The interface to the catalogue is forms-based and is usable without any special training. The system initiates construction of a component descriptor frame representing the request by prompting the user, either for a verb describing the action the component performs, or a noun representing an object manipulated by the component. If the user inputs a verb the system finds a skeleton frame corresponding to the action which conceptualises the verb.

For each frame slot there is a corresponding prompt which the system displays to the user in search of objects that are manipulated by the component. If the request is initiated with an object the user is then prompted for a verb which describes the way in which the object is manipulated. During the request building process the system can be asked for help regarding appropriate responses. The system uses partially completed frames to search the data base collecting together all the known values for 'slots' yet to be filled. These are then displayed to the user for use in responding to the remaining prompts.

An example of the request building process is shown in Figure 12.1. The example shows a window-based interface to the component catalogue running on a Sun work station using the utility program section of the UNIX manual as our experimental catalogue.

The main component catalogue interface tool is shown in the top window, the resulting retrieved components in the bottom window. The main menu is the bottom-left panel (rectangle) in the interface tool. In a previous menu in the session the user has specified that the verb 'send' characterises the function of the required component. The system shows this verb together with its conceptual classification 'communicate' in the text at the top of the menu. The fields in the menu are prompts for objects normally associated with the communicate action — object communicated, source of communication, destination for communication. There are also fields for descriptors of the action and objects, if applicable.

The panel at the right displays known keywords for the menu field at which the cursor/caret is currently placed. Hence bug, date, etc. are known keywords for objects that are communicated. The user can select and stuff these keywords into the menu

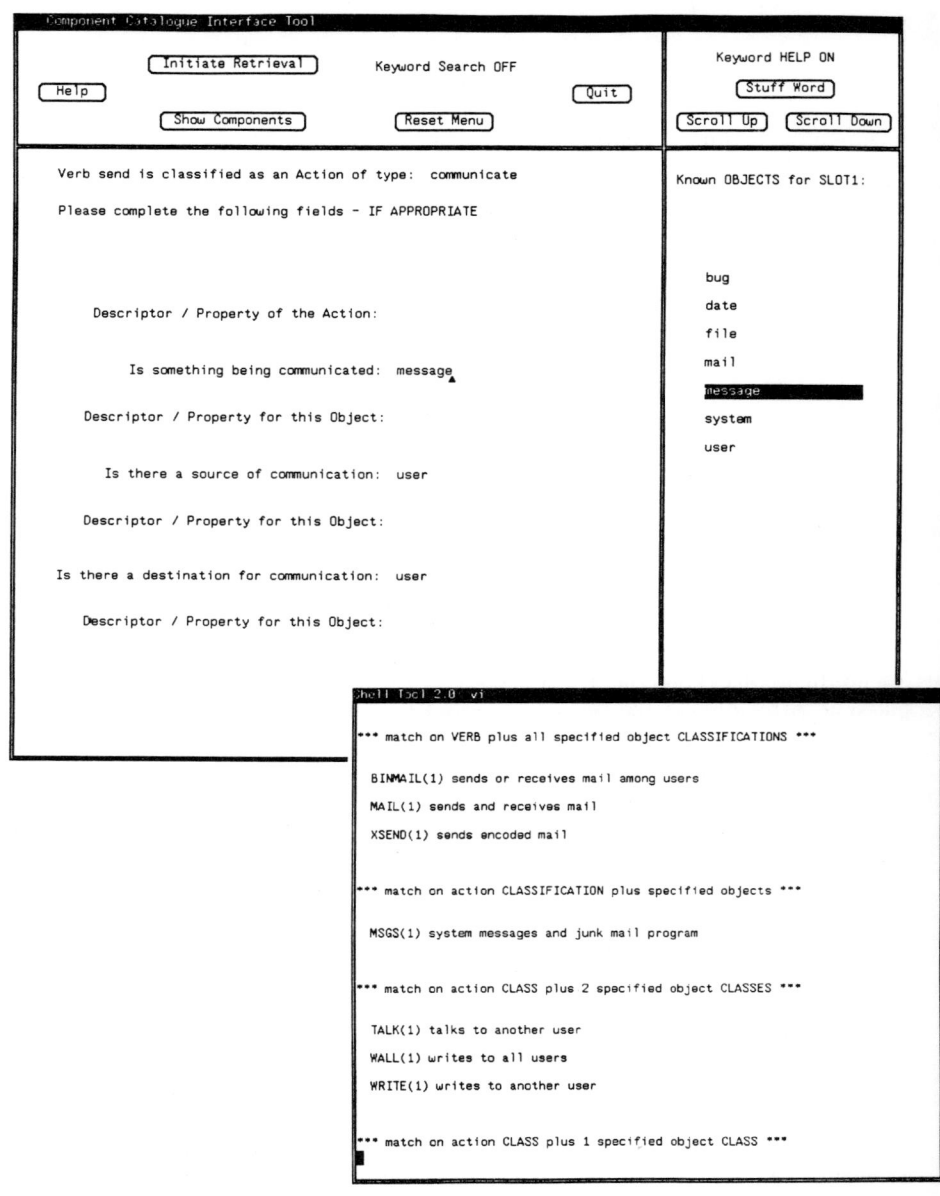

Figure 13.1: The Component Catalogue Interface

13.3. COMPONENT INFORMATION BASE

if they are appropriate for their requirements. This facility is particularly useful since by using known terminology it guarantees that at least one component description will be retrieved.

When the menu is completed to user satisfaction the 'initiate retrieval' button is selected. This causes formation of a software function frame representing the users requirements and initiation of a search to find an ordered set of matches between the request and the component representations in the catalogue.

As requests and descriptions have the same internal representation, namely component descriptor frames, using Prolog's built-in control and search mechanisms means the matching process is only dependent on rules for the best-match of the two. An exact match is required if possible. This is implemented by looking for components that are described using the same verb and nouns as the user specifies. Thereafter a match is sought of actions instead of verbs, then nominals instead of nouns, then, if multiple object slots are filled, single object matches are sought and finally just matches of action or object alone.

In the retrieved components window the components are ordered according to how well they match the users request. The first three components shown are all described using the same verb as the request (send) and for each of the menu fields for which the user has chosen to specify an object, are described using objects that are in the same conceptual classification as the users. For example 'mail' is in the same conceptual class as 'message'. The component 'MSGS' is ranked as a lesser match as it matched on only the conceptual classification of the verb but on all the specified objects. Thereafter 3 components are shown which match on only 2 of the specified object classes (they all communicate between users). The search retrieves all components with a better than keyword-only match. If the 'Keyword Search' switch was changed to ON the search could be forced down to keyword only.

13.3.5 Non-Functional Component Representation

Component descriptor frames have explicit slots for describing primitive functional components. However, earlier in this paper we identified other types of software component such as objects, abstract data-types and sub-systems which cannot be directly described in this way. In general, these components are multi- part components and, at the lowest level, their parts are describable as functions. The approach we have adopted to describe non-functional components involves considers them to be collections of simpler components and we have included in their representation information which allows the retrieval software to find those component collections.

A good example of a component collection is the 'curses' package provided with UNIX for the management of different terminal types. This package is made up of about 60 individual functions and each of these can be described using a component descriptor frame. Each descriptor frame includes a link to the frame which describes the 'curses' package itself so, by retrieving any one of the 'curses' functions, the entire package is discovered. Similarly, an abstract data type is recorded as a collection of descriptor frame with a frame for each type of operation. Finding one of these, reveals the entire collection.

The frame structure which we have adopted is flexible so that it is not necessary for all slots in all frames to be filled in. Thus if a component is actually an abstract data type rather than a function, the function slot would be unfilled but the object slot would be filled with the type implemented by the component. Furthermore, all component descriptor frames include two lists of references. These are references to sub-components such as the operation functions on an abstract type and references to super components which are component groupings.

For example, consider the following Ada package specification:

```
generic
type ELEM is private ;
package Linked is
   type LIST is private ;
function Head (L: LIST) return ELEM;
function Tail (L: LIST) return LIST;
   function Is_null (L: LIST) ;
function Add_to_front (L: LIST ; V: ELEM)
                                  return LIST;
function Delete (L: LIST ; V: ELEM)
                                  return LIST;
private
type LIST is access ;
end Linked ;
```

The component descriptor frame representing this component would be structured as follows:

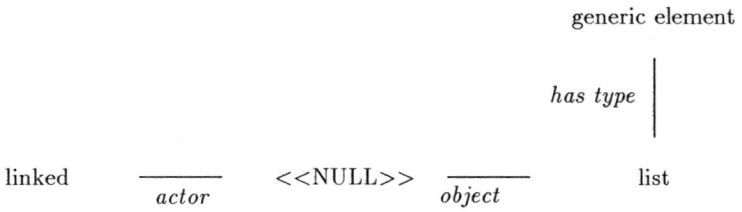

A simple request which filled in a query form with the object field set to List would return this but, normally, we would expect the request to be for a component which carried out a particular list function such as adding a list member. To support this, the above frame and frames for each individual type operation are linked as shown in Figure 12.2. A request which 'hits' a sub-component also causes information about the super-component to be made available to the requester.

At the lowest level, the frame linking allows components which are actually collections of other components to be represented in the catalogue. However, the facility also allows logical component groupings to be established. Thus, all of the components relevant to a particular application domain can be linked so that once one 'hit' has been made, the user may easily find associated components. This is illustrated in Figure 12.3 which shows a a collection of components which are designed to manipulate data structures.

13.3. COMPONENT INFORMATION BASE

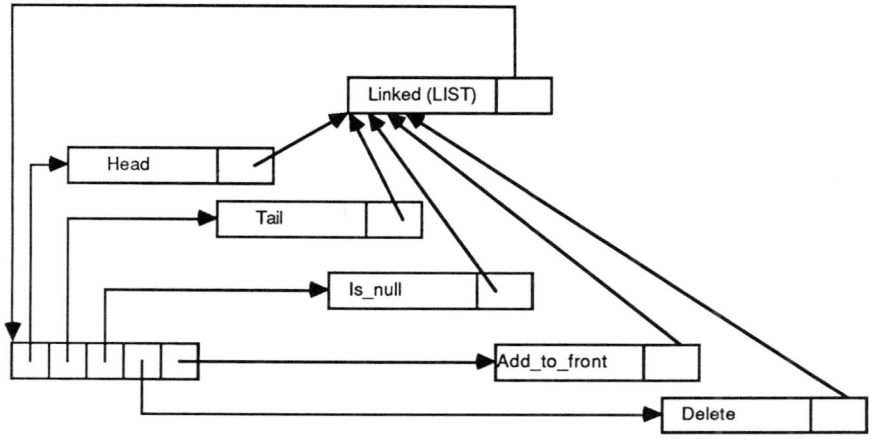

Figure 13.2: Linking of Sub and Super Components

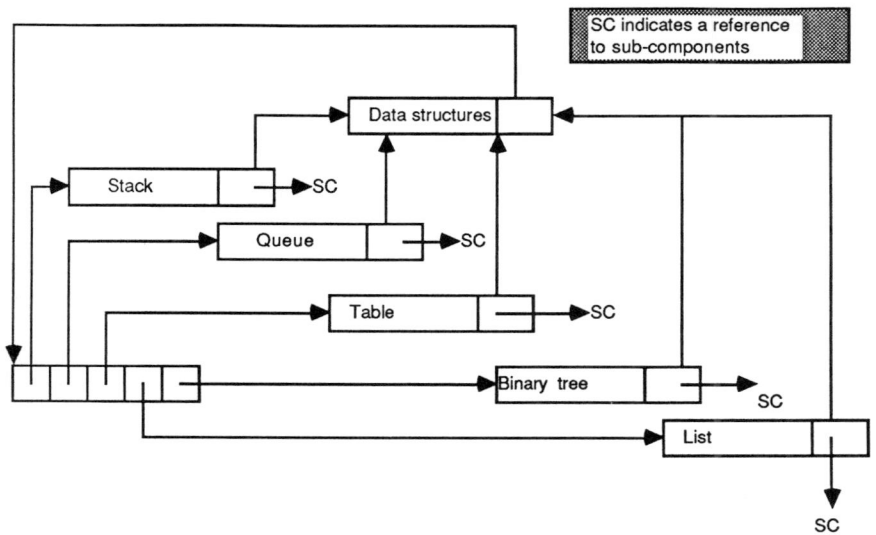

Figure 13.3: Data Structure Components

This linking of frames is one example of the maintenance of frame relationships. here, the relationship represented is 'Has_part' and work is currently underway to determine which other relationships between components can be useful to the reuser. One obvious possibility is a 'Has_attributes' relationship so that all components implemented in the same programming language, for example, can be considered as a single grouping.

13.4 SYSTEM EVALUATION

The evaluation of information retrieval systems is notoriously difficult [65]. Traditionally, information retrieval performance is measured in terms of recall and precision. Recall measures the proportion of relevant material that is actually retrieved. Precision measures the proportion of retrieved material that is relevant. Central to both these measures is the notion of relevance. In general relevance is a subjective notion. In a software component retrieval system the inherent subjectivity of relevance is exaggerated due to the acceptability of close matches.

Ideally, evaluation of the system should involve large numbers of independent users accessing large numbers (thousands) of potentially reusable components in an attempt to use the available components to develop a software system. This is not practicable due to the lack of catalogued components. Any experimentation with limited numbers of components must involve guidance to the users as to what components are available. This guidance inadvertently suggests terminology to be used in component retrieval and this biases any evaluation metrics.

As a consequence of the problems of interpreting relevance and the lack of realistic test situations it is felt that any attempt to deduce experimental results are too subjective to be of value. Instead we suggest the following, openly subjective, arguments for the component descriptor frame representation whilst acknowledging its accompanying weaknesses.

Recall Most importantly a components retrieval system must identify all potentially interesting software components. This is supported by conceptual classification of all specified terminology — thus avoiding problems of keyword mismatch. Relaxing the search to keyword only search, if necessary, should retrieve all components related to a particular notion.

Precision There is little point in retrieving all 'relevant' components if they are hidden among large numbers of irrelevant components. The representation of meaningful relationships between the identified concepts of function and object, together with provision for descriptors, supports more precise descriptions than that afforded by keywords only or boolean combinations of keywords.

Ranking The component descriptor frame representation provides a natural mechanism to implement ranking of components according to quality of match. Ranking helps overcome decisions as to whether or not components are relevant to requests.

Intuitive evidence Although it was not obvious to us initially, with hindsight it is clear that software components characteristically perform functions and that a representation of software components should capture those functions. The work of Prieto-Diaz supports this case.

User interface Component descriptor frames are used to drive a form-filling user interface. Although not influencing the quality of representation this interface actively supports the user in request specification. This is done both by prompting the user to supply keywords that formulate a meaningful representation and by providing suggestions to aid that process.

We recognise the following weaknesses in the representation:

- Applicability to other problem domains. The representation is best suited to problem domains that lack a well defined, generally accepted terminology. For example the NAG library utilises a keyword based classification scheme based on mathematical terminology. Because this terminology is widely recognised and the number of components catalogued is small it seems to be quite satisfactory. A representation such as component descriptor frames may not be suitable for such a domain.

- Developing component descriptor frames is not easy. The task of conceptual classification and identification of stereotypical relationships is a time consuming task. Furthermore it is not a 'once only' process. As new terminology and components are recognised and as initial classifications and relations are experienced necessary revisions will be recognised. However it is our experience that such iterative revisions gradually tend towards stability. These problems are inevitable with any meaningful representation.

- It will always be possible to 'break' the representation. Component data frames may be viewed as a canonical form in which all the systems software component information must be stored. Inevitably some component functions will not fit naturally into such a canonical form.

On the whole a balance has to be struck between the need for meaningful representation, partial matching and ease of use while considering the general applicability of the representation. A representation that has formal semantics associated with it provides meaningful representation but suffers in the other respects. Keywords provide ease of use and general applicability whilst lacking in meaningful representation. We argue that in providing meaningful relationships between conceptual classifications of keywords we strike the required balance.

Our own experience suggests that the catalogue is a useful tool in assisting software reuse. A prototype version has been made available to a large aerospace engineering company for evaluation. They experienced some initial difficulties in tailoring the system to their specialised aplication domain but after this work had been done, they found the catalogue both useful and easy to use.

13.5 CONCLUSIONS

The aim of our work has been to develop a representation for software component descriptions and software component requests which captures their meaning. We described an approach, known as Conceptual Dependency, used in natural language understanding to represent the semantics of the 'understood' text . Following this method we recognised the main concepts of the software component domain, namely the function performed and the objects manipulated by the function. The relationship between the function and objects is represented by what we have termed component descriptor frames.

As a system based around these ideas attempts to capture the meaning of descriptions and requests it has a better capability for matching the two than that provided by independent keywords. In fact, in the worst case, the system behaves as if it were keyword based. We have shown how it is possible to build knowledge about software components into the system. The system is also flexible and extensible. It is a simple matter to add new conceptual actions or conceptual nominals — there is no predefined classification structure into which new classes have to be accommodated.

Although the interface is simplistic it meets our initial requirement in that it is straightforward to use. A form-filling interface, based on the component descriptor frame representation, aids the user in formulating a sensible query. When the user fills in a form, he or she is also presented with help in formulating the appropriate terminology and this has been found to be of immense assistance.

This work on the component retrieval system is now the basis for the development of a more comprehensive reuse support system. This will include facilities for information base browsing, tool support for component cataloguing and will be integrated with automated design tools. Thus, the designer will have reuse information available early in the design process. We believe that early decision making is essential if reuse is to be cost effective and that an integrated component catalogue and design support system is the best way to achieve this.

Chapter 14

Distribution Issues for LAN Based IPSEs

Dave Hutchison, Doug Shepherd and John Walpole

14.1 IPSEs AND DISTRIBUTION

The need for fast response times and a high degree of local processing power to drive sophisticated human computer interfaces has resulted in IPSEs being based on high powered personal workstations. Community working and the consequent communication and sharing of information has led to the interconnection of workstations by a local area network (LAN) [54]. IPSEs are therefore, generally built on a distributed systems base.

There are however, several important differences between distributed and single machine systems:

1. There is the possibility of partial failure in distributed systems due to individual node failures, or network failure. This is far more difficult to deal with than total system failure.

2. Distributed systems are based on an unreliable communications subsystem which can cause the loss or delay of messages.

Because of property (2) it can be shown that there is no accurate global state information available in distributed systems [73, 19, 48]. Therefore, the control of a distributed system must be achieved without full knowledge of the global state. In addition to these problems, the higher level of parallel activity in distributed systems can result in the corruption of data if it is not controlled.

To achieve efficient and reliable operation in a distributed environment the IPSE substructure must meet several requirements.

14.2 SUBSTRUCTURE REQUIREMENTS

IPSE databases should be distributed [106]. The use of a central database was suggested as an initial stage in the development of Eclipse [55]. However, there are several important drawbacks to this approach. Firstly, in terms of system performance, it is difficult to maintain a fast response level if every access to data in the system must go through a central point. In the case of a central database the database becomes a serious bottleneck in the system. The system therefore fails to take full advantage of the high degree of parallelism possible in distributed systems and therefore fails to realise their potential for high performance. Secondly, the use of a central database imposes restrictions on the *extensibility* of the system. Extensibility [74, 6] is the degree to which elements can be added or indeed removed from the system. This is an important issue in the design of a distributed IPSE since it enables the system to grow to meet new requirements, such as changes in the number of development personnel and workstations. Extensibility is restricted by the use of a central database because the database becomes more of a bottleneck as the system grows. Therefore, a *distributed database* is an important requirement for a distributed IPSE.

Another important requirement for a distributed IPSE is concerned with its *availability* [74, 6]. Availability is defined as the degree to which a system can tolerate the loss of an element or the failure of a component and still provide a complete and unimpaired service. Distributed systems have the potential for high availability. This is primarily because resources can be provided redundantly on different machines. To achieve high availability it is important that the system exhibits *redundancy* in terms of both data and control. Redundancy of data can be provided by maintaining multiple replicas of data items on separate machines. Redundancy of control can be provided in distributed systems by ensuring that control is *decentralised* [60]. This implies that there should be no direct dependence on central authority anywhere in the system.

Finally, a distributed IPSE should be no more difficult to use than a centralised IPSE. This can be achieved by ensuring that distribution details are hidden from the ordinary IPSE user. Therefore, distribution issues should be *transparent*. The following types of distribution transparency are defined by Traiger in [125]:

location transparency although data are geographically distributed and may move from place to place, the programmer can act as if all the data were in one node.

replication transparency although the same data item may be replicated at several nodes of the network, the programmer may treat the item as though it were stored as a single item at a single node.

concurrency transparency although the system runs many transactions concurrently, to each transaction it appears as if there were no concurrency in the system.

failure transparency either all the actions of a transaction occur or none of them occur.

As stated by Traiger "Certainly a system that provides transparency is as easy to use as a centralised system".

14.3. PCTE DISTRIBUTION

In an attempt to provide concurrency and failure transparency in database systems and, more recently in general purpose distributed systems the notion of *atomic transactions* has been introduced [130, 68, 30, 45]. Transactions are discussed in detail in section 11.5.

The problem of providing replication transparency in distributed systems is often called the *multiple copy update* (MCU) problem [52, 37]. A solution to the MCU problem for distributed IPSEs is proposed in [91].

To summarise, the distributed IPSE should meet the following requirements:

R1 Distributed database.

R2 Transparent distribution.

R3 High extensibility.

R4 High availability.

R5 Replicated data.

R6 Decentralised control.

The following section presents a brief discussion of PCTE [95] distribution and the degree to which it meets these requirements.

14.3 PCTE DISTRIBUTION

The designers of PCTE regard distribution as one of the system's salient features. Despite this, PCTE distribution is still a long way from meeting the requirements stated above.

In terms of distribution transparency, PCTE provides little more than the illusion of system wide naming at the user level. The requirement for nodes to be autonomous results in each operating system kernel (in this case Unix system V) managing its own local resources and remaining unaware of the distributed environment. This is a direct result of implementing distribution as a layer above the local operating system kernel [90]. Therefore, node autonomy conflicts with the requirement for distribution transparency (R2). In addition, autonomy prohibits the degree of global resource management possible in a distributed environment [6].

The distribution aspects of PCTE also fail to meet the requirement for high availability (R4). Firstly, there is no facility for maintaining multiple replicas of database objects in PCTE. It is possible to replicate system files, but these must be fully replicated and it is assumed (unreasonably) that the information in these files is relatively static. Updates to these files are performed on a predetermined master copy and the changes are then propagated to the slave copies. There is no mechanism provided for recovering from failures, therefore reliable information can only be obtained from the master copy. The increase in availability provided by this mechanism is therefore minimal. Furthermore, the naming structure in PCTE is not replicated and therefore the availability of database objects could be lower than that provided on a single machine. This is due to the fact that access to an object involves resolving a pathname, components of which will typically be stored on more than one node. Hence, the failure of any node which contains part this pathname results in the object becoming unavailable. Secondly, internode cooperation on the global management of the system is severely limited by the layering of distribution above the local operating system kernel. This prevents PCTE from implementing decentralised control (R6).

In conclusion, very little research effort in PCTE has been spent on the design of an adequate distributed base for IPSEs.

14.4 ATOMIC TRANSACTIONS

Distributed atomic transaction mechanisms are complicated. To understand them it is important to distinguish the different problems which they attempt to solve. This distinction is made below, and is presented in more detail in [130].

Transactions should maintain consistency. To maintain consistency in distributed systems the fundamental problems of synchronisation [66, 75] and recovery [66, 4] must be solved. The problem of synchronisation can be further subdivided into the problems of mutual exclusion and event ordering. This distinction in particular is often missed. Once these distinct problem areas have been identified it is possible to classify existing transaction mechanisms according to the techniques which they use to solve them.

Existing synchronisation techniques can divided into three distinct classes: locking [44], timestamps [105] and optimistic [18]. Important distinctions between these techniques are as follows:

- Conflicts are determined on a *per operation* basis in locking and timestamp ordering techniques, and on a *per transaction* basis in optimistic techniques.

- Conflicts are solved by *waiting* in locking techniques, and by *aborting and restarting* in timestamp and optimistic techniques.

- Transactions are ordered explicitly by timestamp and optimistic techniques, since both these assign timestamps to transactions. However, in locking techniques transaction order is determined by the order of access to data.

For all techniques which cause transactions to wait the problem of *deadlock* [46] must be solved. In distributed systems the problem of deadlock is extremely difficult to solve and therefore, it is better to adopt a synchronisation policy which is not susceptible to deadlock.

Existing approaches to recovery can be classified as: logging [44] and shadows [67]. A comparison of the two techniques shows that logging is faster during normal execution, but is slower during recovery [92]. However, many variations of the two algorithms exist and the choice of technique is likely to depend on other considerations.

14.5 IPSE TRANSACTIONS

A comparison of conventional database systems and IPSE databases reveals several significant differences which have serious repercussions for the design of IPSE transaction mechanisms. Firstly, the granularity of objects in IPSE databases is far greater than in

14.5. IPSE TRANSACTIONS

conventional databases. Objects in an IPSE database often contain large amounts of possibly unstructured data, such as text or source code. Secondly, transactions in an IPSE database frequently involve interaction with users in activities such as editing. The combination of these two features makes the duration of transactions in an IPSE database much longer than in conventional databases. For example, a transaction to build part of a software system may involve edits and compilations of large objects. This process could last for several hours or even days. Support for *long term transactions* is therefore an important issue in IPSEs. Both PCTE and CAIS have recognised the importance of long term transactions, but neither project has proposed a satisfactory solution to implementing them. It is shown in section 14.5.1 that the support of long term transactions presents severe problems for existing transaction techniques.

PCTE also recognises the importance of *nested transactions* as a method for increasing the reliability and performance of large transactions. The concept of nested transactions and the special problems they present are discussed in section 14.5.2.

Several other IPSE database requirements also influence the design of the transaction mechanism. In particular, the requirements for version control, configuration control and inter-object relationships, described in chapter 2, are shown (in section 14.5.2) to be very relevant.

14.5.1 Long Term Transactions

The duration of transactions is a very important consideration in the design of a transaction mechanism [45]. Long term transactions have been recognised as an important issue in the design of general purpose databases which wish to support software development, CAD and AI applications [35] and particularly in IPSE databases [95, 129]. However, long term transactions can severely limit the concurrency and therefore the performance of a system. [35] states that:

> Since conventional techniques require the holding of locks until termination of the transaction, concurrency would be drastically reduced.

Because of the duration of long term transactions the objects involved remain unavailable for long periods of time. As a result, other transactions which wish to access/update these objects are either held up or aborted. This severely limits the concurrency of the system. To increase concurrency the partial results of a long term transaction could be made visible before commit time. However, this would cause problems for recovery since, after a failure it would be necessary to undo results which may have been observed by other transactions. Therefore, the transaction would no longer have the property of atomicity. Consequently, it would be impossible to guarantee the consistency of data in the system.

At the heart of the concurrency problem for long term transactions is the need to satisfy the condition of *serialisability* [30]. Serialisability requires that the effect on the database of the execution of several concurrent transactions is the same as if they were executed in some order. It is this requirement to order the execution of transactions which results in the need for transactions to hold on to their resources for the duration of the transaction. If it was possible to maintain consistency and atomicity without having to meet the requirement for serialisability then concurrency could be increased.

A second problem with long term transactions is their high probability of failure. As the length of a transaction in a distributed system increases then the probability of a failure occurring also increases. This raises the question of what action to take after a failure has occurred. Existing systems tend to abort transactions when they restart after a failure. However, a long term transaction may have already involved several hours (or even days) of work by the time the failure occurred. In this case it would be undesirable for the transaction to abort (and hence undo all this work). A far better solution would be to save the current state of the transaction and restart execution at a later time. To provide such a facility the concept of *save point* has been introduced [44]. If a failure occurs during the course of a transaction then on recovery, rather than aborting, it can roll back to the last save point and restarted from there. Save points can therefore be used to ensure the eventual success of a long term transaction [86].

Another important feature of long term transactions is that they must be able to exist across process boundaries. This feature is supported in PCTE and CAIS by representing transactions as objects in the database. A similar approach is taken by the ISIS system [24].

The problem of supporting long term transactions is the most serious drawback of using existing transaction techniques in distributed IPSEs. The following subsections discuss the problems of supporting long term transactions using the existing synchronisation techniques of locking and timestamping.

Locking

Locking techniques are unsuitable for supporting long term transactions because the data items updated by a transaction must remain locked until the end of the transaction. Consequently, other transactions which wish to access these data items are caused to wait for long time periods and the concurrency in the system is drastically reduced.

As well as causing severe concurrency problems long term transactions also exacerbate the problem of deadlock. In [45] it is stated that:

> At least in database applications, the frequency of deadlock goes up with the square of the multiprogramming level and the fourth power of the transaction size.

The multiprogramming level is a function of the length of transactions. A study of the probability of deadlock is presented in [46].

The deadlock problem is compounded further by the fact that deadlock is extremely difficult to detect in distributed systems. Simple deadlock detection techniques which use timeouts are precluded by long term transactions because the timeout value needed to distinguish deadlock from normal waiting is too large to be useful. Other more elaborate deadlock detection techniques are very complex and therefore costly in terms of system performance. Consequently, it is important for long term transaction mechanisms to use a synchronisation technique which is deadlock free.

14.5. IPSE TRANSACTIONS

Time Stamp Techniques

Although synchronisation techniques based on timestamp ordering are not susceptible to deadlock, they are still unsuitable for long term transactions. This is primarily because timestamp ordering techniques also satisfy the serialisability condition. Rather than ordering competing transactions by causing one (or more) of them to wait, timestamping schemes cause one (or more) of the transactions to abort. Therefore timestamp schemes avoid the problem of deadlock at the expense of aborts [45]. When transactions are long term this results in an excessive number of transaction aborts and hence poor system performance.

14.5.2 Nested Transactions

Nested transactions [87, 86] allow transactions to be divided into *subtransactions* which can be executed concurrently. Hence, actions within a nested transaction may actually be transactions (or even nested transactions) at the next lower level of abstraction. A distinction is made between the top level transaction and the subtransactions within a nested transaction. Subtransactions may contain further subtransactions and therefore a nested transaction can be regarded as a tree with the top level transaction at the root. Standard tree and family relationship terminology is often used to describe subtransactions within nested transactions (e.g. child, parent, ancestor, descendant, sibling etc.).

There are several advantages to supporting nested transactions within a distributed IPSE. Firstly, nesting can greatly reduce the execution time for large transactions since subtransactions are executed in parallel rather than serially. Secondly, nested transactions can be used to make long term transactions more robust. This can be achieved by saving the results of committed subtransactions and using them to implement save points (as discussed in the previous section). After the failure of a nested transaction only the subtransactions which have not yet committed must be restarted. Nested transactions also have the advantage that they allow the structure and inter-dependencies of operations within large transactions to be represented. This is particularly useful in distributed IPSEs for activities such as system building where sub-components of software systems can depend on the preconstruction of others.

Nesting does however present some new problems. The first of these is concerned with recovery and is illustrated by the following example from [45].

In a travel agent system a transaction may consist of the following sequence of events:

1. Customer calls travel agent giving destination and dates.

2. Agent negotiates with the airlines for flights.

3. Agent negotiates with car hire companies for cars.

4. Agent negotiates with hotels for rooms.

5. Agent receives tickets and reservations.

6. Agent gives customer tickets and gets credit card number.

7. Agent bills credit card.

8. Customer uses tickets.

The complete nested transaction between the customer and the travel agent includes steps 1 to 8. Each of the steps which involves negotiation with another organisation is also a transaction in its own right, and is nested inside the overall transaction.

Should the customer decide to cancel the trip, the top level transaction must be aborted. Under some circumstances though, some of the sub-transactions (e.g. the flight reservations) may have already committed and their results may have become visible to the outside world. It is important to note that, if this is allowed to happen, the nested transaction will not have the property of atomicity. To abort a nested transaction which allows its subtransactions to make their results visible to other transactions when they commit requires *compensating* transactions. Compensating transactions are started to undo the effects of any subtransactions that have already committed at the time of the failure.

A second problem to be solved with nested transactions is concerned with synchronisation between subtransactions. Concurrent access to data shared between subtransactions must be controlled in the same way as for single level transactions. However, subtransactions of the same nested transaction will often require access to common data items. This leads to an increase in what Gray calls the *multiprogramming level*. As stated earlier: the frequency of deadlock goes up with the square of the multiprogramming level. This makes deadlock a serious problem for nested transactions.

Existing approaches [87, 86, 95] build nested transactions based on locking and have detailed rules for passing locks between child and parent transactions.

To overcome the problem of losing atomicity current implementations force subtransactions to hand up their locks to their parent transaction at commit time rather than releasing them and making their results visible to other transactions. The results of subtransactions are only made visible outside the nested transaction once the top level transaction commits. However, these techniques are susceptible to deadlock.

The following section discusses the relationship between transactions and the other important IPSE functions of version and configuration control.

14.5.3 Relationship with the IPSE Database

A characteristic of IPSEs and more advanced programming environments is their recognition of change as being of fundamental importance. The information held in an IPSE database is frequently undergoing change. In such systems changes to objects are recorded as trees of versions, and version control systems may be thought of as editors of version trees [36]. Traditionally editors save backup copies of objects to allow users to return to the initial version of an object. This is an attempt at making edits atomic. However, this principle could usefully be generalised to encompass the notion of transactions and to make edits to the system's data atomic with respect to failures and other concurrent edits. In this way the consistency of a system's data could be maintained.

A further characteristic of the IPSE database is the need to store relationships between versions of objects in order to form configurations. The IPSE function of

14.6. CONCLUSIONS 215

configuration control and the need to ensure that changes to configurations are carried out consistently is an underlying theme trhoughout much of this book.

The above discussion raises the important question of whether transactions in IPSEs can be integrated with the functions of version and configuration control in the form of a single mechanism. Recent studies [16, 94] have already shown that the use of multiple versions of objects can significantly increase the level of concurrency provided by a transaction mechanism. This is especially true in the case of read-only transactions where all interference between read-only and update transactions can be eliminated [134]. In such systems reads are directed to an existing version of an object whereas updates create a new version.

14.6 CONCLUSIONS

For IPSEs to operate reliably and efficiently in the distributed environment they must exhibit the following features:

- Distributed database.

- High extensibility.

- High availability.

- Replicated data.

- Decentralised control.

- Atomic transactions.

This chapter has concentrated on support for transactions and has detailed an additional set of requirements for transaction mechanisms in distributed IPSEs.

The application of the transaction concept to distributed IPSEs presents a new set of requirements, many of which cannot be met by existing transaction techniques. It has been shown that long term transactions are a characteristic of IPSEs. Long term transactions cause severe problems for existing synchronisation techniques which are based on the notion of serialisability. Consequently, to support long term transactions it is important to investigate the possibility of *non-serialisable* transactions.

It has also been shown that nested transactions are an important issue in distributed IPSEs since they allow the reliability and performance of large transactions to be increased, and they provide support for activities such as system building. However, both long term and nested transactions significantly increase the probability of deadlock. Deadlock is extremely difficult to detect in distributed systems, especially when transactions are long term. Therefore, only transaction mechanisms which are deadlock free are suitable for use in a distributed IPSE.

The IPSE database functions of version and configuration control have also been discussed in relation to transactions, and it has been shown that the use of multiple versions of objects can increase the concurrency provided by a transaction mechanism. Furthermore, it has been shown that transactions, version control and configuration control are all interrelated problems. Consequently, consideration should be given to the integration of transactions with version and configuration control in distributed IPSEs.

The deficiencies mentioned above are emphasised in [45]:

> Our concept of transaction and the implementation techniques we have are inadequate to the task of many applications. They cannot handle nested transactions, long-lived transactions and they may not fit well into conventional programming systems.

Chapter 15

Distributed Systems Management and IPSEs

D. Coffield, Dave Hutchison and Doug Shepherd

15.1 BACKGROUND

PCTE was developed for a local area network based architecture. In common with other evolving distributed systems PCTE will have to evolve to operate over a wide area. This is natural, for as a support environment it may be used within a company over several sites. As shown in the previous chapter, PCTE is deficient in the area of network management and the following sections consider the repercussions of this if PCTE is to be applied over a wider area.

Network management can be split four ways: configuration management, fault management, performance management and event management.

The PCTE documentation promotes the impression that PCTE will have an error free network system to run on top of. This is even more unlikely in a WAN application. Just why this is so is discussed in the next section.

As distributed IPSEs will no doubt have to function over WANs management will become increasingly important. The latter part of this chapter introduces the topic of distributed systems management (DSM) and explains what is involved. Future implementations of distributed IPSEs must take the low level system base and its operation seriously, if the IPSE itself is to be reliable.

15.2 PCTE FROM A WAN VIEWPOINT

The distribution mechanism consists chiefly of the following:

- A work station is represented in the OMS as an object of type station.

- A created station retains its unique station_id until the station is deleted from the network.

- User names/password information is replicated on all nodes.

- Processes have unique process numbers.

- The decision of where to run a process is primitive - there is no support for load balancing.

- OMS objects are grouped into volumes mounted on work stations. Distribution keeps tabs on what's mounted where.

Management of the underlying network system is confined to the Distribution mechanism alone. In effect, a simple sub-set of configuration management has been proposed. This raises the question of whatever happened to the rest of the management architecture. The use of activities (atomic, serialisable transactions) cannot adequately cover the missing parts. For instance, at what stage in a wider PCTE architecture (with multiple work stations) is the failure of a significant node noticed, and what's done about it? At a finer granularity how is the absence of an inaccessible but important object noticed - all objects cannot be replicated everywhere. The PCTE may be transparent to the user but the system administrators need tools to support probing of each node, they need tools to provide easy system updates, to investigate node failures etc. Such tools, which should be part of any network management system, are not present in PCTE.

A LAN based PCTE architecture can become complex relying on the fast intermachine communication which LANs offer. Present day WANs operate at significantly slower rates and are more susceptible to failure than LANs. Consequently any PCTE system running over a WAN will be slower and less reliable. Over an internetwork the communication speeds and reliability will vary with location.

Wide area expansion has consequences for several of the bulleted points, above. Replicating user names and password information around an internetwork and maintaining that information is non-trivial and wasteful of disk space. Management, especially a directory service, would assist with this task.

Keeping process numbers unique is simple - just prefix the PID with the station name, or preferably address (there is a possibility that two stations may have the same name).

Distribution keeps tabs on which objects are located where - that becomes more difficult as the network expands.

15.3 IMPROVING PCTE DISTRIBUTION

This section briefly speculates on what should be added, to provide some support for WAN based PCTE. Again it focuses on management issues.

The statement is made in the PCTE documentation that the ideal PCTE architecture is a local area network with work stations connected to it. Work stations retain their autonomy while participating in a wider PCTE community. A simple network management system based on agent processes, one per node, should be added. The agent processes (nm-agents) are responsible for executing requests from a network management centre (this can effectively be a package callable on any work station by someone with the correct authority) and for exchanging information with each other

15.4. THE SIGDSM WORK

on the health of the network system. Any significant occurrence, or event, can be brought to the attention of a select few nodes, or indeed on all the nodes. The system administrators can then investigate the event.

The nm-agents can communicate using connectionless, lightweight protocols (which fits in with PCTE as is). As the minimum enhancement to PCTE an event management system should be added to at least recognise faults and performance problems and highlight them for the administrators. Also performance management and fault management systems could be added to investigate problems further and perhaps effect a temporary patch while the administrators were informed. The configuration management ought to be enhanced to give the administrators facilities such as file transfers, LAN wide posting and deletion of "messages of the day", software update and installation facilities, topology map capability etc.

As all network information (addresses) are replicated on each node, the basis for a nm-agent management system already exists. For information exchanges broadcasting can be used, and as PCTE is LAN-based this presents no problems. The network management centre as a package provides an interface to the agent based system and allows greater control to be exercised than the agents themselves can execute.

Further additions to the management system would include a simulation tool to investigate the effect of additional work stations on the wider PCTE architecture.

The manager/agent model having been adopted for the local area, PCTE can then be utilised over the wider area PCTE. The notion of domains as geographical areas of responsibility then becomes useful. The larger PCTE can be split into several domains each with its own manager. The managers together provide support for the internetwork PCTE.

We can summarise what has been stated above by saying that PCTE is an evolving distributed system, intended to run over a local area network, that supports little in the way of network management. As a consequence, the reliability and maintainability of the resulting system is in question. If the environment is extended to the wide area then PCTE cannot function successfully without adding management functions. The application of the manager-agent model to the local area can be suitably enhanced and adopted in the wide area environment giving such a large PCTE system greater reliability.

15.4 THE SIGDSM WORK

We have demonstrated above the lack of network management in the Eclipse/PCTE environment and mentioned, without any particular detail, the topic of distributed systems management e.g. [69]. The Lancaster Distribution Group has been actively involved in a Special Interest Group on Distributed Systems Management (SIGDSM). SIGDSM is an independent group from both the industry and the academic sectors. A report has recently been published by the group [85] and the work is also referred to in [20]. The main reason for presenting a summary of the work here is that Eclipse/PCTE is seen to be deficient in many of the areas discussed, and DSM is an area that can only grow in importance as distributed systems become more prominent. No specific parallels are drawn in the discussion between DSM and Eclipse/PCTE. Rather, the reader is invited to consider what is discussed against Eclipse/PCTE and draw his/her own conclusions.

15.5 MANAGING DISTRIBUTED SYSTEMS

Distributed systems management is responsible for the total management of all activities over a set of resources distributed over LANs, WANs and internetworks. It caters for functions that again can be though of as traditional operating system functions but over a much larger area than current distributed operating system designs can handle. The prerequisite for a controlling distributed operating system is completely removed. Indeed, early work with respect to the wide area environment by the COST group (Cooperation Scientifique et Technique, see below) proposed the somewhat radical notion of operating systems providing only an interprocess communication mechanism and a support environment for programmers. In the distributed environment everything else was to be the remit of distributed systems management. If anything, this is an indication that distributed operating systems are another area where ideas are currently changing radically.

Presently, distributed systems management is a supplement to existing systems to assist them to function in a distributed manner. The following sections explain what distributed systems management involves.

Work on distributed systems management has been limited so far and has often been integrated with the design of distributed operating systems; e.g. created to function within a specific environment, typically a LAN. With the growth and convergence of the networking technologies there will be many different varieties of distributed system that cannot, and will not, be controlled by a single operating system. The argument is that a distributed system belonging to an organisation may be constructed from other systems that are distributed in their own right, and there will be many operating systems and a variety of protocols in use throughout the global system. It is this complex issue that distributed systems management attempts to address.

In 1984 the COST 11 bis Distributed Systems Management group produced a report on the subject that has spawned a research project under the COST 11 ter effort involving several European countries [70]. In the UK, an *ad hoc* Special Interest group on Distributed Systems Management (SIGDSM) involving various UK companies and Universities is also addressing the problem [85]. The difference between these two groups is that COST concentrate their efforts on the wide area environment whereas SIGDSM is interested in both the local and wide area environment. The COST report gives the impression that substantial work on this has been done in the LAN area; a belief we would dispute. Certainly systems such as the Cambridge Distributed System were designed with management built in, in the form of resource managers [23], but the kind of environment initially of interest is one where a distributed system has evolved rather than being specifically designed from scratch. Systems currently under design should possess the necessary tools to make management easier. Previous reports have considered whether this was the case as far as Eclipse/PCTE is considered. The discussion here closely parallels the work of the SIGDSM group, although our opinions differ on a few points.

15.5. MANAGING DISTRIBUTED SYSTEMS

15.5.1 Review

The issues that contribute to the difficulty in managing distributed systems can be summarised thus:

- The resulting systems are large and complex.
- There is a substantial diversity of components (both hardware and software).
- Non-deterministic communication delays arise between systems.
- The large number of areas that management itself has to address: configuration, faults, security, performance, accounting, naming, and the users themselves.
- The distinction between management and the normal system functions is often ill-defined.

In addition to management objectives outlined so far, these may be added:

- Optimising use of resources.
- Minimise costs (of the service providers and users).
- Maximise revenues (of the service providers).
- Optimise performance of the service for the users.

These are more traditional (real world) management objectives that can equally apply in a distributed systems environment. Once more, the relative importance of each is determined by the application.

15.5.2 Services

The SIGDSM group had adopted the notion of services to describe a distributed system. The object oriented model was the previous candidate for a descriptive technique by the group but the current instability of the terminology led to the idea of a service. (A service is more abstract than an object. An object was felt to imply a physical "thing", although the object model itself is more general.) A distributed system, therefore, can be thought of as a set of services provided to user, where a service is an abstraction of a set of operations provided to users allowing them to perform a particular function. Services can be divided into application and support services. Mail and databases are examine of application services, and communications and processing are examples of support services. (The earlier discussions on network management in the thesis were, of course, involved with a support service.)

A service type can be considered to have three parts:

- an exported interface defining the syntax and semantics of the operations available to a user, the operations themselves being described in terms of messages or remote procedure calls.

- an imported interface that defines the syntax and semantics of the operations of the service(s) on which this service relies.

- encapsulated components are the hardware and software components used to provide the service (and they themselves may be instances of service types).

A server is a named instance created from a service type and users are the clients of the server (the may be human or computer processes).

15.5.3 Domains

Definition

Distributed systems management is a complex subject and the concept of domains helps to rationalise and break down the management process. Our definition of a domain is "a physical/geographical area over which control can be exercised". Domains can be described in terms of two properties: their structure and their relationships with other domains.

Structure

Domains can be readily discussed from two viewpoints: logical and physical.

Physical domains are easily recognised: wide area, metropolitan area, local area, local area segments, for example.

The domain concept parallels well with physical structures. Physical domains can be staged by size e.g. as above, or to an even finer granularity. Logical domains are more abstract in nature and represent a grouping of physical domains i.e. a logical domain may map onto several physical ones.

The logical and physical split is adequate and most systems can be grouped as such. The SIGDSM group suggested a five way division of domain structure.

Physical as above.

Organisational which maps onto our logical view.

Conformance to a standard where all components of a distributed system which conform to a particular standard form a domain.

Service provider domain encapsulates all the service types and servers used to provide the service.

Security servers that adopt a specific security policy.

Relationships

Having structured domains, the next step is to identify the relationships that can exist between types. There are two main physical domain relationships: disjoint and interacting (Figure 15.1).

Disjoint domains are unrelated, do not cooperate, and share no resources: no interaction. Interfacing domains correspond with each other on task that require it and do so by making use of the management services provided. Typically what is anticipated is an exchange between the management service in the respective domains before the use of the resources required for the actual task itself.

15.5. MANAGING DISTRIBUTED SYSTEMS

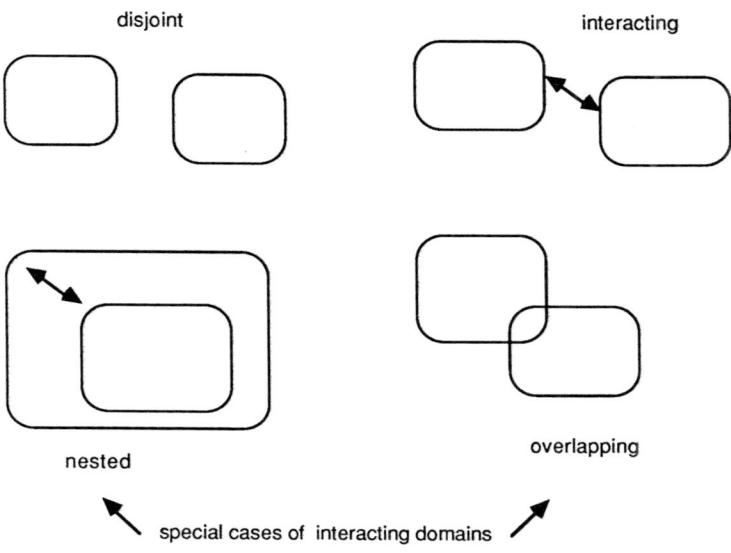

Figure 15.1: Domain relationships

Other domain classes have been proposed (by SIGDSM). These are nested and overlapping domains. Our view is that nested and overlapping domains are special cases of interacting domains. Nested domains exist as a logical view of a specific kind of domain interaction. A management system for a particular domain will be nested in any case. It will be hierarchic in nature, and the sub-domains at each level are nested. Overlapping domains are claimed to be impossible and potentially an untidy concept. It is unlikely that any resource is owned by two or more domains. Rather, it will be owned by one domain and possibly available for use by others. Overlapping domains, where applicable, are therefore a special case of interaction. (This between domain negotiation that occurs when remote resources are sought is not intended to be visible to the user).

Implementation

It is necessary to discuss how domains would be implemented in practice. The system of the previous chapter provides some hints.

First, each resource on a network has a specific owner and is correspondingly recognised to be in a specific domain, largely determined by geographical position. Each domain has a management system that looks after that domain. At the highest level there is a domain manager. Should resourceA/domainA wish to make use of a service provided in resourceB/domainB, the two domain managers must first negotiate and then give or deny permission (Figure 15.2). This negotiation will occur via a specified management protocol executed between the two network or resource managers in the two domains. The manager-agent model is a natural method by which domains may be implemented.

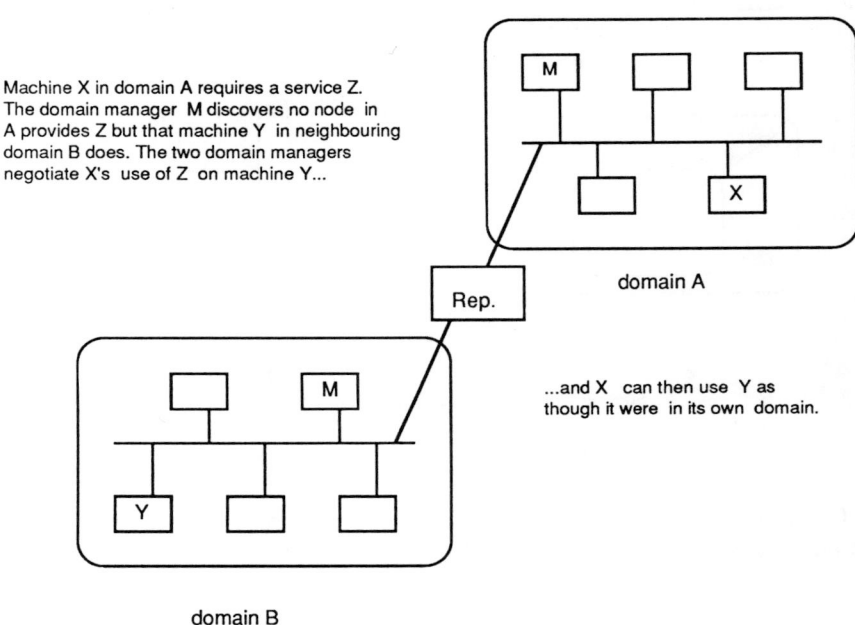

Figure 15.2: Two interacting domains

15.5.4 Management Functions

Having identified what distributed systems management is, this section continues to consider the actual functions of distributed systems management.

The functions of distributed systems management are similar to those of network and processing management. Because the distributed systems definitions appear to capture the functions of the individual network management functions, the logical conclusion is that distributed systems management is th e sum of the other two management classes. The resulting management system is more comprehensive and complex in nature. As many of the functions are similar to those reviewed before only a short discussion on each is presented; differences, of course, will be highlighted.

Configuration Management

Configuration management in a distributed system has greater responsibility than its network management namesake. It does not refer to managing new software versions as part of an applications life cycle. Rather, it involves identifying hardware and software components, installing hardware components, allocating software components to the hardware components, interface bindings, and so on. Importantly, configuration management can be static or dynamic in nature. In the former, the system has to be shutdown and re-installed, whereas in the latter it can be done as the system is running.

A large amount of state information is required for effective configuration management.

Name Management

Users require a lookup service to identify where resources within a distributed system are located. Human users prefer symbolic identifiers with which to do this. A name server maps between the symbolic and real identifiers, such as names to addresses. Name management is the management of the naming strategy within the appropriate name space. Tasks to be performed include:

- name space structuring i.e. the format of names.

- name allocation names have to be unique at some point in a system. Users should be allowed to have their own aliases for a server, should they wish to do so.

- name registration.

Performance Optimisation

Performance management was mentioned earlier. A related function is performance optimisation. Optimisation involves monitoring the system, obtaining feedback on its usage, identifying weaknesses and exercising control to correct these. Typical weaknesses include processing bottlenecks, communication delays, high error rates. Ultimately, optimisation is the responsibility of the service administrator, who must ensure that users obtain the best possible service from the system.

There are tradeoffs between various objectives. Increasing the reliability of a system by providing redundancy, and using fault tolerant processing techniques, may result in additional overheads and reduce performance in terms of delay and throughput.
Some areas where performance can be optimised include:

- The communication system forms the backbone on which any distributed system is totally dependent. Objectives here would be to reduce communication delay and increase traffic throughput. Parameters that can be manipulated include: packet retry timeouts, routing algorithms, number of buffers in individual nodes, and even the transport protocol used.

- Processing can be affected by the allocation of software components to computers and the objective is to obtain an equitable distribution of resources to software components. Memory usage, processing time, process priority, I/O overheads and communication delays should all be considered on allocation.

- Reliability indicates the ability of a system to work without failure. This can be improved by component redundancy of critical parts.

Security

Security is an issue that has not been specifically covered so far but is one that should be considered carefully in real world applications of distributed systems. Objectives are to maintain the confidentiality and integrity of information stored in, and communicated between, the system nodes. The integrity of the service itself, along with suitable access control and authentication is important. The mechanisms to achieve each of these would include the use of encryption, passwords, and access control lists.

Security management functions are responsible for the handling of encryption keys (including their regeneration at frequent intervals), user registration and authentication, access control and trace files of activity for security audit purposes.

Domains are a particularly useful concept from the security viewpoint.

Accounting

On moving from a local area environment, accounting functions become important. Distributed systems running over LANs, WANs and internetworks will use sub-services that both the service and sub-service providers have to account for. Users will require suitable information on the services they use. There are two views of accounting: the users view and the servers view. The users need to be able to control their use of resources that have been allocated and used by them and the servers need to charge for the services supplied.

Other functions

Other major function of distributed systems management include: monitoring of resources and activities, fault handling and the human interface aspects. All these have been covered in previous chapters and the mechanisms are similar for distributed systems management.

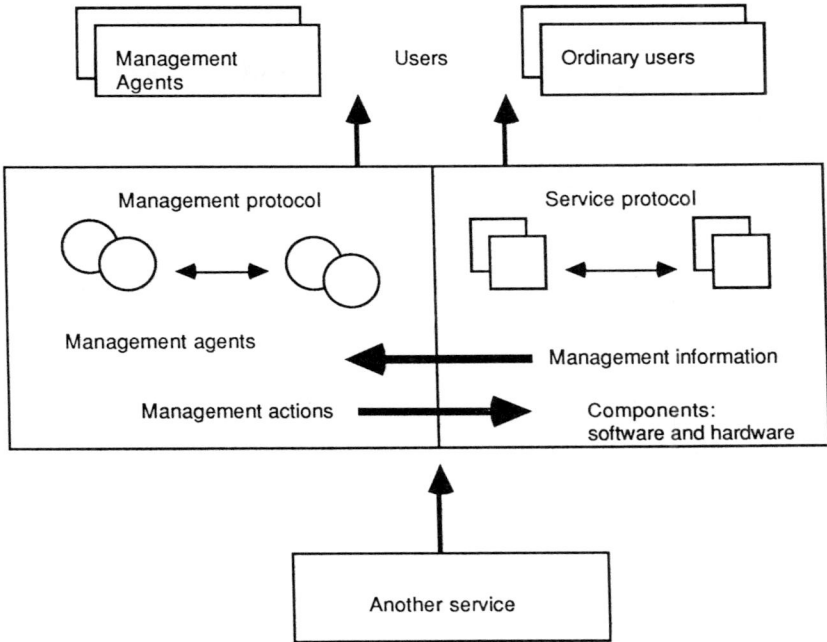

Figure 15.3: The service model from a management viewpoint

15.5.5 The Model

Based on the concept of services a model can be derived of both the service type and, at a higher level, distributed systems management. Figure 15.3 is a refinement of one of the SIGDSM diagrams. It highlights the internal mechanisms of one service type and demonstrates how that service type may make use of the facilities of another and indeed be used by another. A good example of this would be electronic mail. If the central box in Figure 15.3 represents an instance of a mail service then the lower service type could be the communications service and the users, at the top of the diagram, could include a file transfer service.

How distributed systems management is achieved can be imagined from this diagram. Management agents do most of the work but, importantly, applications within the system must be capable of exporting certain management information for use by other services, and importing it for their own use, if necessary. For this to work successfully, individual services would be less distinct than they tend to be at the current time. As an example, on a UNIX system, rather than have both a mail *daemon* (i.e. a dedicated server process performing a specific task) and an file transfer daemon, have a single daemon responsible for both activities; consider mail to be special case of file transfer or vice versa (after all, both are concerned with the transfer of data from source to destination).

One criticism of Figure 15.3 lies in the separation of the service protocol and the management protocol, within a single service. the service protocol itself carried management information so the clear division made in the diagram is a little misleading. The diagram also gives some implication of the existence of layering in the system. This is not necessarily the case.

15.5.6 Load Balancing

Load balancing, e.g. [76], may not seem a natural item for consideration in a distributed IPSE. However, we can note here that if sufficient management is present in the system then load balancing is easily added (at lest across homogeneous systems). The information collected by the management system is a suitable basis for load balancing.

15.6 SUMMARY

Network management and distributed systems (distributed operating systems, especially) have so far been distinct research areas. By presenting the functions of distributed systems management it is hoped that a similarity between the two areas can be seen.

The distributed systems community, including distributed IPSEs, need management as part of their developing systems. As networks form the backbone of these distributed systems, network management should now be considered an integral part of distributed systems development. Even distributed operating systems should possess management interfaces and allow a higher level management system access, if the distributed operating system is part of some wider level management system access, if the distributed operating system is part of some wider distributed system. Research should now be carried out with these aims in mind. As far as future distributed IPSEs are concerned more attention needs to be paid to the lower level system base rather than just the development of sophisticated user interfaces and software engineering tools.

Chapter 16

Achievements and Lessons

Frank Bott

While some of the Eclipse partners had previous experience of collaborative projects, none had been involved in a project like Eclipse, an R&D project with six partners, spread across the UK, and some 200 man years of effort. The opportunities which such a project presents are tremendous but so is the potential for catastrophic failure.

16.1 COLLABORATION

That Eclipse succeeded in meeting its objectives and avoided the many potential dangers can be put down to four principal factors:

- an enthusiasm for the project, a willingness to collaborate and mutual respect, on the part of all the partners;

- the involvement of all partners in the central technical issues;

- a strong central design team;

- strong programme management and quality management where appropriate.

It is easy to dismiss enthusiasm, mutual respect and willingness to collaborate as factors which are outside management control. This is not true. Much can be done to cultivate these characteristics within a collaborative project — most of all, perhaps, good imaginative management can ensure that the quota of goodwill, with which most projects start, is not dissipated in the inevitable frustrations and debates which arise later.

At the stage of forming a consortium, there is often a temptation to try to persuade an organisation to participate because its known expertise or its reputation will enhance the standing of the consortium. It is a mistake to try too hard. Unless the organisation in question shows enthusiasm when first approached, it is unlikely to be an effective contributor. Furthermore, a willingness to collaborate depends on a certain degree of humility, an acceptance that the other participants have much to contribute. Prestigious organisations, academic or industrial, do not always demonstrate this quality.

In Eclipse, the regular consortium meetings and the involvement of all partners in the workshops at which central technical issues were discussed were crucial to maintaining the spirit of collaboration. So, too, were the regular visits to the individual sites by the programme manager and the chief designer. (These are features of Eclipse which the partners have tried to introduce into other large collaborative projects in which they are now involved.) The result was that the staff of the different partners came to know each other well, to respect each other's expertise and to enjoy each other's company — collaboration was seen to be fun!

16.2 PLANNING

The initial plans — and the proposal — had seriously underestimated the need for a central design *team*. Provision for a Chief Designer had been made but it had been expected that he would be able, by himself, to coordinate all the design work, that work itself being undertaken by the different project teams. This proved unrealistic. As a consequence, it was necessary to undertake a major replanning exercise some way into the project.

The resources required for programme management and, in particular, quality management (including configuration control) had also been underestimated. Funding bodies should perhaps take note of the fact that large collaborative R&D projects are just as demanding in these respects as other large projects and should encourage proposers to make appropriate provision.

Programmes like Eclipse involve technical uncertainties; over the life of the project, the sponsor's goals may change as may the circumstances and objectives of the participants. Further, if the research element of the programme is to have any real effect on the development side, one must be prepared to change direction as important research results become available. This all means that the initial plans — and, to some extent, even the objectives — of such a programme are much more volatile than those of more routine development projects.

With hindsight, therefore, we have realised that such replanning exercises will always be necessary in a large R&D project. Much disruption, much anguish and much damage to morale would be avoided if provision for them were included in the initial plans. Indeed, the fact that a replanning exercise is itself planned could reduce any tendency to replan too often on a piecemeal basis.

There was pressure on the project at the start to achieve as uniform a pattern of spending as possible and, in particular, to make expenditure in the first year as nearly equal to expenditure in the second and third years as could be managed. The reasons for this — deriving from government budgeting practice — were well understood by the programme management but the result was that resources were used in the first year of the project which could have been much more effectively and efficiently deployed in the subsequent years. An R&D programme like Eclipse cannot be suddenly switched on and immediately reach full speed.

16.3 TECHNICAL ACHIEVEMENTS

The overall technical achievement of Eclipse is to have constructed and demonstrated a second generation IPSE which is open in the sense that tools from other suppliers can be comparatively easily incorporated; it also meets the requirements of Stoneman. We believe that Eclipse is, for the moment, unique.

Within the overall achievement, a number of important technical lessons were learned or confirmed and major technical advances were made.

- The 'granularity' problem — how to represent efficiently both fine-grained and coarse-grained structure in a database — afflicts any team working in the area of tool support interfaces or software engineering environments. The Eclipse two-level database offers a proven pragmatic solution to this problem.

- The value of defining interfaces at the highest reasonable conceptual level was spectacularly demonstrated by the way in which the PTI definition enabled us to undertake the totally unforeseen replacement of SDS-2 by PCTE.

- The importance of spotting future trends in hardware and software development can hardly be over-emphasised. When we wrote the proposal, we were considering supporting Eclipse on a VAX 11/750 with dumb terminals. In the early days of the programme, we nearly committed ourselves to a work station which would have proved a blind alley. A great deal of effort was expended before Sun work stations were chosen and the choice caused some financial embarrassment. Nevertheless, with hindsight, it is clear that the expenditure was abundantly justified.

- Building Eclipse on top of PCTE has demonstrated the viability of PCTE as a standard tool support interface.

- The Eclipse approach to the user interface, through the use of a uniform metaphor (control panels) and standard components has proved very successful. The resulting interface has achieved a high level of consistency and shown itself to be applicable over a wide range of tools.

- The production of high quality tool sets to support development methods demands a lot of highly skilled resources. The generic tools (especially the design editor) developed in Eclipse simplify this task considerably. The wide applicability of these tools has been demonstrated by their use for MASCOT 3, LSDM and the CDL tool sets.

- The capture and editing of design is much harder than the capture and editing of diagrams but Eclipse has demonstrated that it can be done and that the tools which do it need to be active, i.e. they must check the design at appropriate moments and consult the user about how to fix problems.

- The MASCOT 3 tools establish a new standard for design method support tools and demonstrate the advantages of implementing such tools within an IPSE.

- The LSDM tool set has shown that an IPSE has as much to offer in the development of information systems as it has in the development of embedded systems.

- CDL and its support tools show how interfaces can be treated as first class objects and hence how software reuse in an Ada environment can be integrated with detailed design.

16.4 CONCLUSION

There is still much work to be done on Eclipse. Many facilities which one might expect to find are missing and many others are present only in a rudimentary form. Much has been already been done to improve the quality of the weaker parts of the system but there are still areas where further improvement is required. However, all this work is in hand. The impetus provided by the Alvey programme has been sufficient to allow us to create a product good enough to excite commercial interest; funding has therefore been forthcoming for the development of tailored versions of Eclipse for specific clients and to support specific design methods. Eclipse can now fairly claim to be the first production quality, open IPSE. The Eclipse project demonstrates how effective a managed, collaborative R&D programme, such as Alvey, can be in promoting the development of products up to the point at which commercial exploitation can take off.

Bibliography

[1] S. Abiteboul and R. Hull. IFO: A formal semantic database model. *3rd ACM SIGACT-SIGMOD Symp. on Principles of Database Systems*, 1984.

[2] A. Alderson. A space-efficient technique for recording versions of data. *Software Engineering Journal*, 3(6), 1988.

[3] A. Alderson, M. F. Bott, and M. E. Falla. The Eclipse object management system. *Software Engineering Journal*, 1(1):39–42, 1986.

[4] J. E. Allchin and M. S. McKendry. Synchronization and recovery of actions. *Operating Systems Review*, 19(1), 1985.

[5] J. E. Archer. Design of the Rational environment. In A.N. Habermann and U. Montanari, editors, *System Development and Ada*, volume 275 of *Lecture Notes in Computer Science*. Springer Verlag., Berlin, 1987.

[6] G. S. Blair. *Distributed Operating System Structures for Local Area Network Based Systems*. PhD thesis, University of Strathclyde, Glasgow, 1983.

[7] B. Boehm, M. H. Penedo, E. D. Stuckle, R. D. Williams, and A. B. Pyster. A software development environment for improving productivity. *Computer*, 17(6):30–42, 1984.

[8] M. F. Bott, A. Elliott, and R. J. Gautier. Ada reuse guidelines. Technical Report ECLIPSE/REUSE/ADAGUIDE/RP, Software Sciences Ltd, Macclesfield, 1986.

[9] M. F. Bott and M. D. Tedd. Saviour: A software construction tool. *DECUS Proceedings*, 7(1):43–50, 1981.

[10] M. F. Bott and P. J. L. Wallis. Ada and software reuse. *Software Engineering Journal*, 3(5), 1988.

[11] R. T. Boute and M. I. Jackson. A joint evaluation of the programming languages Ada and CHILL. In *Proc. IEE 4th Int. Conf. on Software Engineering for Telecomms Switching Systems*, pages 214–220, 1981.

[12] P. Buneman, R. E. Frankel, and R. Nikhil. An implementation technique for database query languages. *ACM Transactions on Database Systems*, 7(2):164–186, June,1982.

[13] R.M. Burstall and B. Lampson. A kernel language for abstract data types and modules. In *Proc. Symp. on Semantics of Data Types, Sophia Antipolis*, volume 173 of *Lecture Notes in Computer Science*. Springer-Verlag, 1984.

[14] J. N. Buxton. *STONEMAN: Requirements for Ada Programming Support Environments*. United States Department of Defense, Washington, 1980.

[15] M. Caplinger. Structured editor support for modularity and data abstraction. In *Proc ACM SIGPLAN Symposium on Language Issues in Programming Environments*, pages 140–147, Seattle, WA., 1985.

[16] W. J. Carey and W. A. Muhanna. The performance of multiversion concurrency control algorithms. *ACM Transactions on Computer Systems*, 4(4), 1986.

[17] J. Cartmell. Formalising the network and hierarchical models of data - an application of categorical logic. In *Category Theory and Computer Programming*, volume 240 of *Lecture Notes in Computer Science*. Springer-Verlag, 1986.

[18] S. Ceri and S. Owicki. On the use of optimistic methods for concurrency control in distributed databases. In *Proc. Sixth International Conference on Distributed Data Management and Computer Networks*, 1983.

[19] K. M. Chandy and L. Lamport. Distributed snapshots: Determining global states of distributed systems. *ACM Transactions on Computer Systems*, 3(1), 1985.

[20] D. Coffield. *Network and Distributed Systems Management: Issues, Architectures and Implementation*. PhD thesis, University of Lancaster, 1987.

[21] L. L. Constantine and E. Yourdon. *Structured Design*. Prentice Hall, Englewood Cliffs, NJ, 1979.

[22] F. J. Corbato, M. Merwin-Daggett, and R. C. Daley. An experimental time sharing system. *Proc. Spring Joint Computer Conference (AFIPS)*, 21:335–344, 1962.

[23] Daniel H. Craft. Resource management in a distributed computing system. Technical Report 73, Computing Laboratory, University of Cambridge, 1985.

[24] J. W. Davison and S.B. Zdonik. A visual interface for a database with version management. *ACM Transactions on Computer Systems*, 4(3), 1986.

[25] F. DeRemer and H. H. Kron. Programming in the large versus programming in the small. *IEEE Transactions on Software Engineering.*, SE-2(2):80–86, 1976.

[26] V. Donzeau-Gouge. Document structure and modularity in Mentor. In *Proc ACM SIGSOFT/SIGPLAN Software Engineering Symposium on Software Development*, 1984.

[27] A. Elliott. The Eclipse Public Tools Interface. Technical report, Software Sciences Ltd., Macclesfield, 1987.

[28] A. Elliott and R. D. Alexander. MASCOT 3 and Ada: An approach to real time systems based on reusable components. *Ada User*, 8(Supplement):S41–S46, 1987.

[29] D England. Graphical prototyping of graphical tools. In *Proc HCI'88 (to appear)*, Manchester, 1988.

[30] K. P. Eswaran, J. N. Gray, R. A. Lorie, and I. L. Traiger. The notions of consistency and predicate locks in a database systems. *Communications of the ACM*, 19(11), 1976.

[31] EURAC. EURAC: Requirements and design criteria for tool support interfaces. Software Sciences Ltd., GIE Emeraude and Selenia, 1987.

[32] M. E. Falla. The Gamma software engineering environment. *Computer Journal*, 24(3):235–242, 1981.

[33] M. E. Falla and D. Burns. The software development system. In *Proceedings of Datafair 1973*, pages 116–173, London., 1973. British Computer Society.

[34] S. I. Feldman. MAKE - a program for maintaining computer programs. *Software - Practice and Experience*, 9:255–265, 1979.

[35] D. H. Fishman, D. Beech, H. P. Cate, E. C. Chow, T. Connors, J. W. Davis, N. Derrett, C. G. Hoch, W. Kent, P. Lyngbaek, B. Mahbod, M. A. Neimat, T. A. Ryan, and M. C. Shan. Iris: An object-oriented database management system. *ACM Transactions on Office Information Systems*, 5(1), 1987.

[36] C. W. Fraser and E. W. Myers. An editor for revision control. *ACM Transactions on Programming Languages and Systems*, 9(2), 1987.

[37] H. Garcia-Molina and D. Barbara. The cost of data replication. In *Proc. ACM 7th Data Communications Symposium*, Mexico City, 1981.

[38] R. J. Gautier. CDL and its tools. Technical Report ARU/WP/RJG/3, Dept. of Computer Science, UCW, Aberystwyth, 1986.

[39] R. J. Gautier. Guidelines for the use of Ada in reusable software components. *Ada User*, 8(Supplement):S27–S32, 1987.

[40] R. J. Gautier. A language for describing Ada software components. In S. Tafvelin, editor, *Ada Components: Libraries and Tools*, pages 75–85, Cambridge, 1987. Cambridge University Press.

[41] R. J. Gautier, H. E. Oliver, and M. B. Ratcliffe. A component description language for Ada. Technical Report ARU/WP/RJG/10 Issue 2, Dept. of Computer Science, UCW, Aberystwyth, 1987.

[42] J. A. Goguen. Parameterized programming. *IEEE Transactions on Software Engineering*, SE-10(5), 1984.

[43] A. Goldberg. *Smalltalk-80: the Interactive Programming Environment.* Addison Wesley., Reading, Mass, 1984.

[44] J. N. Gray. Notes on data base operating systems. In *Operating Systems - An Advanced Course*, volume 60 of *Lecture Notes in Computer Science.* Springer Verlag, 1978.

[45] J. N. Gray. The transaction concept: Virtues and limitations. In *Proc. Conference on Very Large Databases*, 1981.

[46] J. N. Gray, P. Homan, R. Obermarck, and H. Korth. A straw man analysis of probability of waiting and deadlocks. In *Proc. 5th International Conference on Distributed Data Management and Computer Networks*, 1981.

[47] J. A. Hall, P. Hitchcock, and R. Took. An overview of the ASPECT architecture. In J. McDermid, editor, *Integrated Project Support Environments.* Peter Peregrinus, London, 1985.

[48] J. Y. Halpern and Y. Moses. Knowledge and common knowledge in a distributed environment. *Advanced NATO Institute on Logic and Models for the Verification and Specification of Concurrent Systems*, 1:110–130, 1984.

[49] S. Hardy. A new software environment for list processing and logic programming. In *Artificial Intelligence: Tools, Techniques and Applications.* Harper and Row., New York, 1984.

[50] B. Hayselden. Implementing the PCTE user interface on Sun workstations. In *ESPRIT '87 Achievements and Impact.* North Holland, Amsterdam, 1987.

[51] M. Higgs and P. Stevens. Developing an environment manager for an IPSE. In I. Sommerville, editor, *Software Engineering Environments.* Peter Peregrinus, London, 1986.

[52] E. Holler. Multiple copy update. In *Distributed Systems - Architecture and Implementation: An Advanced Course*, volume 105 of *Lecture Notes in Computer Science.* Springer Verlag, 1981.

[53] S. Horwitz and T. Teitelbaum. Generating editing environments based on relations and attributes. *ACM Transactions on Programming Languages and Systems*, 14(4), 1986.

[54] D. Hutchison. Local area networks: An introduction. *Software and Microsystems*, 2(4), 1983.

[55] D. Hutchison and J. Walpole. Eclipse: A distributed software development environment. *Software Engineering Journal*, 1(2), 1986.

[56] P. H. Huyck and N. W. Kremenak. *Design and Memory - Computer Programming in the 20th Century.* McGraw Hill, New York, 1980.

[57] E. L Ivie. The programmer's workbench. *Communications of the ACM*, 20(10):746–753, 1977.

[58] K. Jackson. MASCOT 3 and Ada. *Software Engineering Journal*, 1(3):121–135, 1986.

[59] M. A. Jackson. *System Development*. Prentice Hall, Englewood Cliffs, N.J., 1982.

[60] E. D. Jensen. Distributed control. In *Distributed Systems - Architecture and Implementation: An Advanced Course*, volume 105 of *Lecture Notes in Computer Science*. Springer Verlag, 1981.

[61] JIMCOM (Joint IECCA and MUF Committee on MASCOT). *The Official Handbook of MASCOT: MASCOT II Issue 2*. RSRE (Computing Policy and Standards Section), Malvern, 1982.

[62] JIMCOM (Joint IECCA and MUF Committee on MASCOT). *The Official Handbook of MASCOT: MASCOT 3.1 Issue 1*. RSRE (Computing Policy and Standards Section), Malvern, 1987.

[63] S. C. Johnson and M. E. Lesk. Language development tools. *Bell Systems Technical Journal*, 57(6), 1978.

[64] T. Capers Jones. Reusability in programming: A survey of the state of the art. *IEEE Transactions on Software Engineering*, SE-10(5), 1984.

[65] ed. K. Sparck Jones. *An Information Retrieval Experiment*. Butterworths, London, 1981.

[66] W. H. Kohler. A survey of techniques for synchronisation and recovery in decentralised computer systems. *Computing Surveys*, 13(2), 1981.

[67] B. Lampson and H. Sturgis. Crash recovery in a distributed data storage system. Technical report, Xerox Palo Alto Research Centre, 1979.

[68] B. W. Lampson and E. E. Schmidt. Organising software in a distributed environment. *SIGPLAN Notices*, 18(6), 1983.

[69] Lancaster Distribution Group. Report on wide area communications. Technical report, Computer Science Department, University of Lancaster, 1987.

[70] ed. A. Langsford. Distributed systems management in wide area networks. Report of the COST11 bis dsm group. Available from the editor at Computer Science and Systems Division, AERE Harwell, 1984.

[71] D. B. Leblang and G. Mclean. DSEE: Overview and configuration management. In J. McDermid, editor, *Integrated Project Support Environments*. Peter Peregrinus., London, 1985.

[72] W. G. Lehnert. *The Process of Question Understanding*. Lawrence Erlbaum Associates, Inc, 1978.

[73] G. LeLann. Distributed systems - towards a formal approach. In *Proc. of IFIP Congress*, Toronto, 1977. North Holland.

[74] G. LeLann. Motivations, objectives and characterization of distributed systems. In *Distributed Systems - Architecture and Implementation: An Advanced Course*, volume 105 of *Lecture Notes in Computer Science*. Springer Verlag, 1981.

[75] G. LeLann. Synchronization. In *Distributed Systems - Architecture and Implementation: An Advanced Course*, volume 105 of *Lecture Notes in Computer Science*. Springer Verlag, 1981.

[76] M. Lionel, Chong-Wei Xu Ni, and Thomas B. Gendreau. A distributed drafting algorithm for load balancing. *IEEE Transactions on Software Engineering*, SE–11(10), 1985.

[77] G. Longworth and D. Nicholls. *SSADM Manual Version 3*. National Computing Centre, Manchester, 1986.

[78] T. G. L. Lyons. The public tools interface in software engineering environments. *Software Engineering Journal*, 1(6):254–258, 1986.

[79] T. G. L. Lyons and M. D. Tedd. Recent developments in tool support interfaces. *Ada User*, 8(Supplement):S65–S72, 1987.

[80] T. G. L. Lyons and M. D. Tedd. Technical Overview of PCTE and CAIS. *Ada User*, 8(Supplement):S73–S78, 1987.

[81] K. Marzullo and D. Weibe. Jasmine: A software system modelling facility. *ACM SIGPLAN/SIGSOFT*, 22(1), 1987.

[82] Mascot Suppliers Association. *The Official Definition of MASCOT*. RSRE, Malvern, 1978.

[83] S. McGowan. Fortune - a documentation support tool. In *Proceedings of CAP Technical Conference 1986*, London, 1986. CAP (Industry).

[84] R. Milner. The standard ML core language. *Polymorphism*, II(2), October 1985.

[85] ed. Morris Sloman. Distributed systems management. report of the COST11 bis DSM Group. Available from the editor at Department of Computing, Imperial College, London., 1986.

[86] J. E. B. Moss. Nested transactions: An approach to reliable distributed computing. Technical Report MIT/LCS/TR-260, MIT Laboratory for Computer Science, Cambridge, Mass, 1981.

[87] J. E. B. Moss. Nested transactions and reliable distributed comuting. In *Proc. 2nd Symposium on Reliability in Distributed Software and Database Systems*, 1982.

[88] National Computing Centre. *STARTS Debrief Reports No 1: SDS*. Manchester, 1983.

[89] J. R. Nestor, W. A. Wulf, and D. A. Lamb. IDL - an interface description language: Formal description. Technical Report CMU-CS-81-139, Carnegie-Mellon University Computer Science Department, Pittsburg, 1981.

[90] J. R. Nicol. *Operating System Design for Distributed Programming Environments*. PhD thesis, University of Lancaster, 1986.

[91] J. R. Nicol, G. S. Blair, W. D. Shepherd, and J. Walpole. An approach to multiple copy update based on immutability. In *Proc. IFIP Conference on Distributed Processing*, 1987.

[92] B. M. Oki, B. H. Liskov, and R. W. Scheifler. Reliable object storage to support atomic actions. *Operating Systems Review,(special issue)*, 19(5):147–159, 1985.

[93] M. A. Ould and C. Roberts. Defining formal models of the software development process. In I. Sommerville, editor, *Software Engineering Environments*. Peter Peregrinus, London, 1988.

[94] C. H. Papadimitriou and P. C. Kannellakis. On concurrency control by multiple versions. *ACM Transactions on Database Systems*, 9(1), 1984.

[95] PCTE. A basis for a portable common tool environment: Functional specifications (4th edition), 1986.

[96] A. Poigne. Algebra categorically. In *Category Theory and Computer Programming*, volume 240 of *Lecture Notes in Computer Science*. Springer-Verlag, Berlin, 1986.

[97] T. T. Pressburger and D. R. Smith. Knowledge-based software development tools. In Sommerville, editor, *Software Engineering Environments*. Peter Peregrinus, London, 1988.

[98] R. Prieto-Diaz. *A Software Classification Scheme*. PhD thesis, University of California, Irvine, 1985.

[99] M. B. Ratcliffe. Evaluation of prototyping systems. Technical Report ECLIPSE/REUSE/PROTO/SURVEY, Dept. of Computer Science, UCW, Aberystwyth, 1985.

[100] M. B. Ratcliffe. Component design editor II. Technical Report ARU/WP/MBR/7, Dept. of Computer Science, UCW, Aberystwyth, 1987.

[101] M. B. Ratcliffe. Component design editor: User guide. Technical Report ARU/WP/MBR/6, Dept. of Computer Science, UCW, Aberystwyth, 1987.

[102] M. B. Ratcliffe. Report on a workshop on software reuse. *SIGSOFT Software Engineering Notes*, 12(1), 1987. Reprinted in "Tutorial:Software Reuse:Emerging Technology", ed W.Tracz, pub IEEE Comp. Soc. Press, ISBN 0-8186-0486-3.

[103] P. Reid and R. C. Welland. Project development in view. In I. Sommerville., editor, *Software Engineering Environments,*. Peter Peregrinus., London, 1986.

[104] T. Reps. *Generating Language-Based Environments*. MIT Press, Cambridge, Mass., 1984.

[105] D. J. Rosenkrantz, R. E. Stearns, and P. M. Lewis. System level concurrency control for distributed database systems. *ACM Transactions on Database Systems*, 3(2), 1978.

[106] J. B. Rothnie and N. Goodman. A survey of research and development in distributed database management systems. In *Proc. 3rd International Conference on Very Large Databases*, Tokyo, Japan, 1977.

[107] R. C. Schank. Conceptual dependency: A theory of natural language understanding. *Cognitive Psychology*, 3:552–631, 1972.

[108] P. W. Sellars. IPSEs in commercial data processing. In J. McDermid, editor, *Integrated Project Support Environments,*. Peter Peregrinus, London, 1985.

[109] D.W. Shipman. The functional data model and the data language DAPLEX. *ACM Transactions on Database Systems*, 6(1), March 1981.

[110] H. Simpson. The MASCOT method. *Software Engineering Journal*, 1(3):103–120, 1986.

[111] B. Skwiersky. Review no. 8706-0482. *ACM Computing Reviews*, 28(6):320, 1987.

[112] J. D. Smart. A man-machine interface management system for UNIX. In *Uniforum Conference Proceedings*, Anaheim, 1986.

[113] J.M. Smith and D.C.P. Smith. Database abstractions: Aggregation and generalization. *ACM Transactions on Database Systems*, 2(2), June 1977.

[114] R. A. Snowdon. CADES and software system development. In H. Hunke, editor, *Software Engineering Environments,*. North Holland, Amsterdam, 1981.

[115] I. Sommerville and R. Thomson. SySL - A System Structure Language. Technical report, Software Technology Research Group, University of Strathclyde, Glasgow, 1985.

[116] I. Sommerville, R. Welland, and S. Beer. Describing software design methodologies. *Computer Journal*, 30(2), 1987.

[117] T. A. Standish. An essay on software reuse. *IEEE Transactions on Software Engineering*, SE-10(5), 1984.

[118] V. Stenning. An introduction to ISTAR. In I. Sommerville, editor, *Software Engineering Environments*. Peter Peregrinus, London, 1986.

[119] M. Stephens and K. Whitehead. The Analyst - a workstation for analysis and design. In *Proc. 8th International Conference on Software Engineering*, London, 1985.

[120] M. D. Tedd. The Sapphire project: Building confidence in PCTE. In *ESPRIT '87 Achievements and Impact*. North Holland, Amsterdam, 1987.

BIBLIOGRAPHY

[121] D. Teichrow and A. Hershey. PSL/PSA: a computer-aided technique for structured documentation and analysis of information processing systems. *IEEE Transactions on Software Engineering*, SE3:41–48, 1977.

[122] W. Teitelman and L. Masinter. The InterLisp programming environment. In D. Bairstow, H.E. Shrobe, and E. Sandewall, editors, *Interactive Programming Environments*. McGraw Hill, New York, 1984.

[123] R. M. Thall. The KAPSE for the Ada Language System. In *Proc. AdaTEC Conference on Ada,*, pages 31–47, 1982.

[124] W. F. Tichy. Software development control based on module interconnection. In *Proc. 4th Int. Conf. on Software Engineering*, pages 29–41, Munich, 1978.

[125] I. L. Traiger, J. Gray, C. A. Galtieri, and B. G. Lindsay. Transactions and consistency in distributed database systems. *ACM Transactions on Database Systems*, 7(3), 1982.

[126] UK Department of Industry. Ada Based System Development Methodology Study: Study Report, 1981.

[127] UK Department of Industry. United Kingdom Ada Study Final Technical Report, 1981.

[128] UK Ministry of Defence (PE). MASCOT 3 with Ada, 1987.

[129] United States Department of Defense. Common APSE Interface Set (CAIS), 1986.

[130] J. Walpole, G. S. Blair, D. Hutchison, and J. R. Nicol. Transaction mechanisms for distributed programming environments. *Software Engineering Journal*, 2(5), 1987.

[131] D. L. Waltz. An English language question answering system for a large relational database. *Communications of the ACM*, 27(7):526–539, 1978.

[132] D. L. Waltz and B. A. Goodman. Writing a natural language data base system. In *Proc. 5th International Joint Conference on Artificial Intelligence*, pages 144–150, 1977.

[133] A. Wasserman. USE a methodology for the design and development of interactive information systems. In H.J.Schnieder, editor, *Formal Methods and Practical Tools for Information Design*, pages 31–50, Amsterdam, 1978. Elsevier.

[134] W. E. Weihl. Distributed version management for read-only actions. *IEEE Transactions on Software Engineering*, SE-13(1), 1987.

[135] M. V. Wilkes, D. J. Wheeler, and S. Gill. *Programming for a Digital Computer*. Addison Wesley, London, 1953.

[136] A. Wills. Structure of interactive environments. In I. Sommerville, editor, *Software Engineering Environments*. Peter Peregrinus, London, 1988.

[137] M. Wood and I. Sommerville. An information retrieval system for software components. *Software Engineering Journal*, 3(5):198–207, 1988.

Index

Index

Ada, 3–6, 8–10, 14–16, 29–31, 35, 97–107, 109, 110, 112–121, 123, 125–128, 130–133, 138, 140, 142, 143, 165, 168–170, 182–185, 187, 188, 191, 202, 232
ADI, 94
AI, 13, 116, 155, 159
Algol68, 4
ALS, 7
Alvey, 6, 7, 9, 19–24, 26, 27, 31, 32, 37, 109, 110, 115, 142, 143, 232
Apple Macintosh, 69, 70
Applications Interface, 76–79
APSE, 3, 4, 6–8, 97
ASPECT, 7
AUTO-MATE, 148, 156

BIS/IPSE, 7, 12

C, 11, 35, 65, 73, 89, 98, 143, 145, 158–160, 165, 180
CADES, 2, 3
CAIS, 8, 121, 211, 212
CAIS-A, 8
CASE, 7
CCTA, 5, 145, 148
CDE, 186, 187
CDL, 16, 131, 181–188, 231, 232
Cedar, 163, 164
CHILL, 4
CICS, 145
COBOL, 2, 145
CODASYL, 43
collaboration agreement, 19, 23
configuration control, 9, 11, 12, 14, 27, 30, 35–37, 40, 65, 66, 97, 98, 100, 103–105, 107, 117, 141, 142
Coral, 2, 111, 112
CORE, 17
CTSS, 2

data model, 3, 52
DATA-MATE, 148
DBI, 35, 37, 57–62, 64, 67, 111
DDL, 52, 53, 55, 56, 59, 159, 187
derivation network, 4
desigm editor, 75
Design Editor, 14, 231
design editor, 15, 16, 27, 29, 31, 76, 85, 86, 89–95, 110, 116, 125, 129, 131, 133, 136, 138, 143, 155–158, 160, 187
DRL, 116, 132, 133, 142, 244
DRL, 116
DSEE, 7
DSM, 217, 219

EDSAC 1, 1
Emeraude, 8, 11, 32–34, 37
ESPRIT, 8, 11
exploitation agreement, 23, 24

FDL, 13, 73, 75, 76, 78, 130, 136, 159
FORTRAN, 98, 180
Fortune, 17
Foundation, 4, 6, 25, 27, 28, 31, 32, 34–37, 128
FSD, 57, 67

Gamma, 4
Garnet, 32, 37
GDL, 14, 85–89, 92–95, 125, 136, 156, 157, 159
GENOS, 7
granularity, 30, 31, 231

IADS, 15, 102, 103, 105, 106
IDL, 5, 29, 30
IDLE, 5, 30, 31, 35, 37, 39, 41–47, 52–55, 57, 67, 187
impact analysis, 4, 30, 104, 105, 116, 128, 141, 142

INDEX

Intel, 97, 99, 100, 102
Interlisp, 4, 9, 70
IPSE, 1, 3–12, 16, 25, 26, 29, 32, 85, 130, 152, 158, 165, 173, 190, 191, 207–217, 228, 231, 232
IPSE 2.5, 7
ISIS, 212
ISM project, 7
ISTAR, 7, 12
ITI, 110

Jasmine, 180
JSD, 5, 6, 17, 86, 89, 94

KAPSE, 3, 8

lex, 89
local area distribution, 11, 207
LSDM, 5, 6, 14, 15, 94, 95, 145–148, 152–156, 158–160, 187, 231, 232

Make, 164, 178–180
MAPSE, 3
MASCOT, 5, 6, 14, 15, 55, 75, 89, 94, 98, 109–117, 119–128, 130–133, 136, 140–143, 148, 183, 231
MCHAPSE, 4, 5, 25
MIDL, 5, 29, 30
MMIMS, 73

National Computing Centre, 3, 4

OBJ, 181, 183, 184
OMS, 32, 34–37, 39, 48, 57, 217, 218

Pascal, 4, 111, 112
PCTE, 8, 9, 11, 12, 25, 32–34, 36, 37, 39–42, 46, 48, 50–55, 57, 58, 65, 67, 70, 73, 103, 104, 110, 120, 121, 123, 124, 126, 132, 133, 141, 143, 145, 153, 154, 159, 160, 187, 209–212, 217, 218, 220, 231, 245
PCTE, 110, 120
POPLOG, 9
Project MAC, 2
Prolog, 190, 201
PSL/PSA, 3
PTI, 9, 14, 26, 36, 187, 231

RAPID/USE, 181, 183

rational APSE, 7
RSRE, 3, 4, 111, 148
RTL2, 2, 111, 112

Sapphire, 8
Saviour, 4
SDS, 3, 27
SDS-2, 3–5, 27, 28, 32, 34–37, 110, 141, 231
SEE, 3
Shapes Editor, 14
SIGDSM, 219–223, 227
Smalltalk, 70, 76, 175
SSADM, 5
Star, 70
Stoneman, 7, 9, 10, 97, 231
Sun, 10, 11, 15, 27, 28, 31, 32, 36, 37, 69, 91, 100, 116, 145, 156, 158, 159, 186, 190, 199, 231
SunWindows, 73
SySL, 163–165, 168–173, 175, 176, 178–180

TeleSoft, 97, 99–102

UI, 15
UNIX, 2, 7, 8, 10, 11, 26, 27, 32, 33, 35, 37, 41, 48, 58, 61, 70, 81, 83, 89, 94, 100–102, 106, 154, 158, 159, 164, 168, 175, 178–180, 190, 196–199, 201

VAX, 2, 4, 8, 100, 231
VMS, 4, 8, 100

wide area distribution, 217

yacc, 89